Teaching English *as a* Foreign *or* Second Language

A Teacher Self-Development and Methodology Guide

Second Edition

JERRY G. GEBHARD

Ann Arbor
The University of Michigan Press

Copyright © by the University of Michigan 2006
All rights reserved

ISBN 0-472-03103-1

Published in the United States of America
The University of Michigan Press
Manufactured in the United States of America

∞ Printed on acid-free paper

2009   2008   2007   2006   4   3   2   1

No part of this publication may be reproduced, stored in a retrieval system, or trans-
mitted in any form or by any means, electronic, mechanical, or otherwise, without the
written permission of the publisher.

A CIP catalog record for this book is available from the British Library.

Library of Congress Cataloging-in-Publication Data

Gebhard, Jerry Greer.
　　Teaching English as a foreign or second language : a teacher self-development
and methodology guide / Jerry G. Gebhard.—2nd ed.
　　　　p.cm.
　　Includes bibliographical references and index.
　　ISBN-13: 978-0-472-03103-0 (pbk. : acid-free paper)
　　ISBN-10: 0-472-03103-1 (pbk. : acid-free paper)
　　1. English language—Study and teaching—Foreign speakers. 2. English
teachers—Training of. I. Title.

PE1128.A2G38 2006
428.0071'1—dc22   2005054949

*This second edition is dedicated
to my wife, Yoko Kato Gebhard,
on our twenty-fifth wedding anniversary.*

Acknowledgments

I sincerely thank Maria Saryuz Sarska, Dong Xu, and Tim Conrad for assisting me with research during the development of the first edition of this book. I also want to thank Tom McClaren for assisting me with research on technology, Theresa Tseng for her feedback and research into technology, and both Theresa and Qisi Zhang for helping me to update the appendixes on publishing companies and journals for the second edition. I also thank John Fanselow, Thomas Farrell, Pamela Friedman, Barbara Hill Hudson, Joe O'Connor, Judi Moy, and Lilia Savova for reading and commenting on the first edition of the book at different stages in its development, as well as Nancy Bell and Amy Minette for reading and giving thoughtful feedback on Chapter 3 in the second edition.

I thank the administration at the American Language Institute (ALI) at Indiana University of Pennsylvania (IUP) for their consent to observe and photograph classes; Mary Beth Mahler, Zubeyde Tezel, and Trikartikaningsih for inviting me into their classes; the students in their ALI classes for being so very cooperative. I also want to thank Tim and Kerry Conrad for their ongoing support.

I also thank the many graduate students in the Ph.D. Program in Rhetoric and Linguistics for commenting on chapters in the first edition, students in the Ph.D. Program in Composition and TESOL on chapters in the second edition, and students in the MA TESOL Program for feedback on both editions.

Finally, I would like to thank Kelly Sippell for her support and patience as I recreated this book into a second edition.

Contents

I'm an English Teacher!?
> —Remark made by an unprepared teacher

Introduction: A Self-Development and Methodology Guide

The Audience for This Book

This book is a teacher development and methodology book. It can be used by those of you who are learning to teach English as a foreign language (EFL) and English as a second language (ESL) as a part of your pre-service teacher education program. It can also be used as a teacher development text in in-service teacher development programs as a source for experienced EFL/ESL teachers who would like to refresh their knowledge and improve their teaching. In addition, this book can act as an exploratory text for those who are simply curious about teaching EFL/ESL or by those who have accepted an EFL/ESL teaching position without the benefit of a formal teacher education program and are unprepared to take on all of the responsibilities of being a teacher.

The Purpose and Content of This Book

This book provides ways for you to work on the development of your teaching and classroom practices. It offers ways that you, as an EFL or ESL teacher, can develop your teaching through a process of exploration. This book also provides discussion on the different English teaching settings around the world and teaching issues associated within them. It also provides discussions, examples, and illustrations of how EFL/ESL can be taught as interaction among people; how classrooms can be managed; how teachers and students can make use of authentic teaching materials, media, and technology; and the significance of culture for both students and teachers. In addition, this book shows how EFL/ESL teachers teach students to comprehend spoken English, to converse in English, to read for meaning, and to process writing.

This book is based on questions EFL/ESL teachers, including myself, have asked about teaching and learning over a number of years, and each chapter begins with a set of questions related to the content of that chapter. As such, one way to use this book as a part of your development is as a reference for ideas based on the questions posed at the beginning of each chapter and answered within it. This book also has a list of recommended sources at the end of each chapter and includes references to professional books and articles as well as EFL/ESL textbooks. The appendixes contain information on publishing companies and academic and practical journals on teaching EFL/ESL. These additional sources will help further your own development as an EFL/ESL teacher.

The end of each chapter includes a set of self-development tasks that are an integral part of this book. The purpose of these tasks is to offer opportunities to work on your development as an EFL/ESL teacher by observing, talking about, and writing about teaching. I encourage you to spend time on these tasks. I realize that finding the time to do these tasks is not necessarily easy because of busy teaching schedules. However, I encourage you to find the time to systematically think about your teaching in new ways and to stretch your imaginations through the teacher development tasks.

I want to point out that this book is not, and was never meant to be, a book that neatly fits into what is known as "reflective teaching." I point this out because one reviewer (Rodgers 1998) mistakenly reviewed the first edition of this book alongside two other books that are clearly within the "reflective teaching" category. The reviewer took issue with the book; as she put it, "A reflective book it is not" (p. 611). As the title tag *A Teacher Self-Development and Methodology*

Guide indicates, this book was created so that readers can work on their own development as teachers by understanding what other teachers, including me, believe about teaching and do in their classrooms. In short, reflection is an important part of learning to teach, and I do offer chances for teachers to reflect on teaching in this book. However, the focus of this book is much broader in scope than just reflection on teaching.

Comments about the Second Edition

My approach to this second edition was based primarily on feedback from readers, including those who took the time to write formal published reviews in journals, students in my TEFL/TESL Methodology class, and people I have met at conferences or online who offered feedback on the book. I have taken this feedback to heart, and I have done my best to incorporate what I have learned from you, the readers, into this edition.

The basic structure of the book has not changed. It still includes three parts. The first provides background to my understanding of self-development, as well as ways you, as teachers or prospective teachers, can explore teaching to work on your development. Part 2 still includes knowledge and experience related to teaching language, and Part 3 is about teaching language skills.

However, while maintaining the same three parts, I have used readers' feedback to make several changes in the book. To begin, I have added an additional chapter, EFL and ESL Teaching Settings (Chapter 3), to Part 1 to highlight the variety of teaching settings where English is taught around the world—teaching EFL in K–12 schools, in public language institutes, and in the private business sectors; and teaching ESL in such settings as K–12 schools, university intensive language programs, and in refugee programs. I have also revised Chapter 2, Exploration of Teaching, by providing a wider view of ways teachers work on the development of teaching beliefs and practices.

As with the first edition, Parts 2 and 3 include a variety of example activities, materials and media, and teaching strategies/ techniques for use in the classroom. However, in line with my discussion on teaching contexts, I include examples across a wider range of teaching settings, such as in K–12 ESL, ESL intensive language institutes, Peace Corps, and university EFL classrooms.

The second edition maintains the use of the discussion on exploration of teaching from Chapter 2 by providing teacher self-development tasks at the end of each chapter. I have also updated and expanded the Recommended Teacher Resources sections at the end of each chapter so that interested readers can locate up-to-date articles and books to help them to continue to develop their skills. Likewise, I have updated the information on journals and on publishing companies in Appendixes A and B. The endnotes for each chapter have also been updated and expanded.

As the world becomes ever-more technologically advanced and teachers need to make use of modern technology, discussions of technology have been added throughout the book. In Chapter 6, EFL/ESL Materials, Media, and Technology, I include a technology continuum related to teaching, which ranges from very low technology (e.g., writing in the air or using sticks to write on the ground), traditional technology (e.g., using chalk and blackboards and paper and pencils), to electrical technology (e.g., overhead projectors, VCRs, audio-cassette players and radios) through very modern technology (e.g., satellite television, high-speed Internet, and e-mail). Of course, not all teachers and students have access to high technology, and it's important to note that high technology does not equal a more advanced culture or better learning opportunities. Any technology can be useful to teachers depending on how they use it. Examples are provided as to how teachers in different settings can make use of different levels of technology. In addition, the chapters on teaching language skills include ways teachers can make use of modern technology, including examples of creative activities.

Part 1

Self-Development, Exploration, and Settings

Teachers themselves . . . must become the primary shapers of their own development.

—Lieberman 1992, vi

The Self-Developed Language Teacher

- Does self-development make a difference?
- What factors are central to teacher self-development?

Does Self-Development Make a Difference?

To emphasize the concept of self-development, I begin this book by illustrating its advantages. To do this, I invite you to enter two different EFL classrooms. The first is the classroom of a teacher (Yoshi) who has not had the opportunity to work on the development of his teaching. The second is that of a teacher (Kathy) who has taken on the responsibility for her own development. I emphasize that both teachers can gain much by paying regular attention to their teaching and aspects of how they teach.

Yoshi's Class

After attending high school in the United States and earning bachelor's and master's degrees in geography from an American university,

Yoshi accepted a position with a corporation in Japan, his home country, where he has been employed for the past six months. Because of his strong language skills, his job includes editing and translating letters, contracts, and other documents in English. A second part of his job is to teach English to two groups of business people for 90 minutes three mornings each week as part of an education program for company employees. These students range from intermediate through advanced levels. Yoshi enjoys the editing and translating part of his job. However, he has become a little discouraged with his responsibilities as an EFL teacher. Let's take a look inside one of his classes.

Nine men and two women are in class today and sit at a conference table. Yoshi, in his usual lockstep fashion, begins by telling them to open their books to page 52. The text covers topics about contemporary world issues, such as world hunger, population control, and drug trafficking. The class is on Chapter 4, which is about the plight of refugees around the world. As he did with the first three chapters, Yoshi reads the introductory paragraphs aloud. After he finishes, he asks the students if they have any questions, and as usual, there aren't any questions.

He then plays a tape that accompanies the text, a short lecture about the common problems refugees have. When the lecture ends, Yoshi reads questions from the text to the class about the content of the tape. He asks, "What's one of the problems refugees have in common?" One student gives the response, "They are hungry." Yoshi smiles and says, "Very good. What's another problem?" The students willingly answer his questions, and all use English.

Next, Yoshi turns to a reading activity in the same chapter. As he had done with earlier chapters, he asks each student to read aloud from the text. As they do, Yoshi stops them to correct their pronunciation. After each student reads, Yoshi paraphrases the meaning and explains vocabulary words to them. Some students write down their understanding of the meaning in Japanese.

When they finish, Yoshi asks the students to answer the text comprehension questions about the reading selection, and a few of the students answer his questions while the rest sit silently or look up words in their bilingual dictionaries. Yoshi expands on each of the answers, sometimes offering Japanese translation. At the end of the hour, he gives a homework assignment to memorize words in the Expand Your Vocabulary section of their textbook.

After the students leave, Yoshi reflects on the class. He is happy that he uses English most of the time and that the majority of the students are willing to speak English with him and seem quite content with the class. However, he feels frustrated that the students told him that they did not have time to prepare for class and do not ask questions. He also is disheartened because he rarely breaks from his routine way of stepping through each section of the text and because he ends up summarizing the content of the tapes and text, doing nearly all of the talking in class. Except for a few golden moments, the only time the students talk is when he introduces grammar and pronunciation drills or directly asks them questions. He realizes that his Geography degrees have not prepared him to be a language teacher, and he wonders how he might change his way of teaching. As he leaves the classroom, he considers the idea of going to the bookstore to look for books on teaching English.

Kathy's Class

Kathy graduated from college with a bachelor's degree in history. Before going on to graduate school, she wanted to gain some life experience, contribute something of herself to others, and visit places she had read about in her history books. Kathy was lucky enough to be selected as a Peace Corps volunteer and was sent to Hungary to teach English. After her initial intensive training in aspects of cultural assimilation, language, and EFL teaching in Hungary, she was sent to teach EFL at a high school in an industrial town where she is presently the only volunteer.

The class we will consider here is titled Fourth-Year English. The students in this class are considered to be fairly advanced and have gained a fairly high level of competence in using English. They seem to enjoy Kathy's lessons, which usually combine listening, speaking, reading, and writing.

Kathy raced to the classroom five minutes early to put pictures on the wall of people using various gestures and to put this message on the board:

> Study the pictures on the wall. What do you think the gestures mean? Feel free to talk with your neighbor, but be sure to speak in English.

She did this for two reasons. First, she is bothered by how long it usually takes to begin class. Second, she wants to explore how she can get students to speak English spontaneously with each other. Her objective on this day is to see if students would silently read the message on the blackboard, study the pictures, and start to talk in English.

As students enter the classroom, they are chatting in Hungarian. But they soon see Kathy pointing to the message, and they silently read it. Before long the class fills with talk, but Kathy has mixed feelings. A few of the students are using English, but others continue to use Hungarian. Kathy gets their attention and points to a picture of a man with a wrinkled brow and wide eyes, who is tilting his head and shrugging his shoulders. She asks, "How about this picture? What does this gesture possibly mean?" One student volunteers, "It mean 'I don't know'?" Kathy accepts this and goes on to the next picture. After the students give their interpretations, Kathy tells the class they will spend the next few class periods considering their own and others' nonverbal behaviors—such as eye contact, gestures, and the use of space—as well as different ways to express meaning in different cultures.

Kathy then has students select pieces of hard candy from a bag, telling the students with the cherry flavor to form a group in the back, those with lemon to group to the right, those with grape in the front, and those with lime to the left. After the students settle, she gives each group a set of statements about nonverbal behavior and asks them to decide if they are true or false. The students are silent at first as they study such statements as, "During a conversation in Japan, the proper place to focus one's eyes is on the neck of one's conversation partner, while in Saudi Arabia it is proper to gaze directly into the person's eyes."

As they work on this task, Kathy circulates among the groups. She does not tell them the answers, even when they coax her. The room is full of laughter, but Kathy also notices that students are speaking more than the usual amount of Hungarian today. She also notices their English language errors and wonders how she might give students more feedback on their language use.

Kathy next gets their attention and goes through the list of statements. Students ask her questions and react to each other's opinions. In the end, they discover that all the statements are true. One student claims she has tricked them.

Kathy then hands out a short article on nonverbal behavior she learned about at a workshop for language teachers. She tells the students to read the first three paragraphs silently, after which she has a student volunteer to paraphrase the meaning. The article is about kinesics (the study of gestures, eye contact, and posture). She then passes out five small gold stars to each student. The students are instructed to read the article twice and to paste the stars during their second reading next to ideas in the reading they find most interesting. Kathy tells the students that they cannot use a dictionary for this activity and that they should try to guess the meaning of an unfamiliar word from the context. She points out that if they are stumped, they can call on her, as she jokingly calls herself a "walking dictionary."

As Kathy walks out of the class, she has mixed feelings about the lesson. Her exploration with the message and pictures seemed somewhat successful; she started the class quickly, and some of the students used English. The students also stayed on task during the class, and they appeared to enjoy it. But many of the students used Hungarian during group work. She was also concerned that she did not give them feedback on their language. "Perhaps if I gave them more feedback, they'd want to use more English," she murmured to herself.

Comparison between Yoshi's and Kathy's Teaching

As you've undoubtedly noticed, there are some obvious differences between Yoshi's and Kathy's styles of teaching. While Yoshi goes through his lessons in a more or less "lockstep" fashion, mostly following the text, Kathy designs her own lessons and brings innovative ideas into her teaching. Yoshi follows a course program in which he leads into a topic with a tape, followed by a reading selection, comprehension questions, another reading, and discussion questions. He rarely breaks from the step-by-step progression in the course text, even when he senses the students are not showing interest or comprehending the content. He does his best to explain the meaning of the text, but he does not break from it. Nor does he engage the students in negotiating the meaning of the text with him or each other. He is the center of the lesson and all instruction. He feels secure in having the text to follow, and although at some level he senses that his lessons could be greatly different, he does not break away from his lockstep way of teaching.

In contrast, Kathy doesn't seem to rely on one way of teaching. Rather than making herself the center of attention, she consciously looks for ways to make the class a community of learners in which students feel free to communicate with each other in English, to ask her and classmates real questions, and to assume some of the responsibility for their own learning. She is trying to focus the learning on the students.

In recognizing these differences, it is worth asking why Kathy explores creative ways to teach while Yoshi does not. One reason is likely because Kathy went through an intensive Peace Corps training program. But this training was relatively brief, and it was meant only to acquaint her with what EFL teachers do in the classroom. Perhaps cultural background has something to do with the difference? Kathy is a native speaker of English who comes from America, while Yoshi has the same native language and cultural background as the students. Although the students want Yoshi, a near-native speaker of English, to use English with them in class, they might be hesitant to speak up in English with someone who also shares the same language and cultural norms/values. It may also be difficult for Yoshi since he likely speaks Japanese with these same people when they are not in class.

The setting may also be a factor. Yoshi teaches in a corporate world, a setting where in many cases students' business responsibilities take precedence over English classes and homework assignments and where students are not required to attend the classes. Kathy teaches at a high school where many of the students are quite motivated to learn English (and other languages).

However, perhaps the most significant reason for the differences is the way they approach their development as teachers. While Kathy is eager to take on the responsibility for her own development, Yoshi is now just realizing the need to do this. Just what has Kathy done to work on her development? The answer is addressed next, as is the fact that although Kathy seems aware of her development, she can learn more about her teaching. As will be discussed in Chapter 2, she could learn to more systematically reflect and act on her reflections through observing herself and others, keeping a teaching journal, and engaging with others in talk about teaching.

What Factors Are Central to Teacher Self-Development?

Several factors affect teacher self-development. First, there is no doubt that development takes *time*. It takes time to observe interaction in our own classrooms and to visit other teachers' classes, as well as to write in a journal and to talk to others about teaching. Preservice teachers have an advantage in that the time factor is built into the teacher education program. Teachers in in-service programs or those working independently on their development have less time. Nonetheless, teachers who believe that development is important need to make a commitment to devote time to their development.

In addition, for teachers who are in the first few years of their teaching career, time is needed to work through stages in their development.[1] Kathy, for example, apparently allowed herself to work through these stages. She was not always confident or able to create and re-create relevant, interesting lessons for the students. The developmental stages of a teacher include going from being dependent on outside sources (such as supervisors and the textbook) and concerned with self-survival ("What do I do tomorrow in class?") and with what kinds of techniques to use, to being concerned with student learning and able to make informed teaching decisions.

Second, development requires an *ongoing commitment*. Development teaching is not something to do only in a teacher education program or at the beginning of a teaching career. Rather, even the most experienced teacher can learn new things about teaching, and development is enhanced when the teacher makes a commitment to ongoing development. For example, although many would call Kathy's teaching skills developed, she continues to think about her teaching and its consequences on students, especially about creating a more learner-centered classroom that engages students in learning to be communicatively competent in English.

Third, development is enhanced through *problem solving*. When teachers recognize problems and work at solving them, they can discover new ways to teach and discover more about about their role as a teacher. For example, Kathy's exploration into getting the class started quickly and her interest in getting students to use more English in class indicate that she continues to generate ways to solve perceived problems in her teaching.

Fourth, development is also enhanced through *exploration for exploration's sake*. Teachers can, indeed, discover much by exploring simply to explore, not just to solve a problem. Such exploration can be based on pure interest—for example, trying an approach that is the opposite of one you love simply to see what happens, or trying a new approach/technique simply because it sounds interesting.[2]

Fifth, development is enhanced by *paying attention to and reviewing the basics of EFL/ESL teaching*. Although Kathy's introduction to the basics began during her Peace Corps training, she has continued to study ways to create opportunities for students to interact in English; ways to manage classroom behavior; and materials and media used to teach EFL. In addition, she undoubtedly considered ways to teach different skills, such as reading, writing, listening, and speaking.

Sixth, development is enhanced by *searching out opportunities* to develop. It turns out that Kathy talks with other teachers about teaching; she reads about teaching; she attends teaching seminars and workshops; and she participates in other activities that give her chances to reflect on her teaching and see new teaching possibilities. In other words, when we, as teachers, teach lessons in different settings, read about teaching, observe our own and others' teaching, write about teaching, and talk about teaching issues and problems, we are provided with opportunities to raise new questions about our teaching, as well as ways to search for answers to these questions. The more activities we experience related to teaching, and the more questions and answers we can come up with through this ongoing process, the more chances we have to develop our teaching beliefs and practices.[3]

Seventh, self-development of teaching beliefs and practices *requires the cooperation of others*.[4] It takes others who are willing to observe us, listen to us, and talk with us about our teaching. We need administrators, students, other teachers, and friends to help us succeed with our development. Without their cooperation, self-development is very difficult as there is neither any source for feedback nor any stimulus for ideas.

TEACHER SELF-DEVELOPMENT TASKS

These tasks can be an integral part of your development as an EFL/ESL teacher. Although some can be done alone, it is to your advantage to gain the cooperation of others. If you are using this book as part of a pre-service or in-service teacher education program, it will be easy to attain the support of other teachers. If you are reading this book on your own, I encourage you to seek out others who will read this book and work on the self-development tasks with you. If you are not yet teaching and are using this book as a way to learn about the field, it will not be possible to do all of the tasks. However, there will still be many you can do, such as the journal tasks.

Talk Tasks

1. What does self-development mean to you? What kinds of things do you believe you can do to work on your development as a teacher? Ask another EFL/ESL teacher these same questions. Discuss what self-development means and the steps you can take to work on your own development.

2. Read this quote from Maxine Greene's work. Do you agree? What does she mean? Talk with other teachers who have thought about her words.

> If the teacher agrees to submerge himself into the system, if he consents to being defined by others' views of what he is supposed to be, he gives up his freedom to see, to understand, and to signify for himself. If he is immersed and impermeable, he can hardly stir others to define themselves as individuals. If, on the other hand, he is willing . . . to create a new perspective on what he has habitually considered real, his teaching may become the project of a person vitally open to his students and the world. . . . He will be continuously engaged in interpreting a reality forever new; he will feel more alive than he ever has before. (Greene 1973, 270)

3. Draw up a plan to work on your development as a teacher. Here are a few questions to get you started. Compare your plans with those of another EFL/ESL teacher who has made a plan. Would you revise your plan based on this discussion? If so, how?

    a. Are you ready to work on your teaching development? How strongly do you want to expand your knowledge of teaching and learn how to explore your teaching beliefs and practices?
    b. How much time are you willing to invest in your development as a language teacher? Can you make a tentative schedule of the time you can devote to this undertaking?
    c. Thumb through this book. Study the contents and the list of questions at the beginning of each chapter. What areas of teaching are you interested in developing right now? What questions capture your interest?
    d. How will you read this book? Will you selectively read chapters? Use the index? Use the questions at the start of each chapter as a way to decide on what to read?
    e. How will you get others involved in your process of development?

Journal Writing Tasks

1. Purchase a notebook that you can easily carry around with you and that has ample space for writing.

2. Write freely in your notebook about what self-development means to you.
3. Create in writing a plan for working on your development. What kinds of things do you plan to do to work on your development as a teacher?

Recommended Teacher Resources

Directory on Professional TESOL Preparation Programs
Directory of Teacher Education Programs in TESOL in the United States and Canada. Alexandria, VA: TESOL, 2005.

Edited Books on Teachers' Experiences in the Classroom
Johnson, K. E., and P. R. Golombek, eds. *Teachers' Narrative Inquiry.* New York: Cambridge University Press, 2002.
Farrell, T. S. C. *Reflecting on Classroom Communication in Asia.* Singapore: Pearson Education, 2004.
Freeman, D., and J. C. Richards, eds. *Teacher Learning in Language Teaching.* New York: Cambridge University Press, 1996.
Richards, J. C., ed. *Teaching in Action: Case Studies from Second Language Classrooms.* Alexandria, VA: TESOL, 1998.

An Inspiring Book
Clarke, M. A. *A Place To Stand: Essays for Educators in Troubled Times.* Ann Arbor: University of Michigan Press, 2003.

Endnotes

[1] Research by Bullough and Baughman (1993), Calderhead (1988), and Fuller and Brown (1975) shows that teachers need time to develop their teaching abilities. Research by Fuller (1969) and Fuller and Brown (1975) suggests that teachers move through stages from self-survival to making informed teaching decisions. Recent research in second language teaching points out how little we know about teachers' thinking in relation to their classroom practices during stages of their development. However, there is some effort (Johnson 1992; Johnson and Golombek 2002; Nunan 1992; Richards 1998; Richards, Li, and Tang 1998) to discover more about the development of teachers' beliefs and thoughts in relation to their teaching decisions and practices.

[2] Fanselow (1987, 1988, 1992a, 1992b) elaborates on how teachers can "try the opposite" as a way to explore their teaching. For

example, if a teacher always teaches from the front of the class-room, she could try teaching from the back. If she always has students read aloud from the text, she could ask them to read silently.

3 My research into teacher development (Gebhard 1990; Gebhard, Gaitan, and Oprandy 1987; Gebhard and Oprandy 1999; Gebhard and Ueda-Motonaga 1992) shows that when teachers have opportunities to process their teaching through a variety of activities, they will explore and sometimes change their way of teaching.

4 Edge (2002) and Fanselow (1988, 1992a) also point out that without the cooperation of others, self-development is difficult.

As we explore, rather than seeking prescriptions and judgments from others, rules [can be] broken that say we teachers must seek alternatives from those in charge, rather than ourselves or our peers, and that we must work alone within our autonomous but isolated and lonely classrooms, rather than with colleagues.

—Fanselow 1987, 7

Exploration of Teaching

- What are ways to explore teaching?
- How can teachers explore teaching through self-observation?
- How can teachers explore their own teaching through the observation of other teachers?
- How can teachers explore teaching through talk?
- How can teachers explore teaching through a teacher journal?
- How does this book provide opportunities for EFL and ESL teachers to explore teaching?

What Are Ways to Explore Teaching?

Some of the ways we, as teachers, can explore our teaching beliefs and practices follow. In this section I briefly discuss these ways,[1] after which I go into more detail on a few ways in particular—the observation of other teachers, self-observation, talking to other teachers, and keeping a teacher journal.

Ways to Explore Teaching

- Read journal articles and books about teaching and learning.
- Read teacher narratives.
- Attend professional conferences.
- Establish a mentoring relationship.
- Put together a teaching portfolio.
- Learn another language.
- Do action research.
- Do self-observation.
- Observe other teachers.
- Talk with other teachers.
- Keep a teacher journal.

One rather obvious way we can develop our teaching is to read professional books and journals on teaching and learning languages. Reading this book, for example, will help you gain knowledge about ESL and EFL teaching. In addition to single-author books, many anthologies are available, and a few are listed in the Recommended Teacher Resources section at the end of Chapter 4. These anthologies cover a variety of topics relevant to the field. For example, *Methodology in Language Teaching: An Anthology of Current Practice*[2] includes chapters by different authors on such topics as lesson planning, classroom management, mixed-level teaching, cooperative learning, task-based language teaching, project work, learning strategies, technologies in the classroom, assessment, and professional development, as well as on teaching pronunciation, vocabulary, grammar, listening, speaking, reading, and writing.

Recently a number of anthologies have been published on teachers' own teaching and learning experiences. For example, *Teachers' Narrative Inquiry as Professional Development*, edited by Karen Johnson and Paula Golombek,[3] includes a collection of highly personal narratives by teachers who inquired about their own experiences in learning to teach. They offer other teachers, especially those new to teaching, glimpses into the realities of teaching. Another anthology, edited by Jack Richards,[4] is *Teaching in Action: Case Studies from Second Language Classrooms*. This book includes 76 case studies written by teachers on topics ranging from teaching in K–12 mainstream programs; affective factors in the classroom; teaching mixed levels and abilities; and teaching writing, speaking, reading, vocabulary, and grammar.

Another way to work on development of our teaching and ourselves as teachers is to attend professional conferences. Thousands of ESL and EFL teachers attend the annual International TESOL Convention, which is usually held in a different major North American city each year. Each state has a TESOL chapter too, and annual—or sometimes semiannual—local conferences are held. These are good opportunities to hear what teachers in your own area are doing in their classrooms, and good opportunities to present your own techniques or action research. It is also possible to attend one of the worldwide affiliate conferences attached to International TESOL. These regional affiliate conferences vary in size from several thousand to a few hundred participants, depending on location. Likewise, the International Association of Teachers of English as a Foreign Language (IATEFL) hosts an international conference, usually in a European country. Participants who attend this conference come from more than 100 different countries. A smaller conference, but of very high quality, is held annually by the American Association of Applied Linguistics (AAAL). Those who attend are usually scholars (including teachers) who are interested in the multi-disciplinary field of applied linguistics. Presentations are on topics such as literacy, discourse analysis, language acquisition, language assessment, foreign and second language pedagogy, and language policy and planning. To learn more about the professional organization TESOL, log on to *www.tesol.org.* To learn more about IATEFL, log on to *www.iatefl.org.* To discover more about AAAL, log on to *www.aaal.org.*

Another way to explore our teaching is through establishing a mentoring relationship with another teacher. Mentoring is sometimes thought of as a new approach to development for language teachers, but in fact, mentoring has a long history.[5] As Eisenman and Thornton point out, "mentoring actually goes back thousands of years to Homer's epic poem, the *Odyssey.*"[6] The concept of mentoring has certainly changed from the days of a wise old sea captain giving guidance to Odysseus's son, Telemachus. Today mentoring is "an interpersonal, ongoing, situated, supportive, and informative professional relationship between two (or more) individuals, one of whom (the mentor) has more experience in the profession, craft, or skill in question."[7]

A teaching portfolio is another additional way to explore and develop our teaching. Some ESL and EFL teacher preparation programs ask graduating students to put together a portfolio so that these teachers reflect on what they have learned in the program and have a collection of work that can be included with job applications. Karen Johnson points out that putting together a portfolio helps teachers make sense of what they have learned, provides chances for them to think about teaching and learning, demonstrates their competencies, and recognizes the complexities of learning to teach.[8]

There are, of course, a number of documents that can be included in a portfolio.[9] Some include papers written for courses, class presentations, professional conference presentations, original teaching materials, reflective journal entries, video- or audiotapes of teaching, reflective observation reports, syllabi, letters of recommendation, reports on observations by others, evaluation reports, vitae, and a statement of teaching and learning philosophy.

Another way to explore our teaching as language teachers is to learn another language. Bailey, Curtis, and Nunan[10] point out several advantages to doing this: First, we can better understand the challenges that the learners face. Second, we can gain more insight into understanding language. Third, by assuming the role of learner, we can gain insight into ways of teaching that seem to work and don't work, at least within our language learning setting.

In Chapter 7, Culture and the Language Teacher, I discuss how native English speakers teaching in EFL settings can also gain deeper insight into the host culture, a way to develop friendships with people who don't speak English, and a much deeper awareness of their own culturally based values and ways of interacting.[11] Likewise, non-native English speakers who are visiting or studying in Australia, Britain, New Zealand, or the United States can benefit in many of the same ways from advanced language study and social interaction with native speakers.

Another approach teachers use to explore teaching is action research, an approach that centers on problem posing. The cyclic process includes posing problems based on what goes on in the teacher's classroom, within a school, or beyond; systematically working through the problem by creating and initiating a plan of action; reflecting on the degree to which the plan works; and then posing a new problem based on the awareness generated from the previous inquiry.[12]

During the past two decades, action research has become more and more popular among language teachers.[13] This form of research allows teachers to investigate and pose problems in their teaching, to work at solving these problems, and generally to gain more awareness of teaching and classroom interaction. This is especially true when teachers have chances to talk about their action research. Ann Burns, for example, has created a forum for teachers to talk about and collaborate on their action research projects in Australia at the local, regional, and national levels.[14] She explains that teachers report they gain much awareness of their teaching after participating in such forums. Likewise, journals have been publishing teachers' action research projects.[15] A number of books have been published for ESL and EFL teachers, such as *Action Research for Language Teachers* by Michael Wallace[16] and *Case Studies in Action Research,* edited by Julian Edge.[17]

Observation is another way to explore and develop our teaching, including observation of other teachers and self-observation. Talking with other teachers about the teaching we observe is also a way to explore new possibilities in our teaching, as is writing about teaching in a journal. I write about each of these four ways to explore our teaching in the sections that follow.

How Can Teachers Explore Teaching through Self-Observation?

As teachers, we can explore through a process of describing, analyzing, and reflecting on our teaching. In this regard, I have been influenced by the work of John Fanselow,[18] whose ideas I have adapted and changed in my own pursuit to gain deeper awareness of teaching.[19] To achieve this aim, I have created the following cyclic process of observation: The first step in the cycle is to collect descriptive samples of our teaching that can be analyzed. This is followed by reflection and multiple interpretations. The next step is to consider how the same lesson could be taught differently and to draw up a teaching plan. Then, by implementing the new plan, the cycle returns to the collection of samples of teaching. Let's take a closer look at each stage in the cycle.

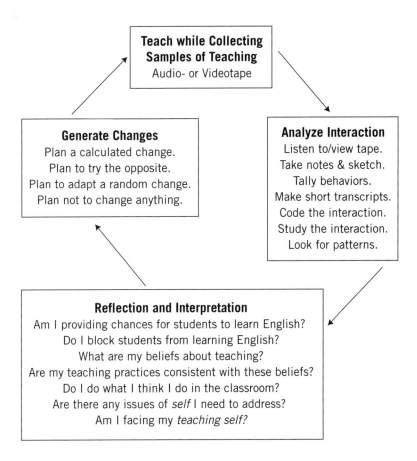

Teach while Collecting Samples of Teaching
Audio- or Videotape

Generate Changes
Plan a calculated change.
Plan to try the opposite.
Plan to adapt a random change.
Plan not to change anything.

Analyze Interaction
Listen to/view tape.
Take notes & sketch.
Tally behaviors.
Make short transcripts.
Code the interaction.
Study the interaction.
Look for patterns.

Reflection and Interpretation
Am I providing chances for students to learn English?
Do I block students from learning English?
What are my beliefs about teaching?
Are my teaching practices consistent with these beliefs?
Do I do what I think I do in the classroom?
Are there any issues of *self* I need to address?
Am I facing my *teaching self?*

Collecting Samples of Teaching

When you collect samples of teaching, you have descriptions of what actually goes on in the classroom that focus attention on some aspect of your teaching. To give you an idea of areas of teaching that can be described, see the chart on page 20 listing some of the exploratory questions teachers have asked. On the left are the initial descriptive questions. On the right are the questions aimed at understanding what happens when a change in teaching behavior is initiated.

Initial Descriptive Questions	Questions: Further Exploration
• How do I give instructions? What do students do after receiving the instructions? Start the task? Ask each other what to do? Ask the teacher to repeat the instructions?	• What happens when I change the way I give instructions, such as when I dictate them? Have students paraphrase them? Project them on an overhead?
• How often do students speak their native language in class? When? What do I do when they use it?	• What happens when I require students to only speak English? When they can't speak any English for ten minutes?
• What is the content of my questions? About study of language? People's lives in general? Students' personal lives? Procedures? Other?	• What happens when I increase the number of questions I ask about students' personal lives?
• How long do I wait after asking a question to get a response?	• What happens when I increase wait time?
• How do I praise students? What words do I use? What nonverbal behaviors? What student behaviors do I praise? How often do I praise?	• What happens when I don't praise students? When I only praise specific accomplishments?
• How much time do students stay on task? What do they do when off task? What triggers going off task?	• What happens when I add a time limit? Decrease time given to finish a task? Give no time limit?
• What are usual seating arrangements in my class?	• What happens when students sit in different seating arrangements?

To collect samples of teaching that address an aspect of classroom behavior it is to our advantage to audio- or videotape classroom interaction. To do this, I suggest you use a small audio-recorder or camcorder. The advantage of an audio-recorder is that it is easy to use. However, some teachers prefer to videotape because it is easy to recognize who is talking and possible to study nonverbal behaviors.

At first the audiorecorder or camcorder may be a novelty, and some students will change their behavior because they are being taped. But it really doesn't take long before students accept it and act normally. I have audio- and videotaped many classes, and it is amazing how fast students accept the recorder, especially if it is treated as a natural part of the classroom setting.

How taping is done often depends on the goals of exploration. For example, if you are interested in the students' reactions to instructions or explanations, the audiorecorder or camcorder can be focused on the students. If you are interested in what happens during group work, it is logical to place the audiorecorder or camcorder on a group of students for a period of time. The idea is to think about the objective of your exploration and to consider how to tape the class to obtain useful samples for later analysis.

Analyzing the Samples of Teaching

The second stage is to analyze the collected samples of teaching, and analysis also depends on the objective of your exploration. For example, if you are interested in knowing the number of questions you ask, you can listen to or view the tape and tally each question you ask, as well as jot down examples of actual questions. You can do the same thing for the number of errors you treat, the number of times students speak English or their native language, and the seconds you wait for students to answer a question.

A second way to analyze the collection of teaching samples is to make short transcripts from the audio- or videotapes. Again, what you decide to transcribe depends mainly on the focus of your exploration. For example, if you are interested in learning how you treat language errors, you might make and study short transcripts of the times errors are treated. If your interest is on learning about the accuracy of the students' language during group work, you can transcribe and study short sections of interaction among students during group work activities. A further step you can take in analyzing interaction is to code a transcript with a category system. Although I do not directly discuss such systems in this book, I recommend two: Communicative Orientation of Language Teaching (COLT) and Foci on Communications Used in Settings (FOCUS).[20]

While it is possible to have a particular focus when collecting and analyzing these descriptions, it is also possible to do the opposite, which I like to call *pure exploration*. Such exploration does not focus on a specific observation objective, but begins with an empty mind. For example, it is possible to tape a class and view the tape, and while doing this, make one-minute transcripts of classroom interaction five, ten, and 20 minutes into the class. These transcripts could then be studied simply to monitor what is happening and when. I think of such exploration as being similar to going for a walk. Usually we have objectives when going for a walk, such as walking to the bank or the grocery store. However, sometimes we can simply take a walk, randomly taking side streets or alleys just to see what is there; when we do this, we often see new things.

Interpreting and Reflecting

After analyzing, we make sense of the descriptions of classroom inter-action. To do this, we focus on several questions. One set of questions I like to ask includes: *How does the interaction in this class provide chances for students to learn the language?* and *How does the interaction possibly block students from learning the language?* Of course, I can narrow the question based on a particular interest. For example, if I am interested in error treatment and have analyzed the patterns of interaction around the treatment of students' oral errors, I can ask, *How does my way of treating students' language errors possibly provide chances for them to be more accurate in their use of English?* and *How does my way of treating their errors possibly hamper their accuracy?* Likewise, if my interest is in understanding my classroom behavior with regard to student talk and questioning behavior, after analyzing the patterns of interaction in the class between the students and me, I might ask, *How does my interaction with students possibly provide chances for them to talk in class, initiate interaction, and ask questions?* and *How does my interaction with them possibly interfere with students' chances to talk, initiate interaction, and ask questions?*

I also ask this set of questions: *What are my beliefs about teaching?* and *Are my teaching practices consistent with these beliefs?* Although it is not necessarily easy to answer these questions, it is well worth the effort. It is possible to give a comprehensive answer to the first ques-tion, taking into consideration theory and research in different fields, such as in second language acquisition, intercultural communication, and sociolinguistics.[21] It is, of course, also possible to narrow the questions to specific aspects of teaching. For example, we can ask, *What are my beliefs about treating students' language errors?* and *Are my teaching practices consistent with my beliefs?*

Reflection can also include this question: *Do I do what I think I do in the classroom?* I have found that most teachers are surprised by the answer to this question. It is not until they have had a chance to describe their teaching and think about it that they realize that what they believe they are doing does not always match what they think they are doing. For example, later in this chapter (pages 28–29) I give an example of how my teaching partner and I realized that the stu-dents in our team-taught class were not aware that we were treating their oral errors although we thought that we were! Likewise, I give an example of a teacher who thought that she was motivating the students by offering praise, while in reality the students were not paying attention to the praise.

Finally, I like to ask this set of questions: *Are there any issues of self I need to address?* and *Am I facing my teaching self?* There are a wide range of issues that teachers might not want to face, more than I can possibly write about here. One example is that some teachers avoid certain issues that trigger negative feelings, such as disciplining students or becoming personally involved in troubled students' lives. Another example is the teacher who struggled in facing the realization that not all students appreciate or accept his friendly, highly personal way of interacting with them.

Jersild points out in *When Teachers Face Themselves* that to gain knowledge of ourselves, we need to find the courage to seek it, as well as the humility to accept what we discover.[22] Such exploration of the self is not easy for some teachers. But, such exploration can be well worth the effort.

Deciding on Changes in Teaching Behavior

The next stage in the exploration cycle is to decide which changes we want to make in our teaching through such questions as: *What do I want to continue to do?* and *What small changes do I want to make in my teaching behavior?* Here I agree with John Fanselow, who has observed that small changes can have big consequences.[23]

One reason to change the way we teach is to solve a problem: Students don't talk; instructions aren't clear; students speak their native language too much. For example, if some students aren't talking during whole-class discussions, the teacher might try group work to see if these students will talk with classmates. If the teacher discovers that students are not understanding instructions when they are given orally, the teacher might write them on the board or on an overhead.

Problem-solving is the usual way that teachers make decisions about what to change in their teaching. However, it is also possible to explore teaching simply to see what happens. This could include doing the opposite of what we usually do or trying something we have never tried before. For example, even if the students understand the oral instructions, it is still possible to write them down and let students read them just to see what happens. If most of our questions are from the text, we can ask questions that are not in the text. There are endless opposite possibilities!

Based on the changes we decide to make, whether calculated to solve a problem or be creative by trying the opposite, the idea is to continue the cycle of exploration while again collecting samples of teaching through audio or video recordings.

**What Teachers Have Done: Examples
of the Observation Process**

The first example illustrates what an ESL teacher did to explore the way she gave instructions.[24] The teacher videotaped her teaching and made short transcripts focusing on how she gave instructions and on what the students did afterward. She discovered that her oral instructions took about two minutes and that many of the students did not understand them. During the start of a group activity, for example, some students asked each other—some in their native language—what they were supposed to be doing. Two students finally asked her to explain the task again. She ended up going from group to group to explain the instructions, and it took five additional minutes before the students were all working on the task.

She reflected on her way of giving instructions and decided that she was not giving the students ample opportunity to comprehend them and was taking up too much class time to clarify them. However, she also saw some value in giving vague instructions; students were given chances to negotiate meaning with her, and to do this, they had to express their ideas in English. To explore different ways she could give instructions and after talking with another teacher for some ideas, she decided to try a few different things, each on different days, and she taped and analyzed what happened when she used these alternative techniques. One day she wrote the instructions on the board and presented them orally. On another day, she dictated the instructions, and on the third day she had students paraphrase the instructions back to her. Through her analysis, she discovered that all three ways worked for this particular class. Although it took longer to give the instructions, students displayed less confusion and began the task soon after the instructions were given. In addition, she discovered that it was possible to turn instructions into a language learning activity.

Another example is the EFL teacher who explored her praise behaviors with pre–teen children.[25] After audio-taping the class, she listened to the tape and tallied the number of times she praised students; she also noted samples of language she used to praise them.

She discovered that she verbalized *very good* quite often, and she identified her frequent use of *very good* as being ambiguous to the students. Because she praised them so often, and sometimes even when they gave wrong responses, she wondered if students knew she was praising them or if they were accepting the praise as empty gestures. She also considered why she praised students and decided that praise was important for them. When genuine, praise can be a motivating factor. But, if students cannot distinguish when and why they are being praised, then it is useless. As such, she decided to implement small changes in her praising techniques. For example, she monitored her use of praise and verbally expressed it *only when* she was genuinely impressed. When students submitted written work, she put happy-face stickers on their work, but *only when* their work was considered outstanding.

After taping and analyzing her praise behaviors again, she knew that she used praise far less frequently and usually at times when students met her high expectations. She also analyzed the quality of the students' written work, and she concluded, after two months, that their work was genuinely improving. Some students even told her that they try harder because they want to see a happy face on their written work.

The next example is from my own teaching. While teaching an American literature course in Hungary, I wondered about the way I used questions in class. To better understand my questioning behaviors, I designed a tally sheet. I audio-taped my class and using the tally sheet, I kept track of the targets of my questions (e.g., to an individual student or the whole class) and the content of each question (e.g., about students' lives, about people and places in general, about language, or about the content of the reading selection). The tally sheet shows what I found.[26]

Tally Sheet: Content and Target of Teacher Questions		
Content of Questions	To Individual	To Whole Class
Questions: Student lives	II	
Questions: People & places		ⅢⅠ ⅢⅠ III
Questions: Language	I	ⅢⅠ II
Questions: Material content		ⅢⅠ I

During my analysis, I discovered that I asked 28 questions during a 25-minute time period; that most of my questions were addressed to the whole class; and that 12 of my questions were about general places and people, 8 about language, and 6 directly about the content of the reading.

Upon reflection, I was not surprised that I asked mostly whole-class questions. However, I was surprised that I averaged more than one question per minute. This discovery was very useful. First, it gave me the chance to reflect on my questioning behavior. As a part of my reflection, I thought about how discussions go on outside classrooms, how all the participants not only answer questions but also ask them and react to each other's responses. Second, I was able to see that my questioning techniques dominated class discussion and prevented students from raising their own questions and reacting to responses. Third, I was able to systematically modify my questioning behavior. In the next seminar, while audio-taping, I consciously asked fewer questions and attempted to achieve more discussion based on a single question. Also, after a student responded to one of my questions, I remained silent or said *uh-huh* in an encouraging way while looking at the other students. If no one reacted or asked a question, I paraphrased what was just said.

After audio-taping and analyzing this second seminar, I discovered that I asked fewer questions, that students asked each other questions, and that students reacted to the responses of others. In short, I was able to achieve my objective—to have students discuss a reading selection in their foreign language.

The preceding examples illustrate how teachers have worked through problem areas in their teaching, but this final example shows how a teacher explored her teaching simply to explore.[27] The teacher, a native Japanese speaker, was teaching an introductory class in Japanese as a Foreign Language to American university students. She was interested in exploring her teaching simply to discover patterns in her teaching behavior, so she audio-taped her class, transcribed short segments of the class, and studied them for recurring patterns of interaction.

She discovered certain patterns of interaction in her classes. She found that most of her teaching consisted of drills and that she followed a lockstep way of teaching. The class was teacher-centered: She asked all the questions, the students responded, and she reacted to these responses. She also reflected on the fact that she asked display questions (e.g., questions for which she already knew the answers) and that the content of the lessons mostly concerned the study of language (i.e., learning about language rather than using language for a communicative purpose).

Based on the patterns of interaction reflected in her classroom, the teacher decided that students did not have ample opportunities to communicate in their foreign language in class. As such, she decided to make a small change in her teaching by doing the opposite of what she usually did. Instead of drilling students on language points, she planned to ask them questions about their lives. She knew that some students were going on a trip to a nearby city, and she decided to ask them about their trip in the foreign language. As an afterthought, she brought a map of the city to class. She then audio-taped her teaching while posing these "life-personal" questions in Japanese and then transcribed parts of the class.

Classroom interaction changed dramatically. Students asked each other questions and reacted to each other's comments. The teacher and students asked questions that they did not know the answers to before asking them. This type of query was not evident in the interaction in the earlier class.

What brought about this change in the interaction? The teacher's purpose was to do the opposite of what she normally did, to ask personal questions to see if the interaction would change in her class, and she did begin her lesson by asking personal questions about where a student went on spring break. According to her analysis, this change was most likely a part of the reason why student interactions changed. However, she also had students show her exactly where they went by using the map. This map also had the apparent consequence (which the teacher was surprised to discover) of allowing the interaction to shift from asking and answering personal questions to studying the map itself. In short, the teacher interpreted the reason for the emergence of student questions and reactions to be the combination of asking personal questions and using the map. It is interesting that the teacher had not predicted that the map itself would contribute to this change in the pattern. This discovery was quite incidental, and such discoveries are one reason to explore teaching.

My purpose in giving these examples of self-observation has been to demonstrate how teachers can explore their own teaching. However, exploration does not have to be limited to looking at what goes on in one's own classroom. It is also possible to explore teaching by observing other teachers' classrooms, the topic of the next section.

How Can Teachers Explore Their Own Teaching through the Observation of Other Teachers?

At first the idea that we can explore our own teaching by observing other teachers may seem contradictory. However, as John Fanselow points out, we can see our own teaching in the teaching of others. When we observe others to gain knowledge of self, we have the chance to construct and reconstruct our own knowledge. Fanselow articulates this in another way: "I came to your class not only with a magnifying glass to look carefully at what was being done, but with a mirror so that I could see that what you were doing is a reflection of much of what I do."[28]

While observing other teachers, it is possible to collect samples of teaching in a variety of ways. We can take fast notes, draw sketches, tally behaviors, and note short transcript-like samples of interaction. As with collecting samples in our own classes, it is possible to audio- or videotape other teachers' classes and photograph interaction. These tapes can be used later to analyze classroom behaviors. I want to point out that I encourage observers and the observed teacher to meet to look at photos, listen to tapes, view videos, study short transcripts, and talk about the class. By doing so, exploration is enhanced for all. The examples that follow and my later discussion (see pages 30–31) on the value of talking about teaching should clarify this point.

Observing Others to Explore One's Own Teaching: Some Examples

This first example involves collaboration between my teaching partner and me. My partner showed consistent interest in error treatment and wanted to gain more awareness of how she treated students' errors. As such, I audiotaped her class and transcribed short segments that centered on how she treated students' language errors. Here's one of these short transcripts:[29]

> *Student:* I have only two sister.
> *Teacher:* Uh-huh.
> *Student:* I have no brother.
> *Teacher:* Two sisters?
> *Student:* Because my mother she dead when I was three years old.
> *Teacher:* She died when you were three?
> *Student:* Yes. She dead when I was three years old.

My partner and I later met to talk, and she was delighted (and a little surprised) to see the way she treated errors. She used rising intonation (i.e., when she asked, "Two sisters?") or asked questions while emphasizing the word she was correcting (as in "She **died** when you were three?"). After appraising her treatment techniques, she decided that the students most likely did not know she was even treating their errors. Instead, they focused on meaning. As a part of our discussion, she also raised a concern over whether or not treating errors was useful. However, at the same time, students were asking her to treat their language errors, and she wanted to comply. As such, she decided that if she did treat the errors, she could at least do so in a way in which the students were aware of being corrected. She read about and discussed error treatment, and subsequently designed and implemented alternative ways to treat errors.

My partner obviously gained awareness from more clearly seeing her way of treating errors, and through the process of observing (and talking) with my partner, I also had the chance to reflect on my own beliefs and techniques for treating errors. I was able to see my teaching in hers; I realized that I often treated errors similarly, and that most likely, students were not especially aware that I was treating specific language errors. By audiotaping and analyzing my teaching, I was able to reconfirm this reflection and develop new ways to treat students' errors.

The second example of the value of observing others teach involves a teacher in Japan who wanted to explore the use of photography as a way to observe teaching.[30] He and I were invited to observe a class at a private language school for young children, and he decided to take his camera. He was able to move freely around the classroom while the students and teacher went about their lesson; as a second observer, I was impressed by the way he was able to fit into the natural flow of the classroom interaction in an unobtrusive way. Surprisingly, after the first few snapshots, the children hardly paid any attention to him.

Later, he created a photographic essay of the classroom interaction, and while looking at the photos with the teacher, he was able to reflect on his own teaching. For example, he noticed how spontaneously the children spoke up in English and wondered how he could get students in his high school EFL class to do this. As a second observer, I was also able to see my teaching in that of the photographed teacher; as I studied the photos, I was impressed by the great number of activities the teacher did with the students, each leading naturally into the next, and I wondered how I could design lessons to do this in my own classes.

How Can Teachers Explore Teaching through Talk?

Talking about teaching can offer chances to learn about and reflect on our own teaching. Talking can indeed be useful. Unfortunately, talking about teaching is not something that normally goes on among EFL/ESL teachers, and when it does, it seems to take on a face-saving nature. As Paul Arcario[31] points out, the way conversations about teaching normally take place begins with the observer giving an opening evaluative remark, such as, "I liked your class." This is followed by a three-step evaluative sequence. In the first step of the sequence a positive or negative evaluation is made, such as "I think the students are talking a lot" (positive) or "Maybe the students don't have enough chances to speak" (negative). These comments lead to a second step, justification (explanation of why the comment was made), and then to the third step, prescriptions about what should be done in the class to improve teaching, such as, "You should do more group work." Arcario points out that this last prescriptive step is more obvious when a negative evaluation is made because there is a perceived problem to be solved.

This usual way of talking about teaching is not especially productive. It is also not necessarily easy to change. But change can be made, especially if we take the time and effort to prepare for the discussions and follow agreed-upon rules that aim at nonjudgmental and non-prescriptive discussion. This was evident from an experience in Japan where I had the pleasure of working with 12 experienced American, Canadian, and Japanese EFL teachers, all of whom taught in different settings (Japanese public and private schools, corporations, and language schools). We planned for and visited some of the teachers' classes in small groups of three or four. After observing, we talked about the class over lunch or coffee. We found both the observations and discussions to be highly stimulating and informative, and part of the reason was our planning. Before each observation, the teacher whose class we were to visit gave us an aspect of teaching on which she or he wanted us to focus attention. For example, one teacher wanted us to focus on the times students speak their native language, another on the amount of time students stayed on task.

We also established rules about how to talk about the teaching we observed. We came to an agreement to stop ourselves from making positive and negative judgments about our own and others' teaching. We made this agreement because judgments take attention away from description of and toward feelings about what is going on. We also agreed not to seek prescriptions about teaching, in other words, what we should do in the classroom. Rather, we worked at generating alternatives based on descriptions of teaching. We looked for possibilities to try out, not best ways to teach. The teachers and I found these two sets of rules to be very powerful. We gained lots of description of teaching, were able to generate alternative techniques for the classroom, and, by the end of our experience together, became far less judgmental in our attitudes toward teaching.

As we did in Japan, I encourage you to talk to other teachers about teaching. To do this, I invite you to plan observation visits, meet to talk about your observations in non-prescriptive nonjudgmental terms, and generate alternative approaches to teaching. However, I also encourage you to talk about issues in teaching, media and materials, technology, and mutual problems, such as with student motivation, unreasonable administrative demands, and working conditions.

How Can Teachers Explore through a Teacher Journal?

We can explore teaching by writing in a journal. The purpose of writing in a journal is to have a place to record our observations of what goes on in our own and other teachers' classrooms, write about our discussions, consider teaching ideas, and reflect on our teaching. However, journals are also a place for us to raise doubts, express frustrations, and raise questions. With this in mind, here's a list of what some teachers include in their journals.[32]

- Quickly written descriptions of classroom interaction collected in their own and other teachers' classrooms, as well as analyses and interpretations of these descriptions
- Tally sheets, transcripts, sketches, and coding as a part of their description and analysis
- Photos (snapshots) and descriptions of what goes on in each photo
- Summaries and reflections on discussions with other teachers
- Lists of alternative ways to teach aspects of a lesson (e.g., different ways to give instructions)

- Stream-of-consciousness writing (to let ideas flow)
- Reflections on language-learning experiences
- Thoughts on beliefs about teaching and learning
- Questions about teaching and learning
- Answers to their own questions
- Summaries and critiques of journal articles and books
- Lesson plans and teaching ideas

Those of us who have maintained teaching journals know how time-consuming it can be. As such, I suggest you only try to keep a journal from time to time. For me, a few weeks a year seems just about right. I also encourage you to carry a journal with you and take the time to write down ideas when they emerge, even while walking down the street or at breakfast. Along with these inspired entries, I encourage you to write entries soon after teaching, while the experiences are fresh. Finally, at the end of a period of time (for instance, two months), I encourage you to take the time to read your entries thoughtfully, look for patterns in your teaching and thinking about teaching, and write an entry on this analysis.[33] Taking time to review past entries is important, since it is through this kind of reflection that we can see ourselves as teachers and view our teaching differently.

How Does This Book Provide Opportunities for Teachers to Explore Teaching?

Since observation as a way to explore teaching can be empowering, in this book I provide a number of opportunities to explore teaching through observation. This book contains descriptions of teaching based on my observations of lessons taught by EFL/ESL teachers and on my own self-observations. By reading this book, you are considering a variety of different observation reports on what EFL/ESL teachers do in their classrooms.

In addition, the Teacher Self-Development Tasks section at the end of each chapter provides a variety of different observation tasks. The purpose of these tasks is to teach a nonjudgmental process of looking at what goes on in your own and others' classrooms. Some of these tasks ask you to audio- and videotape teaching, tally behaviors or make short transcripts, and analyze teaching. The goal of doing these observation tasks is for you to see your teaching differently. It is through awareness of your own and others' teaching that it is possible to see new possibilities.

As you perform these observation tasks, I also encourage you to work through the reflective exploration cycle by collecting samples of your teaching, analyzing these samples, interpreting and reflecting on the analysis, deciding on changes, and implementing these changes while again collecting samples of your teaching for analysis and continuation of the cycle. Throughout this cycle, I encourage you to explore to solve problems in your teaching, as well as to explore for exploration's sake, simply to see what happens.

The tasks in each chapter provide chances for you to talk about teaching. For discussion with other teachers, I offer topics related to the content of each chapter, and I also provide chances for you to generate your own topics based on your interests and needs. I remind you that although talk about teaching may be done in a usual, evaluative, prescriptive way, it may also be done in a nonjudgmental, descriptive, and alternative-generating way.

Finally, at the end of each chapter I provide opportunities for you to write in a journal about your teaching experiences, ideas, observations, and beliefs about teaching. Although I give a variety of writing tasks related to the content of each chapter, I also encourage you to go beyond my suggestions.

As highlighted in Chapter 1, it is through the combination of reading, observing, talking, and writing about teaching that you will gain the kind of knowledge that frees you to raise new questions and ideas about your teaching beliefs and practices, as well as to search for answers to your questions and discover and rediscover the teacher that lies within you.

TEACHER SELF-DEVELOPMENT TASKS

Talk Tasks

1. Review the list of Ways to Explore Teaching on page 15. Talk with other teachers about this list. Which ways capture your attention? Why? Which ways have you already experienced? What was this experience like? Did you discover new things about yourself as a teacher?

2. Answer these questions:

   a. What is a judgment? What words indicate that a judgment is being made? Why do I suggest teachers avoid making judgments about the teaching they observe?

b. What is a prescription? What words indicate a teaching prescription is being made? (For example, "You should. . . ." indicates prescription.) Why do I think prescriptions of teaching are not useful?

c. What is an alternative? What is the value of generating alternative teaching ideas (over prescriptions)?

3. Talk about your experiences as a language learner. How did your past language teachers teach? What did you like or dislike about the way they taught? How do you think your language learning experience has influenced you as a teacher?

Observation and Talk Tasks

1. Arrange to visit a friend's class with at least one other teacher.

   a. Prepare to observe the class by asking the teacher what aspects of teaching he or she wants you to observe. (You might want to study the list of topics given on page 20.) Also consider how you will go about collecting descriptions of teaching that will capture aspects of it. (For example, will you write quick notes, draw sketches, jot down dialogue, tally behaviors, audio- or videotape, photograph?)

   b. Observe the class.

   c. Meet after the class over coffee or lunch to talk about the class. Monitor your way of talking about the class so that your conversations about teaching are nonjudgmental and nonprescriptive. During your conversation, generate a list of alternative ways the teacher could teach aspects of the same lesson differently.

2. Tape-record or videotape interaction in your class. Listen to or view the tape. Select interaction on the tape that interests you. Make short transcriptions of the interaction in dialogue form (using a new line when the speaker changes). Then, meet with another teacher. Together study and talk about the transcripts by working through the following steps:

   a. Analyze the interaction. What is going on? Is there anything in the interaction that captures your attention? What?

   b. Interpret the teaching. Are opportunities provided for students to learn English? Are opportunities possibly blocked?

    c. Decide on a small change. What are alternative ways to teach? Which would you like to try?

    d. Design a new lesson that includes a small change. Implement this change while taping and again analyze what happened.

Journal Writing Tasks

1. Write about your experiences as a language learner. How did your past language teachers teach? What did you like or dislike about the way they taught? How do you think your language learning experience has influenced you as a teacher?

2. Write about your observation and conversation experiences (from doing the Observation and Talk Tasks). Take time to reflect on the experience. What did you learn about teaching? What ideas do you now have about your own teaching? What did you learn about observation and talking about teaching in a nonjudgmental descriptive way?

3. Carry your journal with you. When a teaching idea or reflection comes to you, write it down.

4. The idea of this task is to experience writing about a class over a period of time. Pick one of your classes. Make sure you have a break soon after the class. Just after the class, each time you have taught it, take 15 minutes to write about this class. Use a stream-of-consciousness approach to your writing. In other words, just let the ideas flow. Feel free to add sketches, anything that works for you. After a few weeks, find a place where you can concentrate. Read all your entries. Then, take time to write about what you have learned about yourself as a teacher and how you teach.

Recommended Teacher Resources

Recommended Readings on Ways to Explore and Develop Teaching

Bailey, K. M., A. Curtis, and D. Nunan, eds. *Pursuing Professional Development*. Boston: Heinle & Heinle, 2001.

Burns, A. *Collaborative Action Research for English Language Teachers*. Cambridge: Cambridge University Press, 1999.

Burton, J., and M. Carroll, eds. *Journal Writing*. Alexandria, VA: TESOL, 2001.

Edge. J., ed. *Action Research*. Alexandria, VA: TESOL, 2001.

Edge, J. *Continuing Cooperative Development: A Discourse Framework for Individuals as Colleagues.* Ann Arbor: University of Michigan Press, 2002.

Fanselow, J. F. "'Let's See': Contrasting Conversations about Teaching." *TESOL Quarterly* 22 (1988): 113–20.

Gebhard, J. G., and R. Oprandy. *Language Teaching Awareness: A Guide to Exploring Beliefs and Practices.* New York: Cambridge University Press, 1999.

Richards, J. C., and D. Nunan, eds. *Second Language Teacher Education.* New York: Cambridge University Press, 1990.

Richards, J. C., and T. S. C. Farrell. *Professional Development for Language Teachers.* New York: Cambridge University Press, 2005.

Wallace, M. *Action Research for Language Teachers.* Cambridge: Cambridge University Press, 1998.

Recommended Books on Teacher Reflection

Farrell, T. *Reflective Practice in Action: 80 Reflection Breaks for Busy Teachers.* Thousand Oaks, CA: Sage, 2004.

Richards, J. C., and C. Lockhart. *Reflective Teaching in Second Language Classrooms.* New York: Cambridge University Press, 1994.

Schön, D. A. *Educating the Reflective Practitioner: Toward a New Design for Teaching and Learning in the Professions.* San Francisco: Jossey-Bass, 1987.

Zeichner, K. M., and D. P. Liston. *Reflective Teaching: An Introduction.* Mahwah, NJ: Lawrence Erlbaum, 1996.

Endnotes

[1] Sources with suggestions for exploration of teaching and professional growth are also in Bailey, Curtis, and Nunan (1998, 2001); Gebhard (1992); Gebhard, Gaitan, and Oprandy (1987); Gebhard and Oprandy (1999); and Murphy (2001).

[2] See Richards and Renandya (2002).

[3] See Johnson and Golombek (2002). Also see Farrell (2004) for reflective accounts of classroom communications by teachers in Asia.

[4] See Richards (1998).

[5] See Bailey, Curtis, and Nunan (2001).

[6] Discovered in Bailey, Curtis, and Nunan (2001, 207). See Eisenman and Thorton (1999, 80–81) for the original quote and full article on the topic.

[7] See Bailey, Curtis, and Nunan (2001, 207).

[8] See Johnson (1996).

[9] Karen Johnson (1996) provides a set of portfolio creation guidelines for teacher educators and teachers. Bailey, Curtis, and Nunan (2001) provide an elaborate discussion on the purposes of a portfolio and what can be included.

[10] See Bailey, Curtis, and Nunan (2001).

11 Cherry Campbell (1996) writes about her language learning experience in Mexico where she kept a journal about her socializing experiences in Spanish and what she gained from this experience as a person and teacher.

12 Crookes (1993) writes about how action research extends beyond the walls of the classroom and can become a political endeavor.

13 Those who discuss the process of doing action research in ESL/EFL classes include Bailey and Nunan (1996); Bailey, Curtis, and Nunan (2001); Burns (1996, 1999); Burns and Hood (1997); Edge (2001); Gebhard (2002, 2005a, 2005b); Gebhard and Oprandy (1999); and Wallace (1998).

14 See Burns (1996, 1997).

15 See Farrell (2000) for information on the *PAC Journal,* which publishes action research done by teachers in Asia.

16 See Wallace (1998).

17 See Edge (2002).

18 As a doctoral student at Teachers College, Columbia University, I studied with John Fanselow. I especially appreciate his nonjudgmental descriptive approach to looking at teaching, his use of multiple interpretations of a description, and his creative way of categorizing knowledge and generating alternative teaching behavior. I suggest teachers and teacher educators read his work (1977a, 1983, 1987, 1988, 1992a, 1992b, 1997).

19 See Gebhard (1991, 1992, 2005b), Gebhard and Oprandy (1999), and Gebhard and Ueda-Montonaga (1992).

20 COLT was created by Allen, Fröhlick, and Spada (1984); FOCUS by Fanselow (1977a, 1987).

21 Richards (1998) and Richards and Lockhart (1994) have a rich discussion on teachers' beliefs. I also address beliefs in Gebhard and Oprandy (1999), including how teachers can consider if their beliefs match their teaching practices.

22 See Jersild (1955).

23 See Fanselow (1987).

24 This project was done by Barbara Duncan, who at the time was an ESL teacher at the American Language Institute and an MA student in the TESOL program at Indiana University of Pennsylvania.

25 At the time of this exploration into her praise behaviors, the teacher, Miharu Hiyoshi, a near-native speaker of English, was a student in the Teachers College, Columbia University (Tokyo) MA TESOL program and an EFL teacher at the Yokohama YMCA.

26 This tally sheet was first published in Gebhard (1991).

27 A more detailed account can be found in Gebhard and Ueda-Motonaga (1992).

28 See Fanselow (1992a, 2).

29 This transcript was originally published in Gebhard (1990).

30 The observer-photographer was Yutaka Yamauchi, who at the time was a graduate student in the MA TESOL program at Teachers College, Columbia University (Tokyo) and a private high school EFL teacher.

31 See Arcario (1994).

32 This list is based on my own research into what teachers write about in their journals. There is, of course, other research. Other researchers have focused on journal entries as a way to understand novice teachers' "evolving perceptions of themselves as teachers" (Brinton and Holten 1989, 344), teaching issues and shifting awareness (Holten and Brinton 1995), personal learning experience about power and communication (Esbenshade 2002), and teachers' common concerns and pressing needs (Numrich 1996). Other researchers have looked into the reflective nature of journal writing. Farrell (1998) studied three Korean teachers' journals to consider if "regular journal writing promotes reflective thinking" (p. 92), while Richards and Ho (1998) studied teachers' narratives and questions to interpret "whether journal-writing experiences developed teachers' sense of critical reflectivity over time" (p. 157). Yahya (2000) took her research one step further by studying the ways teaching journals seem to help teachers solve teaching problems, as well as how sharing journals can possibly contribute to teachers' professional growth.

33 Bailey (1990) emphasizes that reviewing entries and looking for salient features in our teaching is crucial to a successful journal experience.

About a quarter of the world's population is already fluent or competent in English, and this figure is growing—in the early 2000s that means around 1.5 billion people. No other language can match that growth. Even Chinese, found in eight different spoken languages, but unified by a common writing system, is known to "only" some 1.1 billion.

—Crystal 2003, 6

EFL and ESL Teaching Settings

- What is an EFL teaching setting? What is an ESL teaching setting? Why are these two terms, *EFL* and *ESL*, not always adequate to describe English teaching settings?
- What are examples of *EFL* and *ESL* teaching settings?
- How are different teaching settings woven into this book?

What Is an EFL Teaching Setting?
What Is an ESL Teaching Setting?
Why Are These Two Terms, *EFL* and *ESL*, Not Always Adequate to Describe English Teaching Settings?

EFL is an acronym for English as a Foreign Language and is studied by people who live in places where English is not a first language, such as in Italy, Saudi Arabia, and Vietnam. ESL is an acronym for English as a Second Language. People who study ESL speak other languages, such as Spanish, Arabic, Chinese, or Swahili as their first or native language. However, they live in places where English is used as the first or native language, such as Australia, New Zealand, Canada, the United Kingdom, and the United States.

Although I am at risk of overgeneralizing, it is possible to point out a few other differences between EFL and ESL settings. To begin, student populations differ. In many EFL contexts, the population is homogeneous in many ways, for example, all sharing a similar history of being Korean, German, or Egyptian. ESL settings, however, for the most part are quite heterogeneous. Students from a great variety of countries can be found in the same ESL classroom. For example, I recently observed an ESL class with students from Italy, Costa Rica, Japan, Korea, Malaysia, Thailand, Bangladesh, the United Arab Emirates, and Turkey.

Further, in EFL settings there are fewer chances for students to use English outside the classroom. Quite often the only understandable English some EFL students experience is in the classroom, although this has been progressively changing due to the spread of technology, such as the Internet and satellite television. In contrast, when ESL students leave the classroom, they can enter any number of situations in which they can hear and use English.

In addition, the goals of learning EFL and ESL are often quite different. In many countries where English is a foreign language, a dual goal for teenagers studying in the educational system is to pass English entrance exams to enter good high schools and universities and, more recently, to be able to use English as a global language. As such, much of the teaching in the junior and senior high schools is directed at being able to analyze and comprehend English to pass entrance examinations and to communicate in English with people from other parts of the world, at least at a basic level. However, the goal is often quite different for young people studying ESL in the United States and other countries where the medium of communication is English. In the ESL setting, the purpose is often tied to literacy. The aim is to use English like a native speaker, including being able to read, write, and interact in English in culturally defined ways.

Of course, there are individuals in EFL settings who want to be literate in English and need to learn English to communicate effectively with others, including those interested in living abroad, doing international business, working as translators, and working in the tourist industry. Subsequently, to meet this need English language programs and teachers provide language-rich experiences for learners within countries that are traditionally thought of as EFL settings. Such programs often offer students lessons on adapting to other cultural contexts while using English and gaining strategies to develop English throughout their lifetimes. Likewise, there are those who study in ESL settings who need to pass entrance exams, for example, students at language institutes who have to pass TOEFL® (Test of English as a Foreign Language) to gain admittance into an American university and ESL students in K–12 settings who have to pass standardized tests given to all students in the public school system.

Such examples certainly illustrate the inadequacy of considering all learners within an EFL and ESL setting as having the same goals and of considering all language programs within these settings as alike. Such overgeneralizations can be quite misleading, even to the point of stereotyping all EFL learners as having certain language learning experiences and all ESL learners as having other experiences.

It also is important to point out, so as not to oversimplify things, that not all English fits neatly into the category of EFL or ESL. This is especially clear when focusing on those populations of people around the world who use an institutionalized second-language variety of English.[1] Such populations use English on a day-to-day basis alongside one or more other languages. Such institutionalized varieties of English are also called *New Englishes*,[2] which function as *intranational languages*, or languages "other than the mother tongue, which is used by nationals of the same country for communication."[3] A New English develops through the educational system where it is often used as the medium of instruction, and within various other institutions, such as government offices. However, the mother tongue is used in most other contexts, such as in interaction with friends and family members.

Such New Englishes have especially developed in countries in Africa (e.g., Ghana, Kenya, Nigeria, Tanzania, Zambia) and Asia (e.g., Bangladesh, India, Pakistan, Philippines, Singapore, Sri Lanka), where there was a need for an official language. Some countries developed English after colonial rule. For example, Kenya was a British colony from 1920 to 1963; English was the official language for several years, but Swahili has since replaced it. Nonetheless, English was maintained, adopted more widely, and has become one of the New Englishes. Another example is in Singapore, where English was introduced as a "unifying medium" alongside Chinese, Malay, or Tamil.[4] As New Englishes developed in each of these countries, they tended to take on some of the language features unique to the users' native language or languages, such as pronunciation, choice of words, and syntactic features. For example, the English used in Singapore has syntactic (i.e., word order), phonemic (i.e., pronunciation of vowel sounds), and lexical (i.e., word choice) features of Chinese and Malay, so much so that it is difficult for many outsiders to comprehend this variety of English when they first encounter it.[5]

What Are Examples of EFL and ESL Teaching Settings?

In this section I consider settings in which EFL and ESL learners study English. EFL settings include public schools (K–12), universities, public language schools, and private language schools. ESL settings include public schools (K–12), university language programs, and refugee/literacy centers. I also consider two settings that do not fit neatly into either an EFL or ESL setting.

EFL Teaching Settings

English is presently taught to EFL students in **public schools** worldwide, and in recent years the trend has been to offer English to younger and younger students.[6] For example, in the recent past, English was introduced to most Japanese students at the age of 13, when they entered junior high school. However, recently the Ministry of Education established a new English curriculum for the public schools that includes teaching English to elementary school students through music, games, and other engaging activities. Other examples include Turkey's recently lowering the start of English from sixth grade to the fourth, Italy's recent School Reform Bill that shifted the start of English to the elementary level, and Saudi Arabia's reform to do the same.

Students' experience varies from country to country. For example, in elementary school in South Korea, teachers devote 40 minutes twice each week to English. Koreans I have talked with say most teachers attempt to teach English through integrative skills of reading, writing, listening, and speaking. They do this by having students experience games, songs, and reading activities, but they also rely on traditional "repeat after me" and simple grammar manipulation activities. In junior high school the time increases to 45 minutes four days each week, and in many of these settings teachers are required to select the text from a list of approved textbooks. The goal also shifts to passing the college entrance exam. As the English part of the exam counts as 80 points from a possible 400 (20 points for students' ability to comprehend spoken English and 60 for reading ability), the emphasis in class is placed more and more on teaching distinct skills of listening and reading as students move through junior and senior high school.

However, unlike in South Korea, students in public schools in Saudi Arabia study English four days each week, 45 minutes per class. Textbooks are designed under the supervision of the Ministry of Education; these texts observe the Saudi traditions of Muslim values and emphasize having students learn to read, write, listen, and speak English. Since English is not tested on the university entrance exam, the junior and senior high school curricula is not geared toward teaching students to pass entrance exams (except for prospective English majors), but rather more toward comprehension and communication.

University EFL settings offer a variety of different English programs. Most universities worldwide require students to take several semesters of a foreign language, and English is either a choice among other languages or required. Most university-wide English programs include courses on grammar, reading, listening, and conversation. Non-native English speakers often teach the reading and grammar-related courses, while native or near-native speakers (often nationals who have studied abroad) are often asked to teach conversation because of a widely held (and often misinformed) belief that only native English speakers can teach students to converse.

Some universities in EFL settings offer English for Specific Purposes (ESP) courses to fill a need within a particular major. For example, students majoring in Hotel Management might be required to take a course on Tourism and English, a student majoring in journalism, a course on English in Mass Communication, and a student majoring in pre-med, a course on reading medical journals written in English. Universities in EFL settings also offer programs for English majors, and there are a variety of different specializations that English majors can pursue. For example, Eötvös Loránd University in Budapest has different English departments, including American Studies, English Applied Linguistics, English Linguistics, and English Studies (Literature).

The number of **public language schools** in EFL settings has greatly increased in recent years. Some of these schools have an assortment of English programs and classes, while others are smaller and more specialized. It is also worth pointing out that although there are some well-established excellent language schools, there are also, unfortunately, a number of schools that have no solid theoretical foundation, hire unqualified teachers, and rely on the textbook to teach the students.

Hess Language School in Taiwan[7] is an example of a respected, fairly large, specialized school envisioned to meet the English language needs of Taiwanese children. Some of the programs at Hess include Step Ahead, their core program that teaches 9- to 15-year-olds listening and basic writing skills; the Jump Series, a game and play-centered class for 4- to 6-year-olds; and Kids Club, an activity-based program designed to give 6- to 8-year-olds a fun experience using English. The school also has a variety of extracurricular activities, including the National Youth Speech and Writing Competition, Magical English Drama Club, and the Hess Family Reading Club.

While schools like Hess are designed to meet children's English language needs, other larger schools market to adults. For example, the American University Association Alumni Language Center in Thailand, better known as AUA, officially began in 1952 "to promote further mutual understanding between the people of Thailand and the United States."[8] It grew over the years to include four branches in Bangkok and 13 branches throughout the country. To date, some 400,000 Thais have studied English at AUA in a choice of three main programs: The Regular Program (15-level multi-skill course), the Intensive Academic English Program (to prepare students to study abroad), and Special Courses, such as TOEFL® Preparation.

In addition to language schools with a variety of programs and courses, there are also schools that have a single program designed to meet a specific need. For example, in Japan there are a large number of cram schools that students attend in the evening and on weekends. The schools specialize in preparing high school students to pass college entrance exams in such subjects as English. One of the most famous of these schools, Yoyogi Seminar, is attended by more than 500,000 students at many branches throughout Japan.[9] These students usually arrive after having spent a full day at school or arrive on a weekend morning. I have observed the lessons given at several cram schools, and I am amazed at how conscientious many of the students are. They sit in long rows in a large room studying English written on a large screen. Using a microphone and small stage, the native English-speaking assistant demonstrates the use of English sentences and the Japanese English teacher explains complex grammar rules and fine nuances of meaning associated with these sentences.

There are also a number of smaller public language schools, such as The Calvary English School in Tokyo. Run by a mother and daughter, this school specializes in offering children chances to learn English in a playful, nurturing atmosphere. The school enrolls groups of seven to ten children, and during their hourly lessons, they provide a wide variety of language experiences. For example, children spell out words using letter-blocks, count forward and backward while pretending to jump rope, listen to children's stories being read from a giant book with pictures, and play word-bingo as they match a picture on a bingo card with the word the teacher gives.

Unlike public language programs where anyone who can pay the tuition can attend, only particular groups of people can attend a **private language program.** These programs are usually established to meet the English language needs of people who work in government positions, such as diplomats and embassy personnel, or the private sector, for example, those who work in the tourist industry (hotel clerks, tour guides), the airline industry (pilots, flight attendants, check-in clerks), oil industry (engineers, technicians on oil rigs), and business (managers headed overseas, those doing international business).

Here's an example of a private language program based on my own experience. Some years ago I worked for Heuristic Associates, a small firm that contracted with Japanese companies, such as Mitsubishi Corporation, to teach small groups of businesspeople (five male students in each class). We taught each group of students four hours daily for 11 months, five days each week. Our goal was not only to see improvement in the accuracy and fluency of these businessmen as they gained communicative competence, but also to prepare them to interact with people from different backgrounds in culturally appropriate ways depending on the context. To accomplish this, we read and talked about cultural beliefs, values, and behaviors, did role-play and culturally based problem-solving activities, and carried out simulations. (See Chapter 9 for examples of such activities.)

Another type of private language program is situated in the home-based school. Although unnoticed by those outside EFL teaching circles, there are so many of these schools that it is worth pointing them out. These private language schools are usually rather small, run by one or two teachers, and often specialized, such as in preparing high school students to pass college entrance exams, giving businesspeople chances to practice conversational English, and preparing people to travel in English speaking settings. Those who start these schools do not usually advertise, finding students through local networking.

An example from my own experience illustrates a typical home school. When I was living in Thailand, I started a small private language school I called Breakfast with Jerry. Three mornings each week, before I left for my regular job, I welcomed three or four Japanese businessmen into my home, and we would sit around the kitchen table. As we sipped coffee and ate pastry, we chatted about international and local news stories, discussed grammar rules, practiced American pronunciation, and talked about and informally role-played how English is used in different social contexts, for example, how American businessmen might set up appointments on the phone and accept and turn down invitations.

ESL Teaching Settings

A wave of immigrants to English-speaking countries such as Australia, Canada, and the United States has created a challenge for the **public school systems** to educate children who are just beginning to learn English. These students arrive with varied educational backgrounds. As Helene Becker points out in *Teaching ESL K–12: Views from the Classroom*, "Some have had extensive schooling in their native countries and are well prepared for the academic challenges ahead. Others arrive underprepared for grade-level schoolwork having had (little) formal education."[10] Jodi Crandall adds that many of the immigrant students who arrive at our schools grew up speaking "nonnative varieties of English that developed during colonization (and) have become institutionalized as second languages in education, government, or commerce, but are rarely the first language of the citizens (with some 60 countries, including India, Jamaica, Kenya, Nigeria, and Singapore)."[11]

Another population in public schools includes Generation 1.5 students. These students are long-term residents of the United States, Canada, Britain, New Zealand, and Australia, and they are usually quite fluent in spoken English. However, many of these students still have language problems, especially with writing and occasionally reading. A problem is that many of these Generation 1.5 students do not want to be labeled as ESL students, and many tend to avoid being grouped with recent immigrants. This often results in a predicament for content-area teachers who do not know how to teach students who have native-like proficiency in spoken English but have ESL features in their writing.[12] (See

Chapter 11 for suggestions on teaching writing to Generation 1.5 students.)

School districts have responded to the needs of K–12 students in a variety of ways. Some have been overwhelmed by the growing presence of students with not only language and cultural adjustment needs, but also in some cases perceptual awareness needs related to the concept of literacy and schooling. Their response has been to place most immigrants in low-track or remediation programs. Unfortunately, as we have discovered,[13] remediation and putting students in low-level classes is the exact opposite of what many of these students need. Such placement simply puts limits on their opportunities to gain the interaction, language, and skills they need to be successful in the new school.

A separate program that addresses students language and academic needs is the *pullout model* in which ESL specialists pull students out of their grade-level classroom for ESL lessons. Pulling students out of their classrooms has certain benefits. As Becker points out, time can be used to address content needs, review lessons to clear up language and concept problems, bond with a person who cares, and provide survival-level oral English and reading instruction for beginning level students.

It is important to point out that pullout programs with little direct connection to what students are studying and doing in their grade-level classroom have been shown to be an ineffective way to facilitate success in school.[14] Indeed, success is more probable if there is continuing communication between the ESL instructor and the grade-level teacher.

Another approach is the *inclusion model* in which the ESL teacher goes into the classroom to work with the ESL students, either as a small group or individually, during classroom instruction; there are certain benefits from this approach. To begin, the inclusion gives the ESL teacher direct access to what is going on in the classroom, the assignments that are being done, and the kinds of challenges these assignments might have for the ESL student, such as fully comprehending the instructions or using the library. In addition, the ESL students can voice their problems and concerns with language and content while class is in process, and the ESL teacher can immediately address these problems.

Unfortunately, it is not always possible for the ESL specialist to be in the classroom, especially if he or she is expected to be with other students in other classrooms or even other schools. Another problem is that of embarrassment. Some ESL teachers working in high school inclusion programs, for example, have told me that some of these older students don't want to draw attention to themselves and their language limitations in front of classmates.

A third approach to teaching ESL students is a *team-teaching model*.[15] Also known as a co-teaching model, the ESL teacher and grade-level teacher team-teach the class. As equal partners, they plan and take turns teaching both native and ESL students. One benefit of the team-teaching model is that the ESL teacher can use ESL teaching strategies to present material to the students. Another benefit of using team-teaching, as Helene Becker puts it, is that the ESL students "perceive themselves as 'students' rather than 'ESL students'; they are not singled out as 'different.'"[16]

K–12 ESL Programs

Newcomer Program: Used when ESL students first arrive, faculty and students join efforts to make the ESL and minority students feel welcome, offer personal-social support, give an orientation to the school, assess language skills, provide survival English for those who need it, and provide cultural adjustment advice.

Pullout Program: ESL specialists pull students out of their grade-level classroom for ESL lessons.

Inclusion Program: ESL specialist goes into the classroom to work with the ESL students, either as a small group or individually, during classroom instruction.

Team-Teaching Program: Also known as a co-teaching model, the ESL teacher and grade-level teacher team-teach the class. As equal partners, they plan and take turns teaching both native and ESL students.

Subtractive Bilingualism Program: The bilingual teacher begins with using the students' native language while developing their second language. As students develop the second language and begin to shift away from identity with the home language and culture, more and more emphasis is placed on using the second language.

Additive Bilingualism Program: Unlike subtractive bilingualism, which is criticized because the goal is to take cultural identity away from the child, additive bilingualism aims at providing students with the opportunity to become fully literate in both their native and second languages.

Some public schools also offer *bilingual programs*, including what researchers call *subtractive bilingualism* and *additive bilingualism programs*. Subtractive bilingualism begins with using the students' native language while working at developing the second language. As students develop the second language and begin to shift away from identity with the home language and culture, greater emphasis is placed on using the second language. Unlike subtractive bilingualism, which is criticized because the goal is to take cultural identity away from the child, additive bilingualism aims at providing students with the opportunity to become fully literate in both their native and second languages. So as not to oversimplify things, it is important to point out that bilingual programs "vary a great deal and often do not adhere precisely to one model or another."[17]

An example of an innovative additive bilingual class is Kerry Conrad's[18] dual-language Spanish/English science class in Utah. Through the support of parents and teachers, Kerry has been able to create a dual-level middle school class consisting of half Mexican immigrants and half native English speakers. This class is taught in a dual-language immersion approach with Spanish and English as medium of instruction alternating daily. What happens inside this classroom is especially interesting. Children not only listen to short lectures by the teacher and read materials in either English or Spanish, they also interact with each other as they ask and answer each other's questions and work on science projects. Kerry has been able to create a supportive trusting learning environment both inside and outside the classroom for these students, who became enabled to explore and learn from their difficulties in cross-cultural, cross-lingual communication as they studied science together in an activity-based, cooperative-learning classroom.

Another group of ESL students are those who travel abroad to study at universities in English-speaking countries. In the United States alone there are close to 600,000 international students enrolled in universities each year.[19] Not all of these international students enroll in degree programs; rather, some first take classes in a **university ESL institute** before going on to a degree program, and some simply come to study at the institute and then return home. Some institutes are quite large, attracting hundreds of students and including numerous kinds of English language programs, while smaller, lesser-known colleges and universities attract a more modest number of students to a single program that aims at meeting their academic and social needs.

A survey of university language institutes in the United States shows a variety of English language programs.[20] The list of English programs at language institutes shows brief descriptions of programs. These programs range from the Intensive English for Academic Purposes program to more specialized programs, usually offered at the larger universities and language programs, including programs such as English for Law and Technology and English.

The most sought-after program, and one offered by all the universities I surveyed, is the intensive English for Academic Purposes (EAP) program. The EAP program is designed to meet the academic and social needs of both undergraduate and graduate students who are seeking admission or are conditionally admitted. There are, of course, many different EAP programs; although they all offer coursework to prepare students to study with American students and professors, each has its own unique curriculum. An example of one such curriculum is the American Language Institute's 14-week EAP program at Indiana University of Pennsylvania.[21]

English Programs at Language Institutes

English for Academic Purposes Program: This program usually lasts a full semester. Students study 20 to 25 hours each week in one of several levels (or in mixed levels), in such courses as reading, writing, listening, oral communications, grammar, pronunciation, English online, vocabulary building, and intercultural communication. At beginning levels the goal is to develop basic language skills; at higher levels students turn to TOEFL® Preparation and more academic subjects, including courses in listening to lectures, research writing, and classroom communications.

English for Business: This program is usually designed for international students who want to gain entrance into an MBA program or business professionals who want to further develop their English.

TOEFL Preparation: Some of the larger language institutes have separate programs just for students who want to raise their TOEFL® score.

Advanced Academic Preparation: Some of the larger institutes offer short (5- to 7-week) programs for advanced learners who will begin their studies at an American university.

Bridge Program: This program offers students the opportunity to be a part-time student in a university degree program while taking support classes at the language institute.

> **English for Law:** A few language institutes offer English for legal professionals and pre-law students.

The ALI staff first assesses each student's language ability, using the TOEFL®, oral interviews, and institutionally designed assessment instruments. The results are studied, and a coursework plan is designed for each student. A student is placed in a group (green, orange, blue) or, if one skill, such as reading, is stronger than other skills, a student might study most subjects with students in a green group but join a higher-level orange group to study reading.

Students study a variety of courses from very basic to advanced, depending on the level. For example, at a basic level students attend a vocabulary lab, an open lab (working with individual tutors), and courses such as World of Words (exploration of the "rich world of words," including developing techniques and strategies for finding, understanding, and remembering words), Communicative Grammar (practice using grammar in communicative contexts), Write from the Start (introduction to writing and composing), Stories of Selves (reading and talking about personal experience stories, as well as writing responses to these stories), and Conversation Partners (meeting and talking with volunteer American students in social settings). Likewise, students with more highly developed English also participate in the Conversation Partners course, as well as attend a vocabulary lab and open lab, but the content is more advanced. They also take courses, each geared toward the ability of the students. For example, students at a mid-level take such courses as Writing about Themes (focusing on the writing process while focusing on themes, such as health, gender and technology, as well as responding to readings on these topics) and Intercultural Communication (exploration of communication across cultures, sensitizing students to issues related to cultural values, culture shock, cultural adjustment, and strategies to communicate with people from different cultures).

ESL is also taught in **Refugee and Literacy Centers** where, depending on the political climate, learners come from a variety of nations. For example, one of my first jobs as an ESL teacher was teaching survival English to refugees in Hawaii, mostly from remote villages in Laos. Some of these students felt totally misplaced and longed to return home. However, they also saw the change as an opportunity for their children, and so they sat in class smiling, even laughing, a few coaxing me to teach them outside on the lawn where we would not be confined by the building walls.

Refugees are indeed a mixed group; they often include doctors, nurses, teachers, businesspeople, construction workers, electricians, hotel managers, soldiers, secretaries, housewives, farmers, and migrant workers, among others. However, they all have one thing in common: They are unable or unwilling to return to their country because they have a strong fear of being persecuted based on their race, religion, nationality, or association with a particular group. They have been forced to flee their homeland, and they find themselves living in another country.

Newly arrived refugees usually attend classes in English, as well as in employment preparation programs. Some refugees move through these programs rather quickly because they already have strong English, strong educational backgrounds, and skills that are in demand. However, like the Laotian refugees from my past, some need years of education simply to survive.

Some refugee programs are government sponsored. One such refugee program is the Colorado Refugee English as a Second Language Program (CRESL). This program has served the adult refugee community in the Denver area and Colorado Springs[22] for the past 20 years. Refugees in their ESL program have come from Bosnia, Sudan, Somalia, Ethiopia, Iraq, Iran, Mayanmar, Vietnam, Russia, and the Ukraine. Like many refugee programs, CRESL has a limited budget, so in addition to regular classes to meet the defined needs of the refugees, CRESL, like other refugee programs I am familiar with, depends on volunteers from the community.

Volunteers in the CRESL program take on a variety of jobs. Many spend hundreds of hours each month helping students learn English and adjust to life in Colorado. Some volunteers assist in the classroom, work one-on-one with students, and tutor small groups outside the classroom. Some volunteers join conversation groups that consist of other volunteers and advanced-level refugee students. They meet in casual settings to chat and share ideas in a friendly, fun, and relaxed setting.

I have categorized refugee and literacy programs together because there is some overlap. While literacy programs are usually larger in scope than refugee programs, they are concerned with the literacy of people born in the country, as well as immigrants. The Greater Pittsburgh Literacy Council, which advertises itself as "a national leader in adult education and family literacy," clearly defines what a literacy center does: "to ensure that adults and families acquire reading, writing, math, English language, workforce skills and computer skills so they may reach their fullest potential in life and participate productively in their community."[23] As such, a literacy center is concerned with the refugee population in Pittsburgh, but it does not concentrate only on the needs of refugees, and their concern goes beyond simply providing ESL lessons to these students.

Related to ESL teaching, literacy centers and refugee programs are similar in some ways. They both provide classes designed to meet the needs of the students, such as classes in survival English for those who cannot communicate in the language. They also train and depend on volunteer tutors to teach refugees. The Greater Pittsburgh Literacy Center advertises: "Volunteer tutors, who are specially trained in English as a second language methods, work with students to improve their English skills. Beyond simple language practice, students have the opportunity to work with tutors who can help with cultural concerns that are not addressed in a classroom setting. Tutors offer valuable insights into the inner workings of our culture to help students deal with the day-to-day issues they confront."

As a participant teacher in the refugee program in Hawaii and an observer of several refugee programs and literacy centers, I have gained a great deal of respect for volunteers and regular ESL teachers in both settings. They are usually very devoted and caring, work long hours, are often quite talented at teaching, and work as volunteers or for low wages. But, most say it is worth it! These people experience the hopes and dreams, the struggles and successes of individuals and complete families. The relationship often goes well beyond simply teaching English, since the students often invite the teachers into their lives and expect the teachers and tutors to reciprocate.

Overlapping Settings

Not all settings fit neatly into an EFL or ESL setting. One such setting is the **international school (K–12).** These schools offer all classes in English to expatriates, nationals who have returned home from living in English-speaking countries, and others. Most of the international schools attract students from a variety of cultural and language backgrounds. As such, walking through the hallways, it is possible not only to hear conversations in English, but also in Japanese, Korean, German, Italian, French, Arabic, Chinese, and other languages, depending on the population of students at the school.

As students need to be literate in English to study in most international schools, many of these schools offer English for Academic Purposes (EAP) classes or tutoring for those who need it. The focus is usually on listening to academic lectures, reading texts and literature, and writing.

What makes such schools interesting from an EFL/ESL perspective is that within the walls of the school, it is more of an ESL setting in which English is used as a medium of communication. However, within those same walls there are also subcultures and multiple languages being spoken, and outside the school English is often not spoken very much at all, as is characteristic of an EFL setting.

Another setting that does not fit neatly into either EFL or ESL is the **university within traditionally EFL contexts** where students with strong English skills can take most of their classes in English. Most of these degree programs are international. However, in many cases the majority of students are natives from the country. In such programs, students are expected to do all coursework in English and interact in English while in the classroom and outside the class (at least with students from other countries). However, although English is used within the walls of the university much like in an ESL setting, students who are from the country will leave the university and speak their native language, something that happens in EFL settings.

One example is Al Ain Men's College in the United Arab Emirates, where they offer degrees in Business, Communication Technology, Education, Engineering Technology, Health Sciences, and Information Technology, and English is the language of instruction for all courses within these majors.[24] Interestingly, professors who teach such courses have told me that many of the students are not fully prepared to take courses in English. However, they also have said that by the time the students graduate, they are competent in reading and listening to English.

Perhaps a better example is Tokyo's Sophia University because it has become highly internationalized over the years. Sophia University has more than 500 foreign students from 54 countries, as well as 99 foreign teachers from 20 different countries.[25] In addition, Sophia maintains a policy of inviting researchers from around the world to teach, head research projects, and give invited lectures. Sophia also has established a global network that allows students to study abroad on international exchange programs and is well known in the fields of International Relations and Foreign Studies and for their highly developed Faculty of Comparative Culture and their Department of International Legal Studies.

How Are Different Teaching Settings Woven into This Book?

Understanding different settings is important, to remind you that teaching English is context dependent. How and what we teach depend very much on the setting. For example, the goals of teaching ESL to immigrant children in an elementary school in the United States are quite different in many ways from those of teaching EFL to elementary school children in Japan. In the U.S. setting, the goal is to fully integrate children into the academic and social system. In Japan, the goal is most likely to give children an appreciation of English, the concept of communication in another language, and a basic understanding of grammar and vocabulary.

I weave in examples, even sections, on how the principles and teaching techniques and strategies are relevant to the different teaching settings I have introduced in this chapter. For example, in Chapter 4 on teaching English as interaction, I give an example lesson from a beginning-level junior high school class in Hungary to illustrate how a Hungarian EFL teacher was successfully able to include communicative activities in her high school class. Likewise, in Chapter 5 on classroom management I include a section on guidelines for facilitating learning in K–12 ESL settings. In short, I include a great variety of illustrations throughout this book, some from my observations of what colleagues do, some from journal articles and books, and some from my own experience, and I have intentionally drawn these illustrations from across many different settings.

TEACHER SELF-DEVELOPMENT TASKS

Talk Tasks

1. I describe a number of EFL and ESL teaching settings. Which settings are you familiar with? Find to be most interesting? Least interesting? Why? If possible, meet with others who have read about these settings. What answers do they give to these questions?
2. I have organized the content of this chapter by discussing characteristics of EFL/ESL settings. Another way to organize this chapter

would be to discuss teaching settings based on social (family, school, peer groups, clubs), ideological (values, beliefs, assumptions), economic, and historical factors that influence teaching. Can you think of examples of how social influences might affect teaching English? How ideological factors might be an influence? How economic factors might affect teaching?

3. ESL students who have recently arrived in the United States sometimes complain if they walk into a classroom to find that their teacher is a non-native English speaker. I have seen this happen at language institutes, refugee programs, and K–12 programs. However, there are obvious advantages that these newly arrived students have overlooked. Why do you think some ESL students complain about having a non-native English speaker as a teacher? What would you say to the ESL students who are complaining?

Observation and Talk Tasks

1. If possible, visit one of the settings written about in this chapter. Talk with those who work or study there. If possible, observe a class. Then, if possible, get together with others who are reading this book. Talk about what you learned about that teaching setting.

2. Find a friend. Together, log on to and talk about the website for International TESOL: *www.tesol.org.* Spend some time exploring what International TESOL is and what the organization can offer you as an ESL or EFL teacher or prospective one. After you are familiar with the organization, locate the Interest Sections part of the website. Study the Interest Sections Overview. Select several Interest Sections from the list of 20 sections (e.g., Higher Education, Elementary Education, Intercultural Communication, Adult Education, ESL in Bilingual Education, Video, Computer-Assisted Language Learning, English as a Foreign Language). Consider how each of the Interest Sections might be a part of different ESL/EFL settings.

Journal Writing Tasks

1. If you were able to visit and talk about one of the teaching settings, as given in the observation and talk tasks, write about your experience in your journal.

2. Reflect on the language learning settings you have experienced as a teacher or learner. As you write, also consider what it must be

like to learn a language in settings that you have not experienced but have read about in this chapter.

3. Using some of the websites given in the Endnotes to this chapter, or by exploring the Internet on your own, explore different teaching settings. Then, write about what you learned from studying about these settings.
4. Write about what you learned from studying the different interest sections on the International TESOL website. How might the different interest sections help inform you about different EFL and ESL teaching settings?

Recommended Teacher Resources

Resources on English

Crystal, D. *English as a Global Language. 2ᵈ ed.* Cambridge: Cambridge University Press, 2003.

Manners, P. *The Global Tongue: English.* Princeton, NJ: Films for the Humanities, 1998.

Resources on EFL Teaching

Bueno, E. P., and T. Caesar, eds. *I Wouldn't Want Anybody to Know: Native English Teaching in Japan.* Tokyo: JPG Press, 2003.

McConnell, D. L. *Imparting Diversity: Inside Japan's JET Program.* Berkeley, CA: University of California Press, 2000.

McKay, S. *Teaching English Overseas: An Introduction.* New York: Oxford University Press, 1992.

Mohamed, J. *Teach English Overseas: A Job Guide for Americans and Canadians.* Vancouver, CAN: English International, 2003.

Moon, J., and M. Nikolov, eds. *Research into Teaching English to Young Learners.* Pécs, HUN: University of Pécs Press, 2000.

Snow, D. B. *More than a Native Speaker: An Introduction for Volunteers Teaching English Abroad.* Alexandria, VA: TESOL, 1996.

Resources for K–12 ESL Teachers

Becker, H. *Teaching ESL K–12.* Boston: Heinle & Heinle, 2001.

Bérubé, B. *Managing ESL Programs in Rural and Small Urban Schools.* Alexandria, VA: TESOL, 2000.

Helmer, S., and C. Eddy. *Look at Me When I Talk to You: ESL Learners in Non-ESL Classrooms.* Portsmouth, NH: Heinemann, 2003.

Hudelson, S., ed. *English as a Second Language Teacher Resource Handbook: A Practical Guide for K–12 ESL Programs.* Thousand Oaks, CA: Corwin Press, 1995.

Kreeft, J., and C. T. Adger. "Special Issue on Immigrant Students in Secondary Schools." *TESOL Journal* 7, no. 5 (1998).

Peregoy, S. F., and O. F. Boyle. *Reading, Writing, & Learning in ESL: A Resource Book for K–12 Teachers.* 4th ed. New York: Addison Wesley Longman, 2005.

Reeves, J. "Like Everybody Else: Equalizing Educational Opportunities for English Language Learners." *TESOL Quarterly* 38, no. 1 (2004): 43–66.

TESOL, "Teachers of English to Speakers of Other Languages. The ESL Standards for Pre-K–12 Students." Alexandria, VA: TESOL, 1997.

Endnotes

[1] I have learned about the complexity of Englishes from reading the work of Kachru (1986, 1989). I first learned about Kachru's work by reading Sandra McKay's (1992) highly insightful book, *Teaching English Overseas: An Introduction.* I also appreciate the issues of "ownership" of English raised by Higgins (2003).

[2] See Platt, Weber, and Lian (1984, 2–3) and McKay (1992, 89–95).

[3] See Smith (1983, 14), discovered in McKay (1992, 90).

[4] See Crystal's (2003) book, *English as a Global Language,* for an historical account of how English became a language of use in countries around the world.

[5] See Wong (1992) for a detailed linguistic analysis of Singapore English.

[6] Much of the information about English language curricula in different countries was obtained through interviews with teachers and school administrators from each country. I would like to thank Theresa Tseng for assisting me with these interviews. Ko (1993) and Jung and Norton (2002) have also done very useful research. I also found a document published by the Korean Ministry of Education (1997) to be quite useful.

[7] To learn more about the Hess Language School, log on to: *www.hess.com.tw/english*

[8] The American University Alumni Association website is worth looking at: *www.auathailand.org*

[9] Yoyogi Seminar is featured in a documentary, *Cram School.* See Sano and Miyano (1988).

[10] See Becker (2001, 69). Short (1994) also writes extensively about the academic backgrounds of ESL students who arrive in U.S. schools.

[11] See Crandall (2003). It is important to realize, as Higgins (2003) has researched, that many of the students from the outer-circle countries who study in K–12 settings have strong identities and ownership issues related to their outer-circle English.

[12] Harklau, Losey, and Siegal (1999) and Thonus (2003) write about serving the writing needs of Generation 1.5 students, including pedagogical practices that have proven to be effective.

[13] Dwyer (1998) explains experiences of students with limited English proficiency placed in low-track high school sections. Many of these students did not reach the more advanced science . and math classes. They experienced less challenging academics, as well as scored lower on standardized tests. Hull, Rose, Fraser, and Castellano (2002) also provide a deeply disturbing under-standing of remediation as a social construct.

[14] See research done by Cummins (1994).

[15] Becker (2001) writes about the team-teaching model in more detail.

[16] See Becker (2001, 64).

[17] See Pèregoy and Boyle (2001, 23). Also see Lessow-Hurley (1996) and Ovando and Cullier (1985) for discussions on bilingual education programs and issues attached to them.

[18] See Conrad (2000) for a detailed description of this dual-level Spanish/English classroom.

[19] This information was obtained from the Institute of International Education: *www.opendoors.iienetwork.org*

[20] I surveyed Language Institutes at the following universities in the United States: Columbia University, New York University, University of Pittsburgh, Fairleigh Dickinson University, Indiana University of Pennsylvania, San Diego State University, Loyola University, The University of Pennsylvania, Marshall University, The University of Tennessee, University of Southern California, California State University, The University of Michigan, and Wichita State University.

[21] A fuller description of the American Language Institute's EAP program at Indiana University of Pennsylvania can be found at this website: *www.ali.iup.edu*

[22] To learn about this refugee program, log on to: *www.refugee-esl.org*

[23] To learn more about the Greater Pittsburgh Literacy Center, log on to *www.gplc.org*

[24] *See www.hct.ac.ae/about/colleges_aamc.html*

[25] These numbers are based on figures for 2004. To learn more about Sophia University, log on to *www.sophia.ac.jp*

Part 2

Principles of EFL/ESL Teaching

Language and learning and teaching can be an exciting and refreshing interval in the day for students and teacher. There are so many possible ways of stimulating communicative interaction, yet, all over the world, one still finds classrooms where language learning is a tedious, dry-as-dust process, devoid of contact with the real world in which language use is as natural as breathing.

—Rivers 1987, 14

Teaching Language as Communication among People

- What is the main goal of a communicative classroom?
- How do EFL/ESL teachers provide opportunities for students to communicate in English?
- What makes a classroom communicative?
- What roles are native and near-native English-speaking EFL/ESL teachers expected to play?
- What problems do some EFL/ESL teachers face when teaching English as communication among people?

What Is the Main Goal of a Communicative Classroom?

The primary goal of a communicative classroom is student development of *communicative competence* in English. At a basic level, this includes development of students' ability to comprehend and produce written and spoken English in communicatively proficient and accurate ways.

Influenced by the thinking of Dell Hymes,[1] Michael Canal and Merrill Swain,[2] and especially Sandra Savignon,[3] communicative competence has four interrelated components—grammatical, discourse, socio-cultural, and strategic competency.

To have *grammatical competency* means to be able to recognize sentence-level grammatical forms, including *lexical* items (vocabulary/words), *morphological* items (smallest units of meaning, such as *re-* meaning again in *remind*), *syntactic* features (word order), and *phonological* features (consonant and vowel sounds, intonation patterns, and other aspects of the sound system).

Communicative competence also includes *discourse competency,* or the ability to interconnect a series of utterances (written or spoken) to form a meaningful text (letter, e-mail, essay, telephone conversation, formal speech, or joke). This includes being able to use both *top-down* (knowledge based on experience and context) and *bottom-up* (knowledge of grammatical forms) processing. (See Part 3 of this book, Teaching Language Skills, for more discussion on top-down and bottom-up processing.) According to Sandra Savignon *discourse competency* also includes text *coherence* and *cohesion.* She defines *coherence* as "the relation of all sentences or utterances in a text to a single global proposition (or topic)."[4] While coherence establishes a global meaning or topic, cohesion provides the smaller structural links between individual sentences, such as in the use of *first, second, next,* and *after this.*[5]

The third component of communicative competence is *socio-cultural competency,* which is the ability to use English in social contexts in culturally appropriate ways. In Chapter 7, Culture and the Language Teacher, the importance of being able to adjust to the way people in different cultures and subcultures interact is discussed. When do people compliment each other? How often? What kinds of things do they compliment? What kind of verbal and nonverbal behaviors do they use? The same kinds of questions can be asked about other functions of language, such as when apologizing, complaining, interrupting, asking for permission, requesting, and turning down an invitation. Developing socio-cultural competency means being able to adapt the use of English to the ways people in any culture interact. For example, if an Egyptian were living in Toronto, then he or she would need to adapt to the socio-cultural rules for using English in Toronto. However, if this same person moves to Tokyo, the socio-cultural rules when using English change. Socio-cultural competency becomes most interesting when people from different cultures, such as people from Taiwan, Korea, and Thailand, interact in a context outside any of their own native cultures, as in rural western Pennsylvania. Do they follow the rules used by Americans in rural western Pennsylvania? Or do they create their own rules based partly on the common features of their cultures?

Finally, communicative competence includes *strategic competency, or* the ability to cope with breakdowns in communication, to problem-solve in unfamiliar contexts when communication fails, and to draw on strategies that help restore communication. Examples of such strategies include knowing how to explain directions by drawing a map, knowing how to ask someone to repeat what she said in different words, paraphrasing to check understanding, and being able to guess the meaning of words (in print or speech) from the context.

How Do EFL/ESL Teachers Provide Opportunities for Students to Communicate in English?

Some EFL/ESL classes are taught in a teacher-centered fashion. Recall Yoshi's class. Interaction is dominated by the teacher who, for example, gives lengthy explanations and lectures, drills repetitively, asks the majority of the questions, and makes judgments about the students' answers. However, to provide chances for students to gain communicative competence, other EFL/ESL teachers see value in getting students involved in interacting in English and in this section, based on a framework provided by Littlewood,[6] I discuss how this can be done.

Some teachers who aim at having a communicative classroom begin lessons with what Littlewood calls "precommunicative activities." Used primarily with beginning- and intermediate-level students, precommunicative activities allow the teacher to isolate specific elements of knowledge or skill that compose communicative ability, giving students opportunities to practice them without having to fully engage in communicating meaning. Littlewood discusses two types of precommunicative activities—structural and quasi-communicative. *Structural activities* focus on the grammar and lexicon (vocabulary) of English, while *quasi-communicative activities* focus on how the language is used to communicate meaning. Quasi-communicative activities are often in the form of dialogues or relatively simple activities in which students interact under highly controlled conditions.

Illustrations of these two types of precommunicative activities in a beginning-level class I observed in Hungary are provided. The teacher's goal was to teach students how to ask about food likes and dislikes. The teacher first taught a grammatical item, the use of the auxiliary verb *do* when used in a yes-no question (a structural activity). She began by giving several examples, such as this one:

Statement: You like (to eat) cake.
Question: Do you like (to eat) cake?

She then led students in a vocabulary-building activity (another structural activity) in which she put large pictures of food items on the wall and matched them with the names of food items she had written in big bold letters on separate pieces of paper. She gave students chances to read the names of food items, say them aloud as a whole class, and copy the names while drawing their own pictures of each item.

In order to work up to a communicative activity, the teacher gave students the sample precommunicative activity handout below. Then the teacher held up a picture of each item (e.g., of a piece of cake), and as she did this, she asked the whole class, "Do you like to eat cake?" The students then shouted out "Yes!" or "No!" depending on their own preference. There was lots of laughter, especially when she asked, "Do you like to eat toilet paper?"

Do you like (to eat) cake?
bananas?
fish?
ice cream?
apples?
toilet paper?
pie?

A precommunicative activity handout.

The teacher then handed out a dialogue that combined grammatical and vocabulary items and added a little new language:

A. Do you like cake?

B. Yes, I do.

A: Do you like bananas?

B: Yes, very much.

A: How about fish? Do you like fish?

B: I don't know. Maybe

The teacher read the dialogue out loud, asked students to repeat it after her, and asked students to practice it in pairs.

Next, the teacher did another quasi-communicative activity by dividing students into pairs and placing a set of pictures of different food items face down on their desks. The students took turns picking a picture from a pile, and, using the picture as a cue, asked each other about their likes and dislikes. The teacher included a few comical items, such as a picture of soap, and a few students made up their own comical items, such as chicken ice cream.

Some teachers follow up precommunicative activities with what Littlewood calls *communicative activities.* To illustrate what communicative activities are and how they are used to follow precommunicative activities, let's return to my observation on food items and preferences. After the structural and quasi-communicative activities, and reviewing basic letterwriting formatting, the teacher asked the students to write short letters to students in one of her other classes. Although the teacher encouraged the students to ask about what food they liked, she also encouraged them to express themselves freely.

There are many other possible examples of precommunicative and communicative activities teachers can have students do in classrooms, and I provide more examples in Part 3 on teaching language skills. The point here is that, as teachers, we can create lessons that get students involved in communicating with the teacher and each other in meaningful ways in English.

If you are teaching students beyond a basic level, it's okay to skip the precommunicative activities. If we begin with communicative activities, students can begin with a task, such as writing and producing their own play, giving oral and written presentations on topics they researched through interviewing and library research, and solving problems in small groups. As students work on these tasks, their attention will sometimes shift to language use—for example, they might ask the meaning of a word or how to express an idea—but the thrust of the lesson is for students to communicate with the teacher and each other in meaningful ways.

What Makes a Communicative Classroom Communicative?

Four closely related factors contribute to making classrooms communicative. The first is reducing the central (and traditional) position of the teacher.[7] However, this does not mean that teachers have to give up control of the class. The teacher can maintain control of what goes on in the classroom while still giving students freedom to initiate communication among themselves and with the teacher[8] (see the discussion in Chapter 5).

Factors contributing to making classrooms communicative include:

- Reduction in the centrality of the teacher
- An appreciation for the uniqueness of individuals
- Chances for students to express themselves in meaningful ways
- Choices, both in relation to what students say and how they say it

Genuine communication is enhanced if there is an appreciation for the uniqueness of individuals in the class.[9] Each student brings unique language-learning and life experiences (both successful and unsuccessful) to the classroom, as well as feelings about these experiences (including joy, anxiety, and fear). As teachers, we need to be sensitive to each individual's background and affective state. To create a classroom atmosphere conducive to communication, we need to understand and accept each student as he or she is, and sometimes this is harder than one might imagine.

Also, providing chances for the students to express themselves in meaningful ways contributes to a communicative classroom. Students need chances to listen to each other, express their ideas in speech and writing, and read each other's writing. Negotiation of meaning needs to become the norm; while negotiating, students need chances to ask for and receive clarification, confirm their understanding, ask and respond to questions, and react to responses. If true negotiation of meaning is going on, students will be fully engaged in using English to understand the meaning intended by others, as well as to express their own meaning as clearly as possible. Negotiation of meaning also implies that students have choices as to what they want to say, to whom they want to say it, and how they want to say it. Throughtout this book I provide a variety of classroom activities that promote such interactions. For example, in Chapter 9 I discuss how students can use games, buzz groups, stories, and problem-solving activities to promote communication. In Chapter 11 I discuss writing activities that do this, too.

What Roles Are Native and Near-Native English-Speaking EFL/ESL Teachers Expected to Play?

Whether you teach in a K–12, EFL/ESL adult, or language institute setting, you will play a variety of roles as an EFL/ESL teacher:[10] drama coach, puppet maker, creative-writing specialist, folksinger, mime, photographer, cross-cultural trainer, public speaker, counselor, film critic, poet, storyteller, discussion leader, team builder, grammarian, jazz chanter, reading specialist, error analyst, gaming specialist, values clarifier, computer program specialist, materials developer, curriculum planner, curriculum evaluator, interviewer, friend, language authority, interaction manager, cultural informant, needs assessor, language model, joke teller, disciplinarian, language tester, text adapter, parent, strategy trainer, artist.

As the list shows, teaching is multifaceted, and much of the complexity involves learning how to assume roles that capitalize on our abilities in English while we take on roles that contribute to creating interaction in the classroom that is meaningful for both teacher and students. In this section I address these two sets of roles:

Roles related to English language abilities

- Language authority
- Cultural informant
- Model English speaker

Roles related to the ability to create meaningful interaction

- Needs assessor
- Classroom manager
- Text adaptor
- Entertainer

Roles Related to English Language Abilities

One role we are expected to play is language authority. We are expected to explain complex rules of English grammar, such as the difference between static and dynamic verbs or adjectives and adverbs. However, this role is consonant with our native or near-native intuitive ability to explain the nuances of English, such as how emphatic stress changes the meaning of a sentence, as in *I went* there, *I* went *there,* and I *went there.* Likewise, we are asked to explain the rules of speaking—for example, when a speaker of English would say *I'm sorry* as opposed to *Excuse me,* or what speakers should say and do during social situations in different cultures, such as at a dinner party or when scheduling an appointment with a doctor on the phone. Sometimes we are expected to explain the fine differences in meaning in readings as well as the rules of writing—for example, how to write a good paragraph, use transitions to connect paragraphs and ideas, and use punctuation.

Students also expect us to speak English with them and to model how it is used to express meaning. For example, some students are curious about our use of humor (or lack of it) and its appropriate use, as well as how we display nonverbal behaviors. In addition, some students expect us to use samples of our speech and writing as a model text for them to study. For example, students sometimes ask me to pronounce a word or sentence as they attempt to approximate the pronunciation.

As native or near-native speakers, we also are expected to take on the role of cultural informant. Students ask questions not only about language behaviors *(What is a normal distance to stand from a stranger in Ireland? What do you say when you greet someone for the first time? How do you let a friend know you are angry with her?),* but also about cultural values, beliefs, and assumptions *(Why do Americans say they value equality but then discriminate against each other? What is traditional about Australia?).*

Students also ask questions about socialization—for example, as it takes place in education, family life, and friendships *(What's dating like in the United States? Could you explain what goes on in a typical American family? What do best friends do together in your country?)*—and even about technology *(Could you explain the New York City subway system?).*

For native English speakers, answering such questions is not easy because most of us are never asked these questions in our own countries. The same is true for non-native speakers who study English in English-speaking countries and who are asked questions about their cultures that are equally difficult to answer. We unconsciously acquire the rules of our native cultures as participants in them. Since we have not had the opportunity to think about our own experiences beyond the normal expectations of those in our home countries, it can be perplexing to be asked questions related to our cultures. However, time, thought, experience, and research can make answering such questions easier.

Roles Related to Creating Meaningful Interaction

A number of educators encourage language teachers to play the role of needs assessor, including learning about students' language-learning history, goals, interests, study habits, learning strategies, and language-learning styles. They suggest teachers interview students, ask them to complete questionnaires, and observe what they do and say.[11]

With small classes, I personally like to use dialogue journals to learn about the students. Dialogue journals are like informal letters written back and forth between the student and the teacher. The journal entries give students chances to communicate ideas in writing; as a result, it is possible to learn what each student is interested in and cares about. Dialogue journals can be a way to discover what really bothers students or to discuss personal topics—for example, why a student is not doing his or her homework or how he or she can overcome excessive anxiety when asked to speak English.

The teacher can also take on the role of text adapter. Quite often, the textbook and the teacher's manual become the teacher's main resource, but the text does not ever provide enough ways to promote the kind of interaction the teacher wants to have in the classroom. To foster genuine interaction, teachers must go beyond the text by adapting materials and activities to the lessons in the text or introducing new activities unrelated to it. We can add such things as role plays, games, movies, TV shows, songs, readings, and news programs. We can have birthday parties, plan trips, tell stories, and interview guest speakers. For more ideas, see Chapter 6 and Chapters 8–11.

Another role the teacher can play to promote interaction is that of classroom manager (see Chapter 5). To manage classrooms, we need to be able to:

- Engineer the amount of classroom talk we do
- Manipulate our questioning behaviors
- Control the way we give instructions
- Orchestrate group and pair work
- Keep learners on task
- Make language comprehensible to students
- Handle affective variables of classroom life

We are sometimes asked to take on the role of entertainer. I have included this role because it is controversial. Some students are good at getting us to tell stories about ourselves and others, tell jokes, and even sing. EFL/ESL students can be a great audience, laughing at jokes, attentively listening, and encouraging us to continue. While some of us will strongly argue that our job is not to entertain, some of us see value in the teacher's role as entertainer because it can lower the students' level of anxiety and increase their level of comprehension.

What Problems Do Some EFL/ESL Teachers Face when Teaching English as Communication among People?

Beginning with this chapter, a section of each subsequent chapter addresses the kinds of problems EFL/ESL teachers report. Here, it's the problems teachers have related to interacting with students. Suggestions on how teachers might resolve these problems are provided.

Problems some EFL/ESL teachers face include the following:

- The bandwagon problem
- The overly anxious problem
- The engagement problem

The Bandwagon Problem

One problem of teaching language as interaction between people can occur in EFL/ESL classrooms when teachers jump on the latest methodological bandwagon. For the phrase *to jump on a bandwagon,* *Roget's Thesaurus* gives the alternatives "to float or swim with the stream; to join the parade, go with the crowd." With this in mind, as Mark Clarke points out, bandwagons are "the 'latest word,' the trendy, the fashionable, the most up-to-date in methods, materials, technique."[12]

As Earl Stevick stated some years ago at a TESOL conference, bandwagons provide confidence, the company of others who believe in the same thing, and useful techniques.[13] Those who are new to teaching often welcome a method of teaching that provides these things. This is only problematic if teachers cannot see beyond the "in way" of teaching, cannot accept the bandwagon as simply other people's prescriptions about teaching based on their personal set of beliefs about the relationship between teaching and learning. If we blindly follow a certain method because it is said to be the best way to teach, we become impervious to other creative ways we can interact with our students, and students with each other. As I discuss in Chapter 2, teachers can be liberated to make our own informed teaching decisions, if we know how to become aware of teaching behaviors, analyze their consequences, and generate new teaching behaviors based on the awareness. Reflecting on our teaching through classroom observation, talking with other teachers, and writing about teaching are far more important to teachers than jumping of the latest bandwagon. While bandwagons provide us with ideas about teaching possibilities, confidence, company, and techniques, they may not liberate us to be able to make our own informed teaching decisions, and they could stop us from genuine interaction in the classroom.

The Overly Anxious Problem

Tom Scovel defines anxiety as "a state of apprehension, a vague fear."[14] H. D. Brown adds that "it is associated with feelings of uneasiness, self-doubt, apprehension, or worry."[15] There are reasons for teachers to think about why students are anxious:[16]

- Inability to pronounce sounds and words
- Not knowing the meaning of words or sentences
- Inability to understand and answer questions
- Reputation of the language class as a place for failure
- Peer criticism
- Not knowing or understanding course goals or requirements
- Testing, especially oral testing
- Previous unsuccessful language-learning attempts
- Encountering different cultural values and behaviors

High levels of anxiety can inhibit students from interacting with the teacher and classmates. I have observed particularly high levels of anxiety in many different teaching settings, but especially in EFL settings where students do not have much experience interacting in English, as well as in K–12 ESL settings where language learners are expected to speak English in front of native speakers. In fact, anxiety can create so much apprehension that some students cannot function normally. Most of us have experienced such debilitating anxiety. The teacher asks a question in the new language; all we can do is sit, hearts slightly racing, mouths slightly open, staring at the book or the teacher, nothing coming to mind. Facilitative anxiety, in contrast, can create just the right amount of tension to bring out the best in us. This is what happens to some actors and public speakers before they appear onstage. It can also happen to students before taking a test, and to EFL/ESL students in situations where they are given a chance to use English.

If students in our classes have high degrees of anxiety that are limiting them, there are things we can do to possibly reduce this. For example, they do not need criticism on their language performance. Rather, we must show understanding: When a student expresses an idea, we can use an "understanding response"[17] by really listening to the student and paraphrasing back what he or she said. Paraphrasing not only can provide a way for the student to reflect on his or her own language in a non-critical way but can also improve understanding. When we consistently and sincerely work at trying to understand students' meaning without expressing verbal or nonverbal judgment of the language used, a positive, trusting relationship between the student and teacher can develop, one that also reduces anxiety about being in a language classroom.

Tom Farrell, who taught university students in Korea and Singapore, suggests that students analyze their own propensity for anxiety through the use of personal diaries. If the student sees value in writing about his or her feelings in a journal addressed to the teacher, the topic of the student's anxiety could be pursued by the teacher or even initiated by the student. As Farrell points out, "This use of a diary can show the students that they are not totally alone in times of emotional distress."[18]

The Engagement Problem

As previously mentioned, promoting interaction in the classroom requires the teacher to step out of the limelight and yield to the students so that they feel free to interact with the teacher and each other. However, this is not easy for some teachers. As Wilga Rivers puts it, "Never having experienced an interactive classroom, [teachers] are afraid it will be chaotic and hesitate to try."[19] Adding to this problem are the students' attitudes. Students quite often come into our classrooms with little experience in initiating and participating in interaction in English. As such, they will also hesitate to interact, afraid that things will become out of control, frenzied, or embarrassing.

To avoid this half-engagement problem, it is our responsibility as teachers to provide an atmosphere conducive to interaction. As teachers, we need to show emotional maturity, sensitivity to the students' feelings, and a perceptiveness and commitment that interaction in English is not only appropriate but also expected and necessary for the students if they want to learn to communicate in English. As Rivers has said, "when a teacher demonstrates such qualities, students lose their fear of embarrassment and are willing to try to express themselves."[20]

TEACHER SELF-DEVELOPMENT TASKS

Talk Tasks

1. The point of this task is to learn about the language-learning history of an EFL/ESL student.

   a. Talk to an EFL/ESL student at an intermediate/advanced level. Find out about his or her language-learning background. What kinds of language-learning experiences has he or she had? What kinds of classroom activities does he or she prefer and not prefer? Why?

   b. Get together with other teachers who have talked with students. Explain what you have learned. Listen to what other teachers have learned.

2. Imagine you are asked to teach a lesson on expressing ability through the use of the word *can*, as in "She can cook Mexican food."

   a. Note ideas for a lesson for beginning-level students that takes them through a set of precommunicative and communicative activities.

   b. Collaborate with other teachers on the design of this lesson.

3. Study the list of roles for EFL/ESL teachers given earlier in this chapter. Which roles do you believe you can easily adopt in the classroom? Which roles might be difficult for you? What additional roles can you add to this list? Compare your answers with the responses of others.

4. I see value in the teacher taking on the role of entertainer. Do you agree? Why or why not? Find out what others think.

Observation and Talk Tasks

1. This task gives you a chance to reflect on your teaching. It involves four steps, and you will need the cooperation of at least one other teacher.

   Step One: Tape-record or videotape a class you teach or another teacher teaches.

   Step Two: Listen to or view the tape. As you do, take descriptive notes, draw sketches, and jot down samples of interactive dialogue. Avoid making judgments about the teaching as being good or bad. Simply describe the activities the students do.

   Step Three: Reflect on the experience. List three things you learned about yourself as a teacher and about teaching. List one or two new things you would like to try out in your teaching.

2. The point of this observation is to consider what happens in the classroom from the student's perspective.

   Visit a class. Sit next to a student. Draw a line down the center of your notepad to make two columns. On one side write down everything the teacher does, including what the teacher asks that student to do. On the other side write down what the student does. For example:

What the Teacher Does	What the Student Does[22]
Tells class to open their books to page 103.	Opens book to page 33.
Calls on a student to answer question one.	Searches page 33 for question one. Looks at classmate's book. Sees she is on wrong page. Flips pages. Is silent. Looks at page. Looks at teacher.
Teacher calls on another student.	

At the end of the observation, consider the class from the student's point of view. Meet with other teachers who have done the same task. Talk about what some students experience in EFL classrooms.

Journal Writing Tasks

1. Reflect on the kinds of roles you play in the classroom. Which roles do you like to play? Which roles are you not comfortable playing? What do you need to learn to play some roles more professionally? What additional roles could you play?

2. Consider the list of problems teachers face discussed earlier in this chapter. Write about some of your experiences related to these problems. Have you solved them yet? What could you do to work through unsolved problems? If you have had chances to talk with others about these same problems, write about what they feel and think about the problem and possible solutions.

3. Reread the first section (pages 63–65) on communicative competence. Write your thoughts on what competence includes.

Recommended Teacher Resources

Teaching Methodology Books

Brown, H. D. *Teaching by Principles: An Interaction Approach to Language Pedagogy.* 2d ed. White Plains, NY: Longman, 2000.

Celce-Murcia, M., ed. *Teaching English as a Second or Foreign Language.* 3d ed. Boston: Heinle & Heinle, 2001.

Larsen-Freeman, D. *Techniques and Principles in Language Teaching.* 2d ed. New York: Oxford University Press, 2001.

Richard-Amato, P. A. *Making It Happen: From Interactive to Participatory Language Teaching.* 3d ed. White Plains, NY: Longman, 2003.

Richards, J. C., and T. Rodgers. *Approaches and Methods in Language Teaching,* 2d ed. New York: Cambridge University Press, 2001.

Richards, J. C., and W. A. Renandya, eds. *Methodology in Language Teaching: An Anthology of Current Practice.* New York: Cambridge University Press, 2002.

Rivers, W., ed. *Interactive Language Teaching.* New York: Cambridge University Press, 1987.

Teacher-Friendly Books on Theory, Research, and Practice

Brown, H. D. *Principles of Language Learning and Teaching.* 4th ed. White Plains, NY: Longman, 2000.

Holiday, A. *Appropriate Methodology and Social Context.* New York: Cambridge University Press, 1994.

Johnson, K. E. *Understanding Communication in Second Language Classrooms.* New York: Cambridge University Press, 1995.

Littlewood, W. *Communicative Language Teaching*. Cambridge: Cambridge University Press, 1981.

Norton, B., and K. Toohey. *Critical Pedagogies and Language Learning*. New York: Cambridge University Press, 2004.

Savignon, S. *Communicative Competence: Theory and Classroom Practice*. New York: McGraw Hill, 1997.

Scovel, T. *Learning New Languages: A Guide to Second Language Acquisition*. Boston: Heinle & Heinle, 2001.

Zamel, V., and R. Spack, eds. *Enriching ESOL Pedagogy*. Mahwah, NJ: Lawrence Erlbaum, 2002.

Endnotes

[1] See Hymes (1971, 1972).

[2] See Canale and Swain (1980).

[3] See Savignon (1997, 2001).

[4] See Savignon (2001, 17).

[5] See Halliday and Hasan (1976). Also see Celce-Murcia and Larsen-Freeman (1999) for examples of cohesive devices.

[6] See Littlewood (1981).

[7] Breen and Candlin (1980), Canale and Swain (1980), Nunan (1988), and Rivers (1987) agree that an interactive classroom requires a reduction in the centrality of the teacher.

[8] Stevick (1978, 1980) discusses the concept of teacher control and student initiative.

[9] I agree with Curran (1976) who focuses our attention on the "whole person" of the student.

[10] This list was generated from my own experience and from reading Altman (1981), Richards and Rodgers (2001), Tudor (1993), and Wright (1987).

[11] Anderson (1988) created a learning-style inventory, while Oxford (1990) asks students to evaluate their own language abilities in reading, writing, listening, and speaking. In addition, Reid (1987, 1995) discusses learning styles.

[12] The dictionary definition was discovered in Clarke (1982). The quote is also from Clarke (p. 439). Clarke has very much influenced my thinking in regard to making my own informed decisions. I highly recommend his original 1982 article, as well as his more recent 2003 book and his 2002 book chapter with Sandra Silberstein.

[13] See Stevick (1982).

[14] See Scovel (1978, 135).

[15] See Brown (2000, 107).

[16] This list was created from the work of McCoy (1979), Oxford (1999), and Alpert and Haber (1960). Also see Ohata (2004) for

similar discussion of anxiety for Japanese college students in the United States.

[17] See Curran (1978).

[18] See Farrell (1993, 17).

[19] See Rivers (1987, 10).

[20] See Rivers (1987, 10).

[21] Teachers can benefit from reading Flaitz (2003), *Understanding Your International Students.*

[22] This activity was originally designed by Robert Oprandy.

Success [in learning a language] depends less on materials, techniques, and linguistic analysis, and more on what goes on inside and between people in the classroom.

—Stevick 1980, 4

Classroom Management

- What is classroom management?
- How can EFL/ESL teachers use knowledge of classroom management to create opportunities for students to interact in English in meaningful ways?
- What can K–12 teachers do to create a learning setting for ESL students?
- What problems do some EFL/ESL teachers have in managing classroom interaction?

What Is Classroom Management?

Classroom management refers to the way teachers organize what goes on in the classroom. As the most powerful person in the classroom, the teacher has the authority to influence the kind of interaction that goes on in the class, and this interaction is created from a combination of many related factors—such as how much the teacher talks and what the teacher says, and how the teacher gives instructions, keeps students on task, and makes language comprehensible to the students. The goal of classroom management is to create a classroom atmosphere conducive to interacting in English in meaningful ways so that students can make progress in learning English.

How Can EFL/ESL Teachers Use Knowledge of Classroom Management to Create Opportunities for Students to Interact in English in Meaningful Ways?

This section discusses how teachers manage classroom teaching so that students have opportunities to interact in English in meaningful ways. I emphasize throughout that classroom management is a personal and creative endeavor in which a complex set of factors are combined and constantly tested through classroom use.

Teacher Talk

When asked to tape-record their teaching, listen to the tape, and total the amount of time they talk, teachers are generally surprised to discover they spend much more time talking than they had imagined. Some teachers will say that too much talk is bad and should be avoided. But this is not necessarily true. As David Nunan points out, "It can be argued that in many foreign language classrooms, teacher talk is important in providing learners with the only substantial live target language input they are likely to receive."[1] When it comes down to it, it is not how much time we spend talking, but rather *the way we use talk* to promote meaningful interaction that is significant. Certain uses of teacher talk lack this purpose and are therefore not productive. Other uses seem purposeful and potentially productive.

Some EFL/ESL teachers mindlessly think aloud in the classroom. Although some students might gain something positive from this authentic language experience, it can confuse students, so some students might stop listening even when the teacher has something important to say. Or, if the teacher gives long explanations about language or long-winded speeches on abstract ideas, some students will become passive learners, accepting English as a subject in which the teacher lectures, sometimes in abstract terms that are beyond comprehension. However, we can elect to use English selectively and purposefully to answer students' questions, give instructions, demonstrate useful reading processes, explain homework assignments, relate an amusing story that students can comprehend, participate in daily interpersonal communications with students in English, and use teacher talk as part of the students' planned listening comprehension experience, such as a dictation.

The Teacher's Questions

Teachers ask a lot of questions. For example, in a study of the frequency of questions asked by elementary school teachers in the United States, Nash and Shiman discovered teachers ask between 45 and 150 questions every half hour.[2] My own observations reveal that EFL/ESL teachers also ask a lot of questions. I observed six expatriate teachers who were all teaching in different contexts in Japan and found they averaged 52 questions every 30 minutes during teacher-initiated activities. Since teachers do ask many questions, understanding questioning behaviors can benefit those who want to stimulate students to communicate in English in meaningful ways.

One way to focus on our questioning behaviors is to consider the purposes of questions (see The Purpose of Teachers' Questions[3] on page 83). For many teachers, one purpose is to ask students to "display" their knowledge. For example, when a teacher holds up a large paper clock and asks, *What time is it?* the teacher is asking students to show they know how to tell time in English. And when the teacher asks, *What is the past tense of* to do? the teacher wants to see if they know this grammatical point.

Another purpose for asking questions is to learn things about students and their knowledge through referential questions. Such questions can stimulate interaction and show genuine interest in the students. For example, if the teacher forgot his or her watch and wants to know the time, he or she would use the referential question, *What time is it?* The same is true if the teacher asks, *Who has been to a museum?*—to know who has and who has not been to one because of genuine interest.

Many of those who advocate an interactive approach to EFL/ESL teaching favor the use of referential questions over display questions. My own belief is that both have a place in the language classroom. Referential questions provide a means through which to bring "real questions" into the classroom. They can also be engaging for students because the questions are aimed at communicating with them, not testing their knowledge. However, display questions offer a way to practice language or to drill students, something some students both like and need, and when students find display questions to be engaging, this is being meaningful to them.

Another purpose of teachers' questions is to check students' comprehension; to do this, teachers often ask, *Do you understand?* Such comprehension checks are not as common outside as they are inside classrooms, and I wonder what real value they sometimes

The Purpose of Teachers' Questions	
Display Question	A question in which the teacher already knows the answer and wants the student to display knowledge. *(What color is your shirt?)*
Referential Question	A question in which the teacher does not know the answer. *(What is your favorite color?)*
Comprehension Check	A question to find out if a student understands. *(Do you understand?)*
Confirmation Question	A question to verify what was said. *(You said you got up at 6:00?)*
Clarification Check	A question to further define or clarify. *(Did you say you got up at 6:00 or 7:00?)*

have. Much of the time, if asked, *Do you understand?* students will reply that they do, even when they do not. Perhaps a question such as, *Who can tell me what I just said?* is more valuable because it not only shows student comprehension, but also gives the student practice in paraphrasing.

Two other purposes of asking questions are to confirm and clarify understanding. For example, *We'll meet at 6:00. Right?* asks the listener to confirm something that the asker believes is true, while *Did you say you like strawberry or chocolate ice cream?* and *I'm a little confused. What time are we going to meet?* aim at clarification. Confirmation and clarification questions are used outside classrooms more often than inside. As such, I encourage teachers and students to confirm and clarify often, if for no other reason than to have more natural, and hopefully meaningful, conversations inside classrooms.

In addition to focusing on the purpose of questions, we can consider the content of our questions (see The Content of Teachers' Questions on page 84).[4] Questions can include three possible content areas: study, procedure, and life. I have observed that many of the questions in EFL/ESL classrooms are about *study*, often on the study of language, such as on some aspect of grammar or vocabulary. Less often, teachers ask questions about content other than language, such as questions about movies, trees, food, or anything that is not about language itself. Questions can also be about *procedures*, such as questions used to take attendance, return papers, and ask about schedules.

Besides study and procedure, content of questions can be about *life*. As Fanselow points out, questions can be general to a group of people (life-general content) or specific to one person (life-personal content). Two examples of life-general questions are *How do people greet each other in Vietnam?* and *What music is popular among teenagers in France?* Examples of life-personal questions are *What is your favorite kind of music?* and *What did you do at the picnic?*

The Content of Teachers' Questions

Study of Language   Questions that ask students about aspects of language. *(What is the past tense of* eat? *What does the word* acculturation *mean?)*

Study of Subjects   Questions that ask students about content other than the study of language. *(How big is the Little Prince? How many countries are there in the world?)*

Procedure   Questions that ask students about procedural matters. *(Did you do your homework?)*

Life-General   Questions about the lives of groups of people. *(Do Japanese women generally like hot tea in the summer? How do Nigerians celebrate birthdays?)*

Life-Personal   Questions about the lives of individuals. *(Do you like to drink hot tea in the summer? How do you celebrate your birthday?)*

Some teachers believe that when we include study (not about language), life-general, and life-personal questions in our classroom interaction, we can provide greater opportunities for meaningful interaction than when our questions focus exclusively on the study of language and procedures. Study questions can involve students in using language to learn about a topic, rather than simply studying about the language itself. Likewise, life-general and life-personal questions can involve students in talking about their culture and themselves.

Finally, as teachers, we can consider "wait time" in relation to creating chances for students to engage in meaningful interaction. On average, teachers wait less than one second for a student to answer a question before calling on this student again or on another student. In addition, teachers tend not to wait after a student gives a response, reacting very quickly with *Very good!* and the like. As a result, a usual pattern of classroom interaction emerges: The teacher ends up asking many questions, only students who can respond quickly do so, and the teacher ends up reacting to the students' responses. However, if teachers wait a little longer (three to five seconds) and offer polite encouragement through nonverbal behavior, this pattern can change. When teachers extend their wait time after asking a question, student participation may increase in the following ways:[5]

- The average length of students' responses might increase.
- Students could ask more questions.
- Students may react to each other's comments.
- The number of correct responses could go up.
- Students might make more inferences.

I encourage you to increase your wait time, but I also caution that simply increasing wait time will not necessarily create changes in classroom interaction. The teacher needs to be sincere in waiting; he or she has to genuinely want to hear the student's answer and what other students think about it.

Setting Up Classroom Activities

In order to manage and promote interactive classrooms, we also need to know how to arrange a variety of classroom activities. We can choose to have students work (1) alone, (2) in pairs, (3) in small groups, or (4) as a whole class.

Look at the example of different seating arrangements on page 86, which shows that we have choices as to how we have students sit in the class. These arrangements also imply that we have choices about the activities students do in class. They can sit in a traditional seating arrangement or in a semi-circle during teacher-class discussions or lectures. They can stand up and walk around as they study, for example, to memorize lines in a poem. They can move their chairs to sit alone or in groups while working on a task. They can sit face to face, for example, as they interview each other; back-to-back as they simulate a telephone conversation; across from each other as they practice a dialogue; in circles as they solve a problem or discuss an issue; or next to each other as they study a reading selection, plan a party, or collaborate on a piece of writing. They can also move around the class as they practice skits or role plays. The point here is that we do not have to limit the students to traditional seating. If our goal is to provide lots of chances for students to use English to communicate meaning, we need to feel free to create seating combinations that make this possible.

Seating Arrangements: Possibilities

Another aspect of setting up classroom activities is how we group students, and there are a variety of ways to do this. One way is to select students in advance of the class based on personality characteristics or abilities and experience. For example, shy students can be matched with shy or talkative students, fluent students with those who are or are not fluent.

Students can make their own decisions about which group to join, or they can be grouped according to different characteristics, such as month of birthdate, color of eyes, etc. However, some students might be sensitive to being grouped in this way. So if you do allow students to group themselves, make sure it is by characteristics they don't control or that may be sensitive. We can also randomly group students, for example, by having them count off—one through four—and having all the ones form a group, the twos another, and so on. Students could also be given pieces of paper with colored dots and grouped by the color of the dot they receive. The same thing is possible with pieces of candy, feathers, coins, or anything that can be used to distinguish members of a group. Teachers can also cut pictures or proverbs into pieces like a puzzle, hand the pieces out randomly, and have students locate others who have the sections of the same picture or proverb.[6] This way of forming groups can also be an icebreaker, a way to reduce students' anxiety about speaking in English.

If the goal is to form pairs, we can simply have students sitting next to each other pair up or have students pair up on their own. We could also have students randomly pair-up through a pairing technique, such as having each student find the person with the other half of a picture. I find students are amused by a pairing technique in which the teacher holds up a set of strings (half the number of strings as there are students in the class), letting the ends dangle. Each student grabs an end. The students holding the ends of the same string form a pair.[7]

Ways to Group Learners

Selectively by the Teacher in Advance
The teacher can group students with the same or opposite characteristics or mix them. For example, shy students could be grouped together or shy and outgoing students grouped.

By Ability and Experience	**By Personality Factors**
Accurate/Not accurate	Shy/Outgoing
Fluent/Not fluent	Front-sitters/Back-sitters
Been abroad/Not been abroad	Stone-faced/Smilers
Use English at work/Do not	Talkers/Non-talkers
Computer user/Non-user	Early risers/Late sleepers

Randomly in Class

By Characteristics	**By Lottery**	**By Location**
Favorite color, favorite rock group or singer, types of books read	Same flavor candy, same colored dot, same end of string, same number, same piece of picture, same line of sentence, same coin	Same side of room, proximity, number after counting (1, 2, 3, 4; 1 . . .)

Other Ways
Students Self-Select
Pick-Up Teams

Giving Instructions

The way we give instructions is another aspect of managing a classroom. It is worth taking time to consider how we can make our instructions clear and at the same time provide opportunities through the instructions for students to interact in meaningful ways. One way is to write the instructions on the board or show them on an overhead projector screen. Another language activity is to dictate the instructions. After giving the dictation, I have students correct their own or each other's papers by comparing their dictation with a written version.

Some ways to give instructions include:

- Writing down instructions and giving them verbally
- Giving instructions verbally and role-playing them, showing the students what they are to do
- Having a student read the instructions, then having a student or two paraphrase them to the class
- Writing down the instructions, letting the students read them silently, then having them tell you what you expect from them
- Dictating instructions then having the students check each other's dictations
- Miming the instructions as students guess what they are supposed to do
- Whispering the instructions as students lean forward in their seats, then having students repeat the instructions to the person next to them in a whisper

Keeping Students on Task

Teachers can group students, provide activities, and explore ways to give instructions, but this is not always enough to keep students on task. In addition, some teachers believe that keeping students on task is an important part of providing students with opportunities for meaningful interaction. However, this is not always easy, even when the students know what to do. For example, as a great number of experienced EFL/ESL teachers can point out, while working on tasks in small groups, students will sometimes have their own discussions on matters unrelated to the task. Personally, I have no problems with this, especially if their discussions are in English and they come back to and are able to complete the task. (Perhaps they even benefit more from their own discussion than from working on the task.) However, students will sometimes use their native language during group or pair work to work through the task or talk about something else. And the students are very clever about this! Groups might use their native language while the teacher is on another side of the room and switch back to English as the teacher gets closer.

There are things we can do to keep students on task. The instructions themselves can be important. Some educators believe that students tend to begin working on a task sooner and work toward its completion when it is clear to them what the task involves.[8] Setting a reasonable time limit for the students to accomplish the task may also keep them on task. If students know they cannot possibly finish the task, for example, if you ask them to answer 20 questions on a long reading selection in 30 minutes, they might stop working on the task.

One thing that works for me is to require an oral or written report as a part of the task. For example, if a group task was assigned to identify the traits of a good student, each group of students would be required to write these traits on the board toward the end of the lesson. If the task was to write a dialogue, the students would be expected to act it out or read it to the class.

Finally, the teacher needs to stay out of the way, letting the students work on the task. This is not always easy to do! Some teachers talk to students while they work. I have seen some teachers, including myself, circling, listening, and finally interrupting students in groups to make a comment or ask a question. Sometimes this keeps students even more intently on their task. But, it can also do the opposite. By the time the teacher leaves, students can be totally off task.

In summary, here are some suggestions for keeping students on task:

- Give clear instructions. Make sure the students know what the goal of the task is.
- Let students know that you expect them to stay on the task.
- Have students work on tasks that interest them.
- Have students work on tasks that they can accomplish in a set amount of time. Let students know how much time they have left to complete the task as they work on it.
- Give tasks that have a product as an outcome. Let students know they are expected to report on their findings or conclusions—for example, to give their solution to a problem or their answers to reading comprehension questions.
- Appoint students to take on roles—for example, as recording secretary, timekeeper, or discussion leader.
- Let the students work on the task. Do no interrupt without first considering your purpose. Let the students ask for your input.

Making Language Comprehensible to Students

As EFL teachers, we can also work at providing opportunities for meaningful interaction by making language comprehensible to the students. If the language used by the teacher or in materials is not comprehensible, students can lose interest, become anxious or frustrated, and sometimes become passive or inattentive. As such, it makes sense to work at making language comprehensible, but how can this be done?[9] I suggest three ways to make language comprehensible to students:

- Simplify speech
- Add mediums
- Negotiate meaning

First, we can attempt to make language comprehensible by simplifying our speech. This includes using a kind of "foreign talk," a simplified register or style of speech.[10] Foreigner talk, as it is sometimes used in the classroom, includes exaggerated pronunciation and facial expressions; slower speech rate; frequent uses of pauses, gestures, and sentence expansion; and completing students' sentences for them. We can also simplify materials, as some writers of texts do. They present students with authentic materials (notes, newspaper articles, textbook excerpts, crossword puzzles, maps, letters, advertisements, etc.), but they also simplify the language to their estimate of the students' level of comprehension.

Second, we can add media, including those that are linguistic aural (speech), linguistic visual (print), nonlinguistic visual (pictures, objects, realia), nonlinguistic aural (bird chirps, the sound of water flowing, the sound of the wind in the trees, etc.), and paralinguistic (gestures, eye contact, touch, distance/use of space, etc.).[11] For example, if the students are to read an authentic restaurant menu and the text (linguistic visual/print) is too difficult for them, the teacher and students can bring in or draw pictures of the food on the menu (adding a nonlinguistic medium), bring in real food items for students to taste and smell (also nonlinguistic), write a short description of different foods (adding more linguistic visual), or act out how a particular food is eaten, such as how to eat a plate of spaghetti with a spoon and fork or Japanese ramen with chopsticks.

Third, we can work at making language comprehensible to students by negotiating meaning. The teacher can open up communication by asking questions that aim at clarification and confirmation. These same types of questions are useful for negotiating meaning for both the teacher and students; when the students work at clarifying and confirming meaning, language can become more comprehensible to them.

Managing an Interactive Classroom:
Questions Teachers Can Ask

To conclude this section on creating opportunities for interaction, I offer the following questions for you to ask yourself.

- How much do I talk in the classroom? What function does my talk serve? Does my talk seem to be productive? Unproductive? Are there times when I do not need to talk?
- What are the purposes of my questions? Do I mostly ask students to display their knowledge, or do I also ask questions to discover and learn about what the students know and do? Do I ask questions to clarify and confirm understanding of what students have said?
- How long do I wait after asking a question for the student to respond? If my wait time is short (about a second), can I expand the time I wait? What happens when I do this?
- What is the content of my questions? Are the majority of my questions about the study of language? Do I also ask life-personal and life-general questions? Questions about the study of things other than language itself? What consequences do questions with different content have on classroom interaction?
- What seating arrangements do I use? Have I explored a variety of arrangements? What happens when I try out different seating arrangements?
- Do the students stay on task during group work? If students go off task, what do they talk about? What language do they use? What are different ways to keep students on task? What happens when I use these ways?
- How do I make language comprehensible to students? Do I simplify my speech? If so, in what ways? Do I add media? How? Do I negotiate meaning? How? What happens when I try different ways to make language comprehensible to students?
- How do I group students? What creative ways of grouping students would I like to try? What are the consequences of different ways of grouping students?
- How do I give instructions? Are my instructions clear to the students? How can I give instructions differently? What happens when I give instructions differently?

What Can K–12 Teachers Do to Create a Learning Setting for ESL Students?

I have been asked by a number of K–12 teachers to suggest ways they can create a flourishing learning atmosphere for ESL students. In response, I decided to include my answer to the question posed above. However, before answering this question, allow me to summarize research findings and teacher observations on how K–12 teachers tend to interact with ESL students.[12]

Most K–12 teachers are at a disadvantage in that they have not had the chance to study stages of second language acquisition and development[13] and are not fully aware that it takes time, opportunities to interact, and much encouragement for ESL students to move from a beginning level to a fully communicatively competent and literate user of English.

Those who have studied the interaction between elementary and secondary teachers and ESL students have also discovered that K–12 teachers without ESL training unintentionally tend to prohibit interaction opportunities for ESL students.[14] They tend to ask ESL students fewer questions than the other students, and when they do ask questions, they are more likely to be about procedures (for example, *Do you understand what you are to do with the paper and paste?*) or questions about facts, rather than asking high-level cognitive questions that provide opportunities for students to think, such as questions in which students have to make inferences by relating two pieces of information. Uninformed teachers tend to underestimate ESL students' abilities to produce extended utterances and are concerned about the amount of time it might take an ESL student to answer a question. In addition, teachers tend to want to protect the ESL students from being embarrassed. Given all these concerns, teachers tend simply not to call on the student.

Those who have studied interaction between teachers who are untrained in teaching ESL students have also pointed out that when teachers, at least in middle and high school settings, talk with ESL students they seldom adjust their language to accommodate comprehension, other than by speaking louder and perhaps a little slower. However, speaking louder does little to improve comprehension. Although not fully backed by formal research, I believe specific adjustments, such as repeating key ideas in different words, decreasing the use of complex sentences and words, increasing the use of gestures, and consistently checking comprehension can help ESL students to more fully comprehend.

A bigger concern in terms of teaching ESL students in a public school is that some administrators place ESL students in lower-track classes. They do this because they assume that these classes will be easier for ESL students so they will have time to develop their language skills. Once they have improved their English, they can be placed in higher-level classes, according to these administrators. However, as Linda Harklau points out, this is the opposite of what most bright ESL students need.[15] Her observations show that interaction in lower-track classes relies heavily on teacher-directed activities and individual seatwork, rather than on interaction-fostering activities that promote comprehension and development of communicative competence. In addition, higher-level classroom students are exposed to a variety of supplemental reading materials, in addition to the required text. In the lower-track classes, teachers tend to focus exclusively on the text, thus limiting exposure ESL students have to language.

A list of some basic things that K–12 teachers can do to manage their classroom behaviors to accommodate ESL students follows. Keep in mind that these suggestions are not prescriptions about how you should teach but ideas based on research, experiences of K–12 teachers, and my own thoughts.[16]

- Pay attention to the social and emotional needs of the new ESL student. As Peregoy and Boyle point out, "You will be laying the foundation for the early stages of language acquisition."[17]
- Adjust speech. When you know that the ESL student's English comprehension is still developing, speak more slowly, reduce sentence and word choice complexity, and increase repetition, pausing, and use of gestures. Speaking more loudly will likely not help comprehension.
- When possible, use realia, photos, and drawings while explaining concepts.
- Take time to check if the student comprehends. Go beyond simply asking, *Do you understand?* Instead, ask specific questions. For beginners, it helps to ask questions that require a *yes, no,* or a single answer. For example: *Let's review. When we mix red paint and yellow paint, we get purple paint. Right? No. Really? Then what color? Orange! That's right!*
- Include ESL students in class discussions. Get to know each student and his or her language abilities. Take calculated

risks by asking questions that require extended answers, if the student seems ready to answer such questions.

- Assign each ESL student a mentor or even a small group of mentors whose job it is to get to know and coach the student and to explain assignments, concepts, and other classroom interactions when needed. Meet with the mentors periodically to talk about problems, successes, and needs.
- Engage students in interaction-fostering activities, such as group work and task-based activities. Encourage the native-speakers to include the ESL students as viable members of the group.
- Encourage administrators to place capable ESL students in higher-track or age-appropriate classrooms. Also encourage them to set up an *inclusion* program that includes an ESL teacher. If a *pullout* program is used, try to arrange for students to leave the classroom during lessons that are not highly relevant. (See Chapter 3, the section on teaching K–12 ESL classes, to learn more about *inclusion* and *pullout* programs.)

What Problems Do Some EFL/ESL Teachers Have in Managing Classroom Interaction?

Problems some EFL/ESL teachers face include:

- The "I never have enough time!" problem
- The "How do I get students to use English in class?" problem
- The "name remembering" problem

The "I Never Have Enough Time!" Problem

I have heard teachers say, "I never have enough time even to do half of what I planned!" Having faced this problem myself, I asked a number of EFL teachers how they save time. Here is what they suggest.

First, build time constraints into lesson plans. This includes estimating how much time it will take to do each step in an activity—for example, to give instructions for a group task, set up groups, and have students work on the task. Likewise, keep track of time. Simply glancing at a watch and mentally noting how much time has gone by can be productive.

Next, when setting up group work activities, simply telling each group where to locate can save much time: "Group one, you are in the corner. Group two, please form up here, near the board. . . ." In addition during pair or group work, let students know how much time they are allotted to complete their task.

Finally, reflect on how much time it took to do different activities and steps in these activities, as well as consider how we might use time differently the next time we do an activity. Keeping a record of use of time (e.g., in a folder with the lesson plan and materials to do the activity) has proven useful to a number of teachers.

The "How Do I Get Students to Use English in Class?" Problem

I have met EFL/ESL teachers who strongly believe in an English-only policy. Some believe that to learn English, students need to interact only in English. When the goal is to get students to use English much of the time—a problematic goal—teachers have tried a number of things. Some put up signs that say, for example, "This is an English-only zone!" Others point at the student and say, "Speak English!" Others initiate a system in which students can cash in poker chips at times they want to use their native language. Still others create a fund in which students give a coin toward a class party each time they speak in their native language.

Personally, I believe these techniques have minimal effectiveness for most teachers who face classroom English-use problems. If students are not motivated to use English in the classroom or are pressured by peers to follow a hidden set of classroom rules that includes interacting in the students' native language, then these more or less superficial techniques to compel students to use English can become novelties that will likely wane in their effect quickly.

If we truly believe that students need to use English to learn English but they are not doing so, we need to negotiate with them why it is important to use English in class. It is important to gain their trust and commitment. They need to want to use English in class because they see value in doing so. We then are more likely to be successful in implementing techniques that focus their attention on using English to learn English.

The "Name Remembering" Problem

To my embarrassment, I never could remember my students' names. Names are important; learning a student's name shows that a teacher is interested enough to know his or her name. I asked people who are good at remembering names what they do, and I read

The Memory Book.[18] First, I discovered that people who remember names really listen to the name and use it as soon as they hear it. They also study the person's face and match the name to the face, making mental notes: "This is Jacinta from India, with long black hair and black eyes."

Surprisingly, simply paying attention to the name and face worked wonderfully for me when meeting individuals. But when faced with three or four classes of new students, I still had problems. So I decided to create ways to learn whole classes of students' names. I had students complete information sheets about themselves and draw their pictures on the sheets. (An alternative is to take photos.) I could then study the sheets and match the drawings with their names.

My initial exploration into better remembering students' names inspired me to develop a number of activities for the first day of each class that focus on learning the names of the students. One activity is to have students interview each other in small groups (or pairs), and I join each group. We meet to learn each other's names and at least three things about each other. We then form a new group to interview each other. After several switches, we form a large circle and list what we learned about each person in the class.

A second activity is a round-robin memory game. The students form a circle, and starting somewhere in this circle, a student will say, "My name is _____, and I like strawberry ice cream." The next student then says, "This is _____, and she likes strawberry ice cream. I'm _____, and I like to read murder mysteries." The next student introduces the first two and adds his or her own name and something he or she likes. This continues until the last person introduces every student. Of course, students can help out, and some students jot the names down as they hear them. The ultimate challenge for me is to be the last person to introduce the students in a class of 25 students.

A third activity is a "cocktail party."[19] I have each student write a variety of information on a large nametag. The information might include, for example, the student's name in the center; a favorite food in the top right corner; a word recently learned in the bottom right corner; a hobby in the top left corner; and, in the remaining corner, the name of a person, dead or alive, whom the student would like to meet. We then walk around the classroom reading each other's nametags and striking up conversations. As I do this, I pay particular attention to the person's name and face.

TEACHER SELF-DEVELOPMENT TASKS

Talk Tasks

1. Study the list of questions in the section Managing an Interactive Classroom: Questions Teachers Can Ask. Put a check next to the questions that interest you. Then study the ones you checked. Choose three questions you would like to explore. Meet with other teachers. Who has similar interests to yours?

2. Study the seating arrangements given earlier in this chapter (page 86). Meet with other teachers. Design a lesson (on the content of your choice) that makes use of at least five different seating arrangements.

3. Study the list of ways I provide to give instructions. How many additional ways can you think of to give instructions?

4. Study the ways to group learners. Talk about which ones you like. Can you add other ways to group learners?

Observation and Talk Tasks

1. Ask a friend or colleague who is also reading this book if you can observe his or her class. Remind each other that your purpose is not to judge his or her teaching or the students but to collect descriptions of how he or she manages classroom interaction.

   a. Before observing, consider what aspect of classroom management you will observe: for example, the teacher's questioning behaviors, the teacher's way of giving instructions, or the teacher's wait time and its consequences on students' behavior. Let the teacher choose the area of teaching on which he or she is interested in gaining descriptive feedback.

   b. After deciding on an area of classroom management to focus on during the observation, consider how you will collect descriptions of teaching (see Chapter 2). For example, will you take photos? Tally behaviors? Jot down sample dialogue?

   c. Observe the class, collecting descriptions. Meet with the teacher (just after the class, if possible). Talk about the class, focusing attention on descriptions of teaching you collected. Avoid making judgments, the good teaching/bad teaching trap.

   d. Reflect on what you have learned. Were you able to see your own teaching in this person's teaching? What does this teacher do that you would like to do? What do you think this teacher might do differently?

2. Work through steps a–d in Question 1 again, this time with you as the observed teacher and your friend or colleague as the class observer.

Journal Writing Tasks

1. Answer the following question: What is the value of observing other teachers and of talking about the observation? If possible, base your discussion on your own experience in observing other teachers and then talking with the teacher about the class you observed.
2. Write what you learned from doing the Talk Tasks in this chapter.
3. Write about your observation experiences from the first Observation and Talk Task in this chapter. Include discussion on what you learned about how to go about studying your own teaching.
4. Select one or two aspects of classroom management you find interesting. Using stream-of-consciousness writing, reflect on your way of managing classroom interaction.
5. Reflect on how past (or present) language teachers managed classroom interaction. What did you like about the way they managed interaction? As a learner, what did you dislike?

Recommended Teacher Resources

Crookes, G., and C. Chaudron. "Guidelines for Language Instruction." In *Teaching English as a Second or Foreign Language, 3ᵈ ed.,* ed. M. Celce-Murcia, 29–42. Boston: Heinle and Heinle, 2001.

Holliday, A. "Teachers' and Students' Lessons." In *Enriching ESOL Pedagogy,* eds. V. Zamel and R. Spack, 17–43. Mahwah, NJ: Lawrence Erlbaum, 2002.

Lewis, M. "Classroom Management." In *Methodology in Language Teaching: An Anthology of Current Practice,* eds. J. C. Richards and W. A. Renandya, 40–58. New York: Cambridge University Press, 2002.

Endnotes

[1] From Nunan (1991, 190).
[2] See Nash and Shiman (1974).

3 The work of Barns (1975), Long and Sato (1983), Brock (1986), and Fanselow (1987) has had a direct impact on the way I understand the purpose of teachers' questions.

4 My ideas on the content of teachers' questions have been adapted from Fanselow (1987) and a personal communication with Fanselow.

5 See Rowe (1986).

6 Maley and Duff (1982) show a variety of ways to group students. I would like to thank the many students in the MA/TESOL program at Indiana University of Pennsylvania who have added to Maley and Duff's original list.

7 This idea comes from Maley and Duff (1982).

8 See Good and Brophy (1987).

9 Krashen (1982, 1985) created the concept of "I + 1." The "I" stands for the student's current stage of grammatical development, and the "1" stands for language that is just beyond the student's present comprehension.

10 "Foreigner talk" was coined by Ferguson (1975).

11 The idea of adjusting mediums to make language more comprehensible comes from reading Fanselow (1987).

12 A number of ESL teachers/researchers have looked closely at the interaction between K–12 teachers and ESL students. Verplaetse (1998) observed how three middle/high school teachers interacted with both native-English speaking and ESL students. Ryan (2004) researched how teachers without any formal ESL training interact with ESL children at an elementary school in a rural southern U.S. setting. Harklau (2002) researched the differences in interaction in ESL and regular high school classrooms, as well as differences in the kind of interaction ESL students experienced when placed in low-track and high-track classes. In addition, there are interesting and useful accounts of ESL students' experiences in mainstream classrooms, including those of Peregoy and Boyle (2005), Bérubé (2000), and Becker (2001).

13 See Brown (2000) and Richard-Amato (2003).

14 See Harklau (2002), Ryan (2004), and Verplaetue (1998).

15 See Harklau (2002).

16 I highly recommend K–12 teachers read Peregoy and Boyle (2005), *Reading, Writing, and Learning in ESL: A Resource Book for K–12 Teachers, 4th ed.,* and Becker (2001), *Teaching ESL K–12: View from the Classroom.*

17 See Peregoy and Boyle (2005, 17).

18 See Lorayne and Lucas (1974).

19 I adapted this activity from Wright, Betteridge, and Buckby (1994).

Reification of textbooks can result in teachers failing to look at textbooks critically and assuming that teaching decisions made in the textbook and teaching manual are superior and more valid than those they could make themselves.

—Richards 1993, 7

EFL/ESL Materials, Media, and Technology

- Who creates the materials available to EFL/ESL teachers?
- What are the advantages and disadvantages of commercial materials?
- What are authentic materials? What types are available?
- What are the advantages and disadvantages of using authentic materials and media?
- How do EFL/ESL teachers use authentic materials and media?
- What kinds of technology do EFL/ESL teachers use?
- What problems do some EFL/ESL teachers have with materials, media, and technology?

Who Creates the Materials Available to EFL/ESL Teachers?

Basically, materials used in EFL/ESL classrooms are created by four groups of people: publishing companies, government agencies, curriculum development teams at the school level, and classroom teachers.

If you teach in a private language school, ESL K–12 program, business, or other settings, you might be using commercial materials such as EFL/ESL texts, audiotapes, a disk with accompanying workbooks, videotapes with worksheets for students, and computer programs. In fact, a large number of commercially made texts and other materials are on the market for teaching reading, writing, listening, speaking, grammar, survival English, K–12, vocabulary building, cross-cultural communication, pronunciation, English for business, TOEFL® preparation, vocational skills, literature, and more. In addition, publishing companies are producing full series of texts for beginner through advanced proficiency levels. (See the list of publishing companies in Appendix B.)

If you teach in a public school in a country with a centralized educational system, you might find yourself teaching with materials produced (or selected) by a government education agency or committee. Some countries establish special committees that either produce their own texts or solicit proposals from teachers to produce texts. After being approved by this central committee, these texts are produced and used in the schools.

If you teach at certain universities, well-established private language schools, some ESL K–12 schools, and corporations with language programs, you could find yourself teaching with locally designed texts and materials. Teachers who have some EFL/ESL teaching experience usually produce these in-house materials. Sometimes the writers of the materials are also members of a team who design the curriculum for the language program. As a result, classroom teachers are sometimes given a day-by-day lesson plan, which includes goals of each lesson, steps in implementing it, and the materials needed to teach it.

If you are among the teachers who are not completely satisfied with the textbook, you probably adapt the text or design entire lessons with materials you create yourself. Examples of such materials are illustrated later in this chapter and throughout this book.

What Are the Advantages and Disadvantages of Commercial Materials?

Using commercial teaching materials saves time. Another advantage, especially for those new to teaching, is that well-organized commercial materials can systematically guide the teacher and students step-by-step through a series of lessons. Accompanying teaching manuals or companion websites also provide lesson plans with some useful suggestions or techniques.

However, there can be disadvantages associated with using commercial materials, especially if the teacher can't select the text to be used. First, there is the possible problem of ideological conflict in teaching beliefs. Texts are usually based on the author's or publisher's ideas about teaching. For example, some text writers believe students should memorize words and grammar rules before they practice speaking, writing, or reading; others think lots of practice in meaningful contexts is significantly more important. Given a prescribed text, teachers feel as if they have to accept the beliefs of the author/publisher. This conflict can have negative consequences on what goes on in the classroom.

Second, when teachers blindly follow their assigned texts, they might be trivializing the experience for the students. And if we teachers accept our role as simply taking students step-by-step through a book, "the teacher's role is marginalized to that of little more than a technician . . . and the level at which we are engaged in teaching is reduced to a very superficial one."[1]

Finally, commercially made textbooks are prepared for a wide audience that is culturally diverse and geographically dissimilar. As such, the "qualities which give teacher-made and audience-specific materials their authenticity and relevance are usually removed."[2] Teachers should read the introduction of the textbooks and determine who the books were written for. Many ESL textbooks shouldn't be used in EFL settings, and the reverse is also true.

What Are Authentic Materials? What Types Are Available?

To move beyond the limitations of a text, many EFL/ESL teachers adapt or create authentic materials and media. But what are authentic materials, and what types of authentic materials are available to us? Basically, authentic materials include anything that is used to communicate. To give you an idea of the scope of what I mean, here is a partial list of some authentic materials EFL/ESL teachers have used.

Authentic Listening/Viewing Materials

silent films; TV commercials, quiz shows, cartoons, news, comedy shows, dramas, movies, and soap operas; radio news, dramas, and ads; professionally audiotaped short stories and novels; pop, rock, country, film, and children's songs; home videos; professionally videotaped travel logs, documentaries, and sales pitches

Authentic Visual Materials

slides; photographs; paintings; sketches; drawings by children; stick-figure drawings; wordless street signs; silhouettes; calendar pictures; pictures from travel, news, and popular magazines; ink blots; postcard pictures; wordless picture books; stamps; X-rays

Authentic Printed Materials

newspaper articles, cartoons, advertisements, movie advertisements, astrology columns, sports reports, obituary columns, and advice columns; travel magazines; science, math, and history books; short stories; novels; books of photographs; lyrics to popular, rock, folk, and children's songs; restaurant menus; street signs; postcards; currency; cereal boxes; candy wrappers; tourist information brochures and tourist guidebooks; university catalogs; department store catalogs; telephone books; world, city, and relief maps; calendars; TV guides; driver's licenses; comic books; greeting cards; business cards; bank checks and deposit forms; grocery coupons; hotel registration forms; pins with messages; bus, plane, train, taxi, and jitney schedules; teletext subtitles for the hearing impaired

Realia Used in EFL/ESL Classrooms

dolls, puppets, currency, key rings, scissors, folded paper, toothpaste, toothbrushes, combs, stuffed and toy animals, wall clocks, balloons, walkie-talkies, candles, fly swatters, string, thread, chewing gum, glue, rulers, tacks, paper clips, rubber bands, trains, aprons, plastic forks and spoons, dishes, glasses, bowls, umbrellas, wallets, purses, balls, phones, fishing reels, furniture, people, cars, bug collections, play money, stones, plants, sand, clay, ink, sticks, jars, coffee cans, chalk, credit cards, hats, Halloween masks, mannequins

What Are the Disadvantages and Advantages of Using Authentic Materials and Media?

As is the case with commercially produced textbooks, using authentic materials and media has disadvantages and advantages. One disadvantage is that it takes time and effort to locate authentic materials. It is also difficult to make authentic materials and media comprehensible to the students. Also, some students will not accept authentic materials and media as being a valuable learning source. For example, students will sometimes reject TV comedy or games as a learning source because they consider them entertainment but view learning as a serious enterprise.

Nevertheless, there are reasons to use authentic materials and media because they "can reinforce for students the direct relation between the language classroom and the outside world."[3] In addition, they offer a way to contextualize language learning. When lessons are centered on comprehending a repair manual, a menu, a TV weather report, a documentary, or anything that is used in the real world, students tend to focus more on content and meaning than on language. This offers students a valuable source of language input, since they can be exposed to more than just the language presented by the teacher and the text.

How Do EFL/ESL Teachers Use Authentic Materials and Media?

Some teachers use authentic materials to get beyond the limitations of a text. They begin with an idea in a text and, based on their understanding of students' needs and interests, locate authentic materials, as well as create additional activities that make use of them. Here is an example of how one EFL teacher did this. While engaged in a textbook activity, students in a functional English class expressed interest in learning how to order food in a restaurant. So the teacher pulled together pictures of food items from magazines, and he had students in groups study a photocopy of an authentic menu (which a restaurant manager graciously gave him) and match the pictures of the food items to some of those listed in the menu. He then had them create their own menus, including pictures of food items they cut out of magazines. The students next wrote their own dialogues about ordering food in a restaurant; they practiced the dialogues and took turns presenting them in front of the class. The teacher also had students simulate being in a restaurant through the use of realia (e.g., plastic eating utensils and food order checks) and role-play cards similar to those shown.

Waiter Your job is to greet customers and to take their food orders. Make sure to write down each order.	*Customer No. 1* Go into the restaurant with a friend. Order from the menu. You want to treat your friend, but you only have $14.80.
Cashier Your job is to read the waiter's written orders, write in the price of each food item, add up the bill, and collect the money.	*Customer No. 2* Your friend wants to treat you to lunch. You are very hungry.

As this teacher's set of activities illustrates, it is possible to adapt lessons to a text using authentic materials. However, some teachers also see the need to go beyond the text and to create their own lessons based solely on authentic materials and media. There are many examples of how EFL/ESL teachers have done this. Garber and Holmes, for example, used authentic video as a means to have students in their French as a foreign language classes write and produce their own commentaries.[4] They prepared four five-minute video segments on everyday themes, showed them to the students without a soundtrack, and asked them to write a commentary based on the video segment of their choice. The commentaries were corrected by the teachers and audiotaped by the students. After more teacher feedback, students rerecorded their soundtracks. They then watched the original video segments with sound and compared their versions with the original.

Another way to use authentic materials is to include them on reading boards.[5] A reading board looks similar to a bulletin board, but it is purposefully designed to promote interaction between the reader and the text. It can include quick quizzes, problems to solve, quotes from famous people, cartoons and jokes, and news items. Teachers who have created reading boards have used Dear Abby advice columns in which the problem is given without solutions (blank space is provided for readers to write in their own advice). Some teachers have used advertisements that ask readers to compare prices and select the best buy on a product, as well as cartoons with blank bubbles, cultural quizzes, crossword puzzles, and funny pictures or photos of classmates under which readers can write in possible captions.

Melvin and Stout show how authentic mixed media can be used in a different way. They describe an activity called Discover a City, in which students use authentic materials as a substitute for a trip to a particular place.[6] Some of the authentic materials include city street maps; tourist brochures; public transportation, shopping, hotel, and restaurant guides; menus from restaurants; cultural publications announcing museum, theater, and other shows; entertainment sections from newspapers; guides to sports and recreation events; samples of currency; newspaper and magazine articles describing aspects of city life; and songs, films, television shows, and literature about the city.

The students begin interacting with the materials and are given specific tasks. For example, they can be asked to pick a time of year for a visit, and based on the season, find recreational things to do and select and determine lodging costs for four days. Then they select two places of interest they want to visit, find the different transportation methods (subway, bus, walking) and routes by which they can get to this place from their selected hotel, and create a budget based on a set amount of money, including hotel, meal, entertainment, and transportation costs. After searching through the materials to accomplish these tasks, students can be asked to create and present itineraries, justify each of their selections of places to visit, compare their itineraries with those of other students to determine whose plan is more expensive, carry out role plays related to things they would be doing in the city, and complete hotel registration forms.

What Kinds of Technology Do EFL/ESL Teachers Use?

When you hear the word *technology*, what comes to mind? For many of us the words *computer, website, satellite,* and *e-mail* do. But, in reality, technology is much more than this. Technology is scientific and industrial know-how or expertise. Every culture uses technology, for example, to run the transportation system, the communications system (such as the telephone), the agricultural system, and other systems that provide people with the means to live. Some countries have advanced technology, with very efficient trains and buses, digital entertainment wired into homes or beaming in from satellites, and modern computerized machinery in the factories. Other countries have quite the opposite technology, with slow-moving trains and buses, televisions with antennas, and labor-intense factories. Of course, there are some countries that are developing, some quite fast, and they have very advanced technology and very old technology within the same country. For example, in some countries a percentage of people (with money) have access to satellite technology in their homes and even cars (digital satellite maps, for example), while others are living in homes without access to the Internet, are walking on dirt roads, and are riding old buses to their destinations.

We can carry this same idea of technology into a discussion of technology as it is used to teach English around the world. Some teachers have access to high technology, such as computers that can surf the Internet at lightening speed, while other teachers will only have access to chalk and a blackboard.

Before going on to map out and illustrate examples of technology, using a continuum from low to high technology, it is important to emphasize that technology is only one aspect of culture. In addition to having a technological system, every culture has a social system, a human communication system, and an ideological system. Even though people in a culture might not have (or want) access to advanced technology, they can still be a highly developed culture in other ways. For example, although some Thai villagers do not have modern technological conveniences, through centuries of experience with Theravada Buddhism, they now have highly developed ideological and social systems.

The technology continuum shows examples of low through high technology used by EFL/ESL teachers. At the one end is some of the most basic technology—those things naturally around us that can serve as teaching tools. For example, when living in a village some years ago in rural northeast Thailand, I made friends with Buddhist monks. They were interested in learning English, and I was interested in learning Thai and about Theravada Buddhism. We taught each other whenever time allowed and in no particular place. We looked at clouds and asked, "What do you see?" We taught each other how to write by using sticks and the earth, and we spelled words in

A Technology Continuum

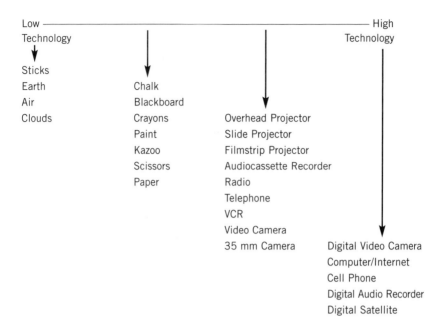

Low ——————————————————————————————— High
Technology   Technology

Sticks			
Earth	Chalk		
Air	Blackboard		
Clouds	Crayons	Overhead Projector	
	Paint	Slide Projector	
	Kazoo	Filmstrip Projector	
	Scissors	Audiocassette Recorder	
	Paper	Radio	
		Telephone	
		VCR	
		Video Camera	
		35 mm Camera	Digital Video Camera
			Computer/Internet
			Cell Phone
			Digital Audio Recorder
			Digital Satellite

the air. I treasure this experience, not only because of the wonderful friends I made, but because I learned that even the most simplistic of things can be useful as teaching technology.

Moving across the continuum to such usual items as chalk, blackboards, paper, and pencils, most teachers simply smile. These are familiar to all experienced teachers. However, teachers are often surprised to learn that they use the board in quite limited ways. See Jeannine Dobbs' *Using the Board in the Language Classroom*,[7] in which 130 board activities are provided.

Most experienced teachers are also familiar with the overhead projector, filmstrip projector, slide projector, audiocassette recorder, video camera, and VCR.[8] (See more about video and audio in Chapter 8.)[9]

One useful technology that is sometimes overlooked by teachers is the radio. However, as a group of elementary school children in Israel discovered, learning to be amateur radio operators cannot only open up our understanding of the world, but also can be an interesting way to develop speaking skills in English.[10] The radio has also been used as a traditional way to conduct long-distance education in some parts of the world. Although video and computers are now used frequently in long-distance English education programs,[11] radio plays a part in more remote and less technologically advanced areas of the world.

Here is an example of how radio has been used in Thailand to teach English. I have a very good Thai friend who lives in a remote part of the country. He loves to learn, and he decided to enroll in a long-distance university degree program. For the first two years he did not attend classes at the university; rather, he read the texts, listened to the radio broadcasts of lectures, and did the assignments from his home. At the end of each semester, he went to Bangkok to take the final exams at the university alongside regular university students. For me, the most interesting part of my friend's experience was the required English Listening-Speaking class. He listened intently to the audiotapes that came with the textbook, and he studied the conversational part of the course by asking himself questions ("Did you have a nice weekend?") and answering his own questions ("Yes, I had fun.")! He even tape-recorded and listened to his English while studying the models in the text. Through such practice he was able to pass the course, including an oral interview! He ended up earning an undergraduate degree with a double major in political science and pre-law and went on to earn a graduate degree at a prestigious university.

Another technology sometimes overlooked is the telephone. Here's an example of how a teacher used the telephone in a creative way. The teacher, Magdolna Lehmann, was teaching English to a group of employees who need to use English at work. Most of the students were confident, but one student was particularly shy, especially about using English in public and on the phone. Magdolna noticed that every time someone spoke English, she handed the receiver to her colleague, saying, "Moment, please." So, Magdolna decided to create lots of chances for this student to speak English on the phone. She not only had the student practice simulated phone calls, but she also designed rather tricky lessons at the office. On a number of occasions, Magdolna asked the shy student's colleagues to leave the office. She then had a friend call the office and ask for Magdolna. At first, the shy student responded, "Please call later." However, the speaker insisted on leaving short messages, and this forced the shy student to communicate with the caller. Of course, after several days, Magdolna and the others confessed that all was not as it seemed! However, the student was not upset and found it easier to answer the phone.[12]

At the other end of the continuum is high technology. Digital technology is developing at a fast rate, and there are some very exciting and creative uses for this relatively new technology. Since I weave a variety of examples of how teachers use computers and other digital technology into other chapters, especially those on teaching language skills, I won't go into great detail here. However, I would like to draw attention to a few examples of how computer technology is being used creatively to teach English.

My first example is about the use of digital video technology at the Marzio School, a private language institute in France. One task of the teachers at the Marzio School is to prepare employees to do business abroad. It became increasingly obvious that students were able to increase their abilities to communicate within the classroom walls, but they were having difficulties with authentic English when talking with people in such places as London, New York, and Texas. With this problem in mind, a team set off for several English-speaking countries, digital video camera in hand, to collect authentic oral materials that students at a beginning level could use to prepare them to travel abroad. The team collected a database of 850 authentic language scenes representing 90,000 lines of speech. Although they had difficulties selecting video clips that are authentic and still comprehensible, they were able to categorize and create listening lessons on a great variety of topics such as greetings, weather, jobs, and family. Related to the use of technology, there were benefits to the fact that digital video was used over non-digital. The students can use the computer program to maneuver quickly as they make decisions about what language they want to experience. For example, in lesson 10—"What's your job?"—students can click on any of 13 interviews. In addition, unlike with traditional video, it is easy for students to listen again and again to the same sentence, skip ahead or back to segments, and go back and forth between different interviews.[13]

My second example is how two teachers, Kerry and Timothy Conrad, made use of computer technology to have students create their own Class Memory Book at the end of the school year. This project not only provided language learning experiences for a class of K–12 ESL students, but also promoted a feeling of belonging for a group of low-income students who do not fit neatly into the mainstream school culture, helped build students' self-esteem, enhanced computer literacy skills, as well as gave the students something they can treasure for years to come. To accomplish this, they began early in the school year by introducing the students to the concept of a memory book. They also had a picture-practice day with a digital camera and worked out a plan for photos taken outside the class throughout the school year. During the year, they discussed and practiced using computer technology to transfer photos, used different computer software programs, and finally processed the Memory Book. The Conrads report that the results of the project surpassed their expectations. The ESL students not only had great satisfaction and enjoyment in creating the book and writing in each other's copies at the end of the year, but they also were able to feel more a part of the larger school community, recognized by the fact that non-ESL students asked for copies of the Memory Book.[14]

My final example is how two teachers, Katharine Isbell and Jonathon Reinhardt, used high technology and task-based learning at Miyazaki International College (Japan) to create opportunities for EFL students to use English to research environmental issues. Their goals were to build students' environmental awareness, develop their computer and academic skills, and increase their English language proficiency. The students were required to work through several projects, the first done by the whole class and later ones done by small groups or individuals. One of the projects was to document changes that occurred to an environment over time by photographing the same location (farm fields, a river, natural areas) once a week for ten weeks. Students kept a written and photographic record of the weekly changes, which they then used to create a website containing a description and a slide show of the recorded changes.[15]

What Problems Do Some EFL/ESL Teachers Have with Materials, Media, and Technology?

Problems some EFL/ESL teachers face include the following:

- The "I am forced to teach from the book" problem
- The "Let the textbook do the teaching" problem
- The "How do I locate useful websites for my students?" problem

The "I Am Forced to Teach from the Book" Problem

Some EFL/ESL teachers are required to follow a particular text, and they find that the administration's policy is stringent. Sometimes, actual lesson plans are provided, and supervisors make sure they are followed. When this happens, teachers can feel helpless in the face of being creative with materials and media. Unfortunately, some teachers give in under the pressure and simply follow the prescribed lessons.

However, other teachers find ways to incorporate additional materials while adapting to the prescribed lesson. They might bring in photos or pictures that correspond to the required reading to make it more vivid. They might have friends record a one-minute natural conversation based on language in a dialogue in the text. Or they might have students spend the last ten minutes of class using Scrabble® letters to spell out words found in their text and make up original sentences from these words. Some teachers also negotiate an "authentic English" day with the students, providing them with a lesson based on authentic materials and media each week.

Whether adapting a lesson or creating a special day every so often, the possibilities for making small changes are endless, and the changes can ultimately have big consequences on the way students interact with each other and the teacher in English.

The "Let the Textbook Do the Teaching" Problem

Following a text has certain advantages. It saves time, and novice teachers can learn something about teaching from following a text, studying the accompanying teaching manual, and using materials from companion websites. But adhering to a text without considering the effects on the students—for example, whether or not they are negotiating meaning with each other and the teacher—can trivialize the experience for the students.

Of course, not all teachers accept the constraints imposed on them by the text. Some teachers want to be more than technicians, doing more than mindlessly following a text and its accompanying materials. They realize that texts are not meant to be blindly plodded through and that teaching guides are only other teachers' ways to teach lessons, which might not be appropriate for their own students. They also realize that much can be gained from exposing students to authentic language materials and media, and they want to make their own informed decisions about how to teach a particular, always unique, group of students.

The "How Do I Locate Useful Websites for My Students?" Problem

There are so many websites that some teachers find it almost overwhelming to know which ones they can recommend to EFL/ESL students. Having faced this same problem, I decided to ask

Internet-using teachers and EFL/ESL students which websites they find to be the most useful. Surprisingly, they came up with many of the same sites. Many said that they like these sites because they are fun to use, useful to learning English, and well established. Based on their recommendations, these websites might be useful to you and your students.

- *www.eslcafe.com* (Dave's ESL Café)—Includes interactive resources, including the ESL Graffiti Wall, ESL Question Page, ESL Idea Page, ESL Message Exchange, ESL Quiz Center, ESL Links Pages, ESL Help Center, ESL E-mail Connection Pages, ESL Discussion Center, and the ESL Job Center.
- *www.eslpartyland.com* (Karin's ESL PartyLand)—Designed for ESL students and teachers, there is a student section and a teacher section. Students can find a variety of interactive quizzes, discussion forums, a chat room, and interactive lessons on a variety of topics. Teachers can find lesson plans, reproducible materials, discussion forums, ideas for communicative practice activities, a chat room, a job board, and links.
- *www.eslwonderland.com* (The ESL Wonderland)—A "jumping off" point for ESL teachers and students who want to find resources for teaching or learning English. It has a multimedia content presented in a learner-friendly manner (text, photos, interactive quizzes).
- *www.eslbee.com* (Advanced Composition for Non-Native Speakers of English)—For EFL/ESL students who want to learn to write academic papers in American schools. The material in this site aims toward high-intermediate to advanced English learners who have never taken a formal English writing course.
- *http://encyclopedia.com* (Encyclopedia.com)—The Internet's premiere encyclopedia. It provides many frequently updated articles. Each article is enhanced with links to magazine and newspaper articles, pictures, maps, and more.
- *www.owcp.net* (Online Writing Collaboration Project)—Designed to promote communication and writing skills. One of the central goals is to help people who are studying English to construct, discover, and transform knowledge as they interact with others. The website includes live tutoring, free courses, and forums.

TEACHER SELF-DEVELOPMENT TASKS

Talk Tasks

1. Locate three different EFL or ESL textbooks. Study the introduction and a chapter or two in each. What are some of the obvious differences in the goals of each book? In other words, what does the author/publisher of each book intend for the students to learn through the use of the book? What kinds of activities are provided? After studying the books, meet with a friend who has also reviewed a few texts. Take turns showing the text materials and discussing the goals of each book.

2. Do you agree that following a text without using additional teaching materials places limitations on the teacher and students and trivializes the learning experience for the students? Explain what you think to a friend.

3. Study the list of authentic printed, visual, and listening materials given earlier in this chapter (pages 103–4). Which do you personally find interesting? Select a combination of three or four items from the lists. Note ideas for a lesson that might use this combination of authentic materials and media. Then meet with another teacher and talk about your ideas for lessons using authentic materials.

4. Review the technology continuum on page 109. Which kinds of technology have you used or would you like to use? How might you use this technology in your teaching?

5. Log on to at least three of the websites for EFL/ESL students described earlier. Which sites do you find to be most interesting? Why? Talk with other teachers about the sites.

Observation and Talk Tasks

The point of this task is to consider how language-learning materials and use of technology can provide or block opportunities for students to learn English. First, pair up with another teacher. Audiotape one of your classes. Then listen to the tape. As you do, transcribe the interaction in the class when students are focused on using materials and/or technology. Study the transcription. Together, list several things you notice about the interaction and answer the following questions: How does the use of the material and/or technology seem to provide opportunities for the students to learn English? How does the use of the material and/or technology seem to block students? How could you use the same materials and/or technology differently?

Journal Writing Tasks

1. Write lesson ideas in which you use a variety of authentic materials and media.
2. Write your reflections on your experiences as a language learner related to the materials you have used. What kinds of materials did you study as a language learner? How did these materials seem to help you to make progress in the language you were studying? How did they possibly hinder progress?
3. Write what you learned from doing the observation and talk task on materials and/or technology and classroom interaction.
4. Do you agree that there is no best technology to teach EFL/ESL and that teachers need to select technology based on the teaching situation? Or are there learning limitations placed on teachers and students who do not have access to high technology? Write your thoughts.

Recommended Teacher Resources

Resources on Course Design and Materials & Media

Graves, K. *Designing Language Courses: A Guide for Teachers*. Boston: Heinle & Heinle, 2000.

Larimer, R. E., and L. Schleicher, eds. *New Ways in Using Authentic Materials in the Classroom*. Alexandria, VA: TESOL, 1999.

Murphy, J., and P. Byrd, eds. *Understanding the Courses We Teach: Local Perspectives on English Language Teaching*. Ann Arbor: University of Michigan Press, 2001.

Quinlisk, C. C. "Media Literacy in the ESL/EFL Classroom: Reading Images and Cultural Stories." *TESOL Journal* 12, no. 3 (2003): 35–40.

Sanderson, P. *Using Newspapers in the Classroom*. New York: Cambridge University Press, 1999.

Wright, A., D. Betteridge, and M. Buckly. *Games for Language Learning*. Cambridge: Cambridge University Press, 1994.

Readings on Technology and Teaching EFL/ESL

Egbert, J., and E. Hanson-Smith, eds. *CALL Environments: Research, Practice, and Critical Issues.* Alexandria, VA: TESOL, 1999.

Hanson-Smith, E., ed. *Technology-Enhanced Learning Environments.* Alexandria, VA: TESOL, 2000.

Healey, D., and S. J. Klinghammer, eds. "Special Issue: Constructing Meaning with Computers." *TESOL Journal* 11, no. 3 (2000).

Henrichsen, L. E., ed. *Distance-Learning Programs.* Alexandria, VA: TESOL, 2001.

Sperling, D., *Dave Sperling's Internet Activity Book.* Upper Saddle River, NJ: Prentice Hall, 1999.

Warschauer, M. "Online Learning in Second Language Classrooms: An Ethnographic Study." In *Network-Based Language Teaching: Concepts and Practice*, eds. M. Warschauer and R. Kern, 41–59. Cambridge: Cambridge University Press, 2000.

Endnotes

1 See Richards (1993, 8–9).

2 See Richards (1993, 6).

3 See Brinton (1991, 456).

4 See Garber and Holmes (1981).

5 Maurice, Vanikieti, and Keyuravong (1989) discuss how they created and used reading boards in an EFL setting.

6 See Melvin and Stout (1987).

7 See Dobbs (2001).

8 See Duncan (1987) for a book on creative ways to use the VCR, audio recorder, slide projector, and other mid-level teaching technology.

9 Although I do not want to elaborate on the use of video technology here, I do want to point out a few useful sources. I gained some useful ideas from reading Migliacci's (2002) article, "New Ways of Using Video Technology in English Language Teaching," Reynolds' (2001) "Video Jigsaw," and Stempleski's (2000) "Video in the Classroom: Making the Most of Movies."

10 See Freund (1997).

11 See *Distance-Learning Programs*, edited by Henrichsen (2001), to learn more about how modern technology is used in long-distance education.

12 For a fuller account of this telephone lesson, see Gebhard, Fodor, and Lehmann (2003).

13 See Marzio (2000) for a more detailed account of the digital video
project.

14 See Conrad and Conrad (2002) for a fuller account.

15 See Isbell and Reinhardt (2002) for a more detailed account of
students' projects and their task-based teaching process.

We speak of cultural adjustment, but the fact is it's not to culture that we adjust but to behavior. Culture, a system of beliefs and values shared by a particular group of people, is an abstraction which can be appreciated intellectually, but it is behavior, the principal manifestation and most significant consequence of culture, that we actually experience.

—Storti 1989, 14

Culture and the Language Teacher

- What is a reasonable working definition of *culture?*
- What cultural adjustment process do most expatriates experience?
- What are the benefits of adjusting to another culture?
- What cultural concepts can EFL/ESL teachers teach students?
- What problems do some EFL/ESL teachers have related to culture and language teaching and learning?

What Is a Reasonable Working Definition of Culture?

Although there are many ways to define *culture,* here it refers to the common values and beliefs of a people and the behaviors that reflect them. At the risk of overgeneralizing, it is possible to talk about common beliefs and values and about how they can differ from culture to culture, as well as the behaviors associated with them.

To illustrate how values and beliefs can vary, let's look at the way people make use of time in two different cultures: mainstream North America and Saudi Arabia. Time, for the average American, is very important. Americans are constantly setting deadlines based on time and will end conversations before they may be finished by looking at their watches and saying, "Oh! Excuse me! I have to go or I'll be late." American English is filled with references to time. Time is something to be on, spent, gained, kept, filled, killed, saved, used, wasted, lost, and planned.

In contrast, Arabs see time as "flowing from the past to the present to the future, and they flow with it."[1] Social events and appointments do not always have fixed beginnings or endings. If a time for an appointment has been set, under many circumstances, it is acceptable to be late, especially if the person is engaged in a conversation. It would be rude to leave in the middle of it, since maintaining friendships and engaging in human interaction are more highly valued than being on time.

The value assigned to equality among people is another way to illustrate different values and behaviors across cultures. For Americans, equality is a highly cherished value. Americans say all people are created equal and that all people have an equal opportunity to succeed in life. These are foundations on which the country was founded. As such, an American ideal is to treat people as equals, regardless of their status. For example, although a custodian and professor at a university may not likely be close friends, they would engage in friendly chat in elevators and hallways, and neither would act in ways to make the other feel personally inferior or superior.[2]

Unlike Americans, the majority of the world sees equality quite differently. Rank, status, and authority are considered far more important. For example, in Thai society there exists the possibility of social mobility (a Thai peasant can end up being prime minister, for instance). However, while in a particular status or class, Thais, including those in the lowest status, tend to accept this condition as part of their fate.[3] Within this system, Thais value well-defined social behaviors that specify the status of each person. For example, in the presence of a professor, a student would not engage in a friendly chat unless addressed, and he or she would be expected to behave in specific ways that show that the professor has a higher status. One way to reflect the other person's higher status is to show *kreang jai*, defined as "a mingling of reverence, respect, deference, homage, and fear."[4] The Thai student would also keep his or her head slightly lower than the professor's while passing him or her.

A final example of how values and behaviors across cultures can differ concerns the value associated with avoiding conflict and maintaining harmony. While some Americans value direct confrontation to solve conflicts, people from Asian countries generally value avoiding confrontations. They have developed subtle, indirect ways to resolve conflict. For example, if a person in Japanese society is upset with someone, he or she will likely not confront the other person directly but will behave in a particular way, such as being unusually silent or ignoring the person, providing the other person with clues that there is a problem.[5] Likewise, Laotians and Thais will avoid direct confrontation by being indirect. For example, if a Thai is angry at her friend, she will be indirect, perhaps by talking with another friend about the problem within earshot of the offending friend. Or she might invite everyone except the offending friend to eat lunch with her. For some Americans, especially males, being indirect would seem dishonest and insincere. Distrust can result. For many Asians, blatant, blunt, direct confrontation would disrupt the highly valued harmony among people.

Quite often, values and beliefs of a group of people have a deep philosophical foundation. For example, traditional Islamic Arab values can be traced in almost every respect to the Koran. The belief that God alone, not humans, can control all events derives from the teachings in this holy book, as does the belief that each person's fate is in the hands of God. Likewise, Theravada Buddhism is at the heart of traditional Thai beliefs. For example, the belief that emotional extremes should be avoided stems from Buddhist teachings.[6]

What Cultural Adjustment Process Do Most Expatriates Experience?

Most of us have mixed emotions about moving to another country. This is true for those of us who have relocated to teach EFL, or in the case of non-native speakers of English, to study and live in English-speaking countries. We are excited about the prospect of a new way of life. We are delighted about discovering obvious differences: the shape of buildings, the products in stores, and the way people dress. However, as we find places to live, begin our jobs or begin to study, and use the transportation system, we feel the impact of the culture on our lives. We discover that we have to think about, even prepare for, the simplest daily activities, such as paying bills, buying food, doing laundry, taking a bus, and using a telephone. These activities soon weigh on us, resulting in culture shock. As one Peace Corps volunteer said: "In a very real sense, all the convenient cultural cushions we have become accustomed to having around are in one moment totally dislodged. You're left flat on your back with only that within you for support."[7]

Some of us exhibit symptoms of culture shock. We may become depressed or nervous and may complain about the food, the weather, housing, and the host people's behavior. We might become physically ill, make irrational comments, have fits of anger over minor incidents, or become very homesick, spending endless hours writing to friends and family.

Some of us react to culture shock by withdrawing. We stay home, sleep, and generally avoid contact with people in the host culture. Some of us temporarily withdraw to the expatriate community to ease the symptoms, seeking refuge from everyday problems by avoiding participation in the host culture. Some end up staying in this safe harbor, since it is familiar and comfortable. However, by surrendering to the seemingly more pleasant world of people like ourselves, we sacrifice dreams; our visions of making friends, learning the language, and living among the people of the host culture becomes blurred. For some of us, what was a pleasant refuge becomes a void in which life can become vaguely unsatisfying.

Although some of us seek refuge in the expatriate community to escape culture shock, others of us continue to endure, despite the discomfort. Instead of withdrawing, we reach out into the larger community, making friends and working out problems as they arise. We reflect on and learn from our experiences, and as we do this, we start to realize that we are adjusting. Everyday life becomes routine. We can get on a crowded bus like a native, give exact change for a purchase, have fun at a party, visit a friend in the hospital, play games that were once foreign to us.

Such adjustments are typified by an understanding that cultural behaviors and values are simply different. We still have cultural stress and problems to contend with, but we become more empathetic, understanding that people in the host culture have been raised in a culture different from our own. Likewise, we "develop a greater ability to tolerate and cope with the external cultural patterns. . . . We acquire alternative ways of behaving, feeling, and responding to others."[8] As we adjust, self-confidence increases, and as we interact freely, a new self-image emerges, a new identity as a participant in the host culture. Quite often, when it is time to return home, some of us are sad to leave, and there are those in the host culture who are sad that we are leaving.

What Are the Benefits of Adjusting to Another Culture?

Although adjusting to another culture can be an arduous experience, there are benefits that make the effort worthwhile. The benefits of successful cultural adjustment include:

- A fuller sense of security
- The possibility of greater success in the workplace
- The possibility of establishing meaningful relationships with people from the culture
- The possibility of gaining fluency in the language of the host country
- A deeper understanding of one's own culture
- A deeper understanding of oneself

Storti points out that when living in another culture, "ignorance is the breeding ground for anxiety."[9] When we attempt to interact with people in the culture without knowing what is expected of us or what to expect, we become apprehensive. However, the more we learn about the culture through our experience, the easier it is to make predictions, and this can reduce apprehension. Another benefit for some EFL teachers is that friendships with local people can develop over the course of living and working in the culture, and indeed, these friendships can become life-long. Related to making friends is learning the language. Although some friendships are developed through the use of English, some can be built on the language of the host country. As we gain confidence through practice (and study) and control over the language, and as the local people get to know us, friendships develop. Although previously isolated, we are now invited to weddings and local religious events, to homes for dinner, and to participate in sports events.

Those of us who have successfully adjusted to the host culture also discover that we have a better understanding of our own culture. When in our own countries, most of us do not necessarily have opportunities to reflect deeply on our cultural selves as profoundly as we do during the cultural adjustment process. Having to face living in a place where values and behaviors are different from our own provides a way to reflect on our own values and behaviors. In short, "once we encounter another frame of reference, we begin to see what we never could before."[10]

Culture shock can be considered a deep learning experience that can lead to a high degree of self-awareness and personal growth. As a former Peace Corps volunteer from Ethiopia says: "It was the rebirth of me. I came away with a totally new concept of life and living, new values, stronger feelings, far richer experiences than I ever would have had in a lifetime in the states."[11]

What Cultural Concepts Can EFL/ESL Teachers Teach Students?

Teachers can teach concepts that not only can bring about appreciation for people and culture, but also can be useful for students when placed in cross-cultural communication situations. In this section I address four of these concepts, and I include activities that aim at teaching these concepts to EFL students. The four concepts are:

- Cross-cultural communication includes adapting behavior.
- Cross-cultural communication involves problem solving.
- To understand a culture, get to know individuals.
- To understand another culture, study your own.

Cross-Cultural Communication
Includes Adapting Behavior

A part of learning to communicate with people from other cultures is knowing how to adapt one's behaviors, including nonverbal and discourse behaviors.

Nonverbal Behaviors across Cultures

Nonverbal behavior includes *kinesics* (facial expressions, gaze and eye management, gestures, touch, and posture and movement) and *proxemics* (the use of space, such as the distance people sit or stand from each other).[12] In this section I point out and illustrate some of these differences, ways in which they can be problematic during interaction, and activities teachers can use to teach students about these differences.

To introduce kinesic differences, I often begin by teaching students that people in different cultures walk differently. Wylie and Stafford, for example, observed that the French walk as if space around them is extremely limited, while Anglo-Americans tend to walk with free-swinging arms at a loose and easy gait.[13] To illustrate how people walk in different cultures, I ask volunteer students to let me follow them around the room, and I match their way of walking. Then, we reverse roles. I walk; they imitate. After doing this, I ask students how important they think it is, while living in another country, to change their way of walking. Some students think I am being silly (or even crazy!). But as the discussion goes on, they hear stories about how foreigners bump into people in crowded streets, trip people, even stop traffic because they are not walking like the people from the culture.

I also give lessons on how people shake hands differently in different cultures. For example, I show students that some Germans use a firm grip, pump the arm, and maintain strong eye contact while stepping closer during the handshake. Some Japanese use a weak grip, no arm pump, and no eye contact. I have students practice these different culturally adapted handshakes, and we talk about why it is important to be able to change the way we shake hands. We talk about the international acceptance of the handshake as a form of greeting between people from different cultural backgrounds, and we discuss how adapting our way of shaking hands when visiting a country shows respect to those we meet. Further, we discuss how misinterpretations can result if we do not adapt our ways. For example, based on a handshake, Americans sometimes misinterpret Germans as too aggressive and the Japanese as shy or passive.[14]

Another area of kinesic behavior that varies from culture to culture is touch. For example, American males touch each other more often and on more body parts than do Japanese males.[15] However, when compared to Arabs, Latin Americans, and Southern Europeans, these same Americans do not touch much at all.[16] Since touch is a very personal behavior, it is well worth making students aware that differences in touching behavior exist. For example, most Thais do not like to be touched on the head by people they do not know very well, and some mothers will become annoyed if someone touches their children's heads. As such, an American might get into trouble if she or he playfully rubs a child's head. Another example is greetings within some Latino cultures. Quite often a greeting can include touching the upper part of the left arm while shaking hands, but when this form of touch is used with a North American, it might be considered too familiar and result in a subtle misunderstanding of intentions.

Related to touch is the use of space and distance, and this can also vary greatly across cultures. According to Edward T. Hall, middle-class white Americans use space according to the following distance definitions:

> *Intimate distance.* From body contact to a separation space of 18 inches. An emotionally charged zone used for love making, sharing, protecting, and comforting.
>
> *Personal distance.* From one and one-half to four feet. Used for informal contact between friends. A "small protective sphere or bubble" that separates one person from another.
>
> *Social distance.* From 4 to 12 feet. The casual interaction distance between acquaintances and strangers. Used in business meetings, classrooms, and impersonal social affairs.
>
> *Public distance.* Between 12 and 25 feet. A cool interaction distance used for one-way communication from speaker to audience. Necessitates a louder voice, stylized gestures, and more distinct enunciation.[17]

People raised in other cultures adhere to different rules. For instance, "for Arabs the space which is comfortable for ordinary social conversation is approximately the same as that which North Americans reserve for intimate conversation."[18] Arabs tend to stand and sit very close, perceiving private space as "somewhere down inside the body."[19] Latin Americans, Greeks, and Turks are also from high-contact cultures and will also stand and sit much closer during everyday social interaction than those from low-contact cultures, such as North Americans, Northern Europeans, and Asians. People from low-contact cultures, when interacting with people who like contact, will back away, feeling very uncomfortable and perceiving the people who like high contact as invading their private space. Those from high-contact cultures might interpret this behavior as being distant and unfriendly.

As teachers, we can provide students with chances to gain awareness of the differences. Showing students clips from films and videotapes that record natural interaction of people from different culture—using intimate, personal, and social space in different cultural contexts—can sometimes bring about awareness. We can also have students from the same cultural backgrounds measure the distance they sit from one another while doing pair work, then compare this with the distance between members of other cultures.[20] Choreographed role plays and dramas can offer another way for students to experience the distance they would encounter in a culture opposite from their own.

Socio-cultural Behaviors across Cultures

In addition to nonverbal aspects of culture, EFL students can benefit from exposure to socio-cultural behaviors that follow the rules of speaking. These include the appropriate ways people interact in social settings, such as how to greet, make promises, approve, disapprove, show regret, apologize, request, complain, give gifts, compliment, invite, refuse an invitation, offer, and thank. The ways people in different cultures do these things are often quite different, although there is some similarity across some cultures.

To illustrate how these behaviors can be different across cultures, let's look at gift giving. In many countries, a person visiting a friend on a special occasion will take a gift. In America, the hostess will open the gift and thank the person. However, in China and Thailand the receiver of a gift will quite often set it aside, not opening it in front of the guest. When I asked a number of Thais why they wait to open the gift, they all responded that they are afraid that they might hurt the guest's feelings if they don't like the gift and this is obvious to the guest. When I asked those with Chinese cultural background why they wait, I consistently got the response that opening the gift would make the guest feel that the host is more interested in the gift than in the friend or friendship.

The way people compliment each other can also differ from culture to culture. North Americans tend to compliment each other often. They compliment a person's new hair cut, clothing, work, home, children, cooking, garden, choice of wine, grades in school—almost anything. In other cultures, people do not compliment each other as often, and the way the compliment is given is often different. In Japan, for example, a compliment will be slightly indirect, such as the one I recently heard, "Your house is very big! It must be expensive!"

The way people react to compliments can also be different. Most North Americans will accept a compliment at face value, while Japanese and Chinese will often react with modesty. For example, an American hostess's typical reaction to the compliment, "This food is delicious!" would be, "Thank you! I'm happy you like it." However, a Japanese hostess would likely react with something like, "Sono hoto nai desu" [That's really not so].

As EFL/ESL teachers, we can teach students that knowledge about ways people interact with each other in culturally defined settings can be useful. We can provide readings and lectures on the topic. (See Recommended Teacher Resources on pages 139–41.) We can also have students do role plays and other activities. However, this is not enough. I believe we also need to teach them the value of problem solving.

Successful Cross-Cultural Communication Involves Problem Solving

Imagine the following scenario. Three people are going to meet in Paris to discuss a business idea. One is a Canadian who has lived in France for 15 years and speaks fairly fluent French. A second is Indonesian and can speak fluent English, but only a little French. A third is French and can speak fluent English. Since all three share English as their common language, much of the interaction will be done in English. But there is still a problem. Which nonverbal behaviors—such as gestures, touch, and use of space—will they use? Which discourse behaviors—such as complimenting, apologizing, complaining, offering, and requesting—will they use? Whose cultural rules are followed? If all act in ways appropriate to their native cultures, how can they avoid misinterpretation of each person's behavior?

I pose these questions to introduce the idea that interacting with people from other cultures can be complex. Simply informing students that there can be differences in culturally based nonverbal and socio-cultural behaviors (and the values associated with them) is not enough. If our goal is to teach students *how* to interact in English in a variety of contexts with other non-native speakers of English, as well as with native speakers, then, in addition to informing students about culturally defined behaviors, we can introduce them to the value of problem solving. It is through problem solving that our students can go beyond simply collecting interesting knowledge about cultures. They can have a way to assess a situation and identify behaviors that they predict will be appropriate to use within this situation.

A Cross-Cultural Problem: American University Dorm Life

Siriporn, a 22-year-old from suburban Bangkok, had secretly dreamed of studying in the United States ever since she was a little girl. As an undergraduate at Thammasat University, she majored in English. Although Siriporn rarely spoke with her conservative merchant parents about going to the United States, they knew about her dream, and they had saved money through the years to send her to America. Siriporn applied to several universities in the United States, and together, she and her parents selected a state university in Pennsylvania.

Siriporn arrived at her American university full of enthusiasm. She wanted to be an excellent student. Studying was the first thing on her mind. She attended all her classes and did her required readings before each lecture. However, Siriporn soon became more and more frustrated. She could not fully follow the lectures, and it took her a long time to comprehend the readings. She would study at the library until it closed and then go to her dormitory room to study some more.

But she had a problem. Her American roommate had many friends, and they all liked to meet in her room to talk and eat. They would simply walk into her room, sit down on her bed, and start to talk, eat potato chips, and play music. Sometimes they would stay up very late, and after they left, she had to clean potato chip crumbs, and even dirt from their shoes, off her bed.

Siriporn thought they were inconsiderate, and she attempted many times to get them to leave so she could study. Twice she walked out of the room in a hurry and without speaking. Another time she politely mentioned to her roommate that she likes to study in the room, but her roommate did not pay any attention to her comment. Another time, while walking with a friend from Japan, she said within earshot of her roommate, "I wish my roommate would not have parties every night." But, nothing Siriporn said or did seemed to make a difference. Her roommate's friends kept coming into her room. She became more and more frustrated, sometimes feeling helpless and angry.

What is the problem? What conflict between Thai and American behaviors and values created this problem? Why do you think Siriporn's ways to solve the problem did not work? How could Siriporn solve this problem?

One way to teach this process is to have students introduce real cross-cultural problems they face. In ESL settings, this is easy to do. Students interact with people from the host culture and with ESL speakers from a variety of cultures. However, in EFL settings this approach is problematic. With the exception of some students, who, for example, work in the tourist industry or in international business, most students do not have daily contact with people from other cultures. An alternative to using real cross-cultural problems is to use imagined or case history scenarios. For example, "A Cross-Cultural Problem: American Dorm Life" is an activity I wrote for America-bound Thai students in which they read and talk about a situation involving an unhappy Thai, work at identifying the problem and the reasons it exists, and generate a list of suggestions that aim at solving the problem.

I suggest teachers write their own problem sets. Problems can be based on knowledge about the students and the types of culturally based situations they might someday face, or they can simply be based on the students' interests. One book that has given me ideas for developing problem sets is *Intercultural Interactions*.[21] It presents a host of situations and problems to solve. Another book, specifically on problem-solving activities based on critical incidents between Chinese and Americans is *Turning Bricks into Jade.*[22]

To Understand a Culture, Get to Know Individuals

It is possible, as I have done in this chapter, to generalize about the cultural values and behaviors of a large group of people. Such generalizations can be useful, for example, to gain a general idea of the differences (and similarities) between people from different cultural backgrounds. However, there is a danger in categorizing a group of people into one single set of values and behaviors since this can lead to stereotyping. Not all British, for example, are reserved. Not all Japanese are indirect. Not all Americans are competitive.

As such, in addition to making generalizations, I teach students the importance of getting to know one person at a time, treating each as a distinct and unique individual. This includes how each individual behaves in different social situations, as well as the values each has. With this in mind, the question is, how can we teach students this concept? One way is to discuss it with them as a whole class; for some students, especially those who already like to personalize their experiences, this can make a difference in the way they perceive learning about people from different cultural backgrounds.

Another way to focus on the individual is to draw the students' attention to the differences among individuals in their own culture and have them relate this knowledge to other cultures. For example, I sometimes do a values clarification activity I call "Who gets to test the drug?" in which students read statements about the lives of seven people, all quite different from each other. One is a homeless drug addict, another is a bright college student, another a middle-aged scientist, another an elderly person who has worked all his life to solve societal problems, and so on. Each person has the same life-threatening disease, and the students are asked to select one of these people to participate in testing a new miracle drug that has the potential of reversing the disease. Students make their own individual choices and then meet in small groups to come to an agreement on their selection of one person to test the new drug.

One reason to do this activity is that it meets criteria, as discussed in Chapter 4, for promoting communication among students. It decreases the centrality of the teacher, provides students with chances to negotiate meaning, and allows them to decide for themselves what they want to say and how they want to say it. However, I also use this activity to show the students how individuals in a culture can vary in their beliefs and values. After the students negotiate who should be given the chance to test the drug, I ask them individually why they selected a particular person. For example, one student might select the scientist because she is doing important medical research, another the student because he is young and has a bright future, another the elderly person because he has contributed so much to society and deserves to be rewarded. I also emphasize that some agree on what they value, while others differ in what they believe is important. I then make the point that it is important to get to know what each person values, rather than making a generalization that all people in a culture believe in or value the same things.

To Understand Another Culture, Study Your Own

A fourth concept worth teaching is that much can be gained from studying one's own cultural behaviors and values. Since acquiring the rules of one's own culture is a fairly unconscious process, students are most likely not aware of many aspects of their own culture. Even everyday behaviors—such as how change is given at a store, or how people greet each other and bid farewell, complain, apologize, compliment each other, and enter and leave a classroom—are usually not apparent to most EFL students. By providing students with opportunities to consider how people interact in their own culture, as well as their own individual values and ways of behaving, they can gain the insight useful to them when encountering people from other cultures. I base this assumption on the idea that by knowing one's own values and behaviors, it is easier to recognize those of others, as well as make necessary changes in behavior when needed. In short, contrasts help.

To teach students about their own cultures, the teacher can design questions that provide students with chances to explain their own culture to the teacher and classmates. For example, a friend who is teaching EFL in Japan sometimes uses the text, *Explain Yourself: An English Conversation Book for Japan*.[23] The entire book consists of different topics, sketches that illustrate the topic, and lists of questions. Topics include the Japanese New Year, sumo wrestling, baseball, funerals, weddings, public baths, university life, temples, and different festivals. Here's a sample of the questions on weddings:

Who pays for the weddings?

Who is usually invited to weddings?

Who sits where? What is the order of the speeches?

What is an *o-miai* (arranged marriage)?

What factors do the two families consider important when arranging an *o-miai*?

What is a bridal school?

My friend pointed out that students not only gain practice in talking about their own culture in English but also raise questions about his culture: "Do you have arranged marriages in the United States? When is a popular time for Americans to get married?" I've also used this idea of explaining one's own culture in ESL settings by having small groups of students prepare oral presentations about their cultures. They collect objects and pictures, read about and consider behaviors and values, and create a presentation.

Another way to teach students about their own culture is to use photos and pictures. For example, by showing Thai students pictures that illustrate the ways Thais sit, it is possible to highlight that in their culture it is impolite to point one's foot at another person (unless they are close friends). By showing pictures of how people in other cultures sit, they can easily recognize the differences, especially noting that people in some cultures sit cross-legged, the foot pointing outward. The students could even practice sitting in other ways, providing a cross-cultural experience for them.

The teacher can go beyond simple behavior by also introducing readings or talking about the values associated with certain behaviors. For example, in the lesson on sitting in Thailand, the teacher could lead a discussion on reasons Thais sit the way they do, making the point that Thais do not point their foot at others because it will disturb the other person's *kwaan* or spirit essence. Many Thais believe that they have many parts to their *kwaan* and any part can escape the body if disturbed, leaving the person less than whole.[24] Thus, Thais do not point the foot (where the worst kwaan are) at someone's head (where the best are) because this could be disturbing. Such knowledge can spark students' interest in values across cultures and deeper cultural knowledge.

What Problems Do Some EFL/ESL Teachers Have Related to Culture and Language Teaching and Learning?

Problems some EFL/ESL teachers face include the following:

- The "I can't seem to adjust" problem
- The "learning the language of the host country" problem

The "I Can't Seem to Adjust" Problem

As discussed earlier in this chapter, EFL teachers (and ESL students and non-native EFL teachers studying abroad) go through a process of cultural adjustment that includes experiencing the loss of the familiar. Things taken for granted at home suddenly require close attention. Taking a bus, buying soap, doing laundry, paying bills, or looking up a telephone number can all require far more effort than was expected. For some, these everyday problems create an emphatic emotional disruption, and it feels like cultural adjustment will never take place. But there are things we can do in a new culture to make the adjustment process easier:

- Give yourself time.
- Identify, accept, and treat symptoms of culture shock.
- Talk with others who have successfully adjusted.
- Learn as much as possible about the host culture.
- Get involved with people in the host culture.
- Study the language of the host culture.

First, we can recognize that cultural adjustment takes time. Adjustment is a gradual process. It will not happen overnight.

Second, it is important to identify, accept, and treat the symptoms of culture shock. To identify the symptoms, it is necessary to step back and reflect on personal feelings and behavior. As I discussed earlier, symptoms include feeling emotionally distressed (homesick, easily angered, depressed, nervous, etc.), complaining about things that affect our lives (housing, food, weather etc.), and withdrawing (sleeping a lot, avoiding people from the host culture, spending all free time with other sojourners). Recognizing the symptoms of culture shock can in itself be therapeutic. But it is also important to accept the symptoms. For example, if I am depressed, I recognize that I am depressed. I simply remind myself that it will not last long. I also do the opposite of what I have been doing as a result of culture shock. If I find I sleep a lot, I try not sleeping so much. If I find I complain too much, I try complimenting.

Third, talking with others who have successfully adapted to the culture can also be useful. It lets others know that our uneasiness, lack of confidence, and everyday problems in getting around and doing simple things is temporary. It is also possible to learn about what others have done to adjust. People usually like talking about their experiences, and most sojourners are more than happy to act as mentors, especially if they have created a happy life for themselves in their second country.

Fourth, it helps to learn as much as possible about the host culture. While some want to know about geography, others are interested in history, art, education, politics, psychology, and religion. I personally like to read translated short stories and novels since they give me a window, as reinvented as it is, into understanding much about the host culture.

Fifth, although not always easy, get involved with people from the host culture. This is very important. It is through daily contact with people in the host culture that we learn about what to expect and how to behave.

Sixth, when we learn the language of the host culture, it is possible to gain an even deeper understanding of the culture and its people, making adjustment not only possible but, at least to me, interesting and even fun.

The "Learning the Language of the Host Country" Problem

The problem of learning the language of the host country is specific to both ESL students and EFL teachers living abroad who want to learn the language of the host country. However, the problem here is discussed with the EFL teacher in mind. Most of us start out with great enthusiasm. However, many give up. It is not because we do not want to become fluent in the language. Most of us dream of gaining great proficiency. Rather, we give up because we get too busy to study the language or find we lack opportunities to actually use the language. We speak English to our students, the office staff, and administrators. We make friends with other EFL teachers and with fluent English-speaking acquaintances from the host culture, and we end up speaking English with them outside the workplace. When we venture out into the country, we meet people who jump at the chance to use English with a native speaker, and we oblige. As it turns out, opportunities to use the language of the host culture become limited. However, some of us are determined, and based on our experience with learning second languages, we agree that learning the language requires a great amount of effort.

Suggestions for learning the language of the host country include:

- Continue studying the language.
- Take on the responsibility for your own learning.
- Create and implement a learning plan.
- Build relationships with people in the community based on appropriate use of the language.

If we want to become fluent in the host country language, we have to devote considerable energy and time to studying it. We start out with wonderful intentions. We join a language class, do our homework, and attend classes regularly. But obligations get in the way, and gradually we attend classes less often. Eventually, we stop going, put the book on a shelf, and tell ourselves we will start again when we have more time. However, studying a language is an ongoing process, and it requires consistent discipline and interest and a willingness to concentrate on studying. Basically, if our goal is to become very fluent and literate in the language, we have to be willing to devote years to this endeavor.

We have to take responsibility for our own learning, which includes creating a plan to learn the language that might include attending classes and collecting and studying language texts. Perhaps more important is our need to have a plan designed to make use of all the resources available to us, including people in the community. For example, to gain spoken fluency, Terry Marshall[25] suggests we (1) decide on what to learn for the day (e.g., how to buy train tickets); (2) prepare an imagined conversation in the target language with the help of a native-speaking mentor/tutor; (3) practice the conversation with your mentor/tutor; (4) communicate the studied language to native speakers by going into the community, finding people, and speaking to them (e.g., at the train station); (5) evaluate our progress.

Having a plan is a start. Implementing it is another matter. Going into the community to find people to use the language with is not always easy. However, it can be done. For example, when I moved to Japan, I purposefully lived in a place where no other foreigners lived, and when approaching the study of Japanese, I used the community. I talked with people at the public bath, the local stores, and the laundry. Being single at the time, I went on dates with women who I knew would be willing to speak Japanese with me. I also joined a yoga club where I could use Japanese, went on weekend hiking trips with a non-English speaking Japanese, and drank a few beers each week at a place where few were interested in speaking English with me. During my lunch hour, I spent ten minutes chatting with a friend in Japanese on the phone, and I used Japanese with a group of American and Australian friends, all interested in mastering the language. I learned a lot from these friends, which is why I support teachers having students speak English with each other in class.

My efforts to find contexts to use Japanese did something unexpected for me. I established a network, becoming a member of several groups within the community—for example, the yoga club, a local restaurant, and the community center. I discovered that as my Japanese got better, my relationships with people in the community became more complex, and that as these relationships became more complex, I needed to learn more Japanese. For example, since I wanted to send New Year's greeting cards to my new friends, just before New Year's I learned how to use ink and a brush to write, as well as the formulaic language I needed. When the yoga club took a trip, I had to learn how to introduce myself to others in public fashion. When a friend's mother died, I had to learn what to say to him. The point is, as it relates to learning the language of the host country, it is important to build relationships with people in the community. Through interaction with them it becomes possible to make progress in the language, because language and culture are inextricably linked.

TEACHER SELF-DEVELOPMENT TASKS

Talk Tasks

1. *Culture* can be defined in many ways. For example, I define *culture* as the shared values and beliefs of a group of people and the behaviors that reflect them.

   a. What merit do you think this definition has?
   b. What are other ways to define culture?

2. Review and discuss my points on teaching cultural concepts to students.

   a. What are the four concepts I discuss? Explain each.
   b. Why do I recommend that EFL teachers teach students cultural concepts? What are the benefits? Do you teach cultural concepts to students? If so, how?
   c. Select one of the cultural concepts. Design a lesson that aims at teaching this concept.

3. Here are three brief research tasks for you. Feel free to do one or more of them.

   a. If you are living abroad, here is a task for you. The way names are listed in telephone books sometimes differs from culture to culture. Locate a phone book. How are the names listed? Are they listed the same or differently from how they are listed in phone books in your native culture? What other differences do you notice?
   b. Each culture has its own special holidays. Go online. Look at holidays in different cultures. See how many different types of holidays you can come up with.
   c. Pick two different cultures. Find out how people in these cultures generally offer guests a drink, such as a cup of tea. Find out how people accept or refuse the offer.

4. Storti provides the following graphic model of the process of adjustment.[26]

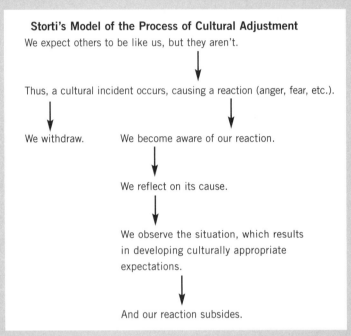

Storti's Model of the Process of Cultural Adjustment

We expect others to be like us, but they aren't.

Thus, a cultural incident occurs, causing a reaction (anger, fear, etc.).

We withdraw.   We become aware of our reaction.

We reflect on its cause.

We observe the situation, which results in developing culturally appropriate expectations.

And our reaction subsides.

Study this model. Notice that there are two possible ways for us to react to a cultural incident. We can withdraw, for example, by moving into the expatriate community, or we can work at adjustment through reflection.

a. Explain what Storti's model means.
b. Talk about the benefits of taking the "reflective" path. You might want to refer to my discussion on the benefits of cultural adjustment (see pages 123–24).
c. Tell stories about your own and others' cultural adjustment.

5. How are people in different cultures polite?

Observation and Talk Tasks

1. Videotape one of your classes. Analyze the interaction by studying how you and the students:

Use eye contact while listening
Touch (or don't touch)
Keep space or distance while standing or sitting

How do your behaviors reflect your native culture? How are students' behaviors different or similar to yours? Meet with other teachers to talk about what you discovered.

2. Try these matching techniques. Then talk to someone who also has tried them. What did you learn from the experience? Consider how matching behaviors can be used as a way for you to learn a language, as well as the value it has for EFL/ESL students.
   a. Sit next to someone who speaks a different language. Match this person's posture, gestures, facial expressions, and breathing. Do this for a few minutes.
   b. Sit in the middle of a movie theater. Do whatever the audience does. Laugh when they laugh. Sigh when they sigh. Sit the way they sit.
   c. Watch people doing things, such as paying for an item at a store, getting a waiter's attention, eating a dish of ice cream, and counting with their fingers. Imitate them. Try to match their behaviors as they did these things.

Journal Writing Tasks

1. Write your ideas about teaching students cultural concepts. If you try out any of the ideas, reflect on how you thought the lesson went.
2. If you now live in a foreign country, or have lived in one, write about your own cultural adjustment process and problems.
3. Write what you have learned from matching people's behaviors. Make a list of possible behaviors you could match.

Recommended Teacher Resources

Readings on Cultural Concepts

Bennett, M. J., ed. *Basic Concepts of Intercultural Communication.* Yarmouth, ME: Intercultural Press, 1998.

Hall, E. T. *Beyond Culture.* Garden City, NY: Anchor Books, 1981.

Samovar, L. A., and R. E. Porter, eds. *Intercultural Communication: A Reader.* 11th ed. Belmont, CA: Wadsworth, 2005.

Scollon, R., and S. W. Scollon. *Intercultural Communication.* 2d ed. Malden, MA: Blackwell, 2001.

Readings on Specific Cultures

Broome, B. J. *Exploring the Greek Mosaic*. Yarmouth, ME: Intercultural Press, 1996.

Crouch, N. *Mexicans and Americans: Cracking the Cultural Code*. Yarmouth, ME: Intercultural Press, 2004.

De Mente, B. *Etiquette: A Guide to Japan*. North Clarendon, VT: Tuttle, 1990.

Flaitz, J., ed. *Understanding Your International Students: An Educational, Cultural, and Linguistic Guide*. Ann Arbor: University of Michigan Press, 2003.

Hu, W., and C. Grove. *Encountering the Chinese: A Guide for Americans, 2d ed.* Yarmouth, ME: Intercultural Press, 1999.

Klausner, W. *Reflections on Thai Culture. 4th ed.* Bangkok, THA: The Siam Society, 1993.

Kohls, L. R. *Learning to Think Korean: A Guide to Living and Working in Korea*. Yarmouth, ME: Intercultural Press, 2001.

Matsumoto, D. *The New Japan: Debunking Seven Cultural Stereotypes*. London: Nicholas Brealey Publishing, 2002.

Ness, G. *Germany: Unraveling an Enigma*. Yarmouth, ME: Intercultural Press, 2000.

Nydell, M. K. *Understanding Arabs: A Guide for Westerners. 3d ed.* Yarmouth, ME: Intercultural Press, 2002.

Richmond, Y. *From Nyet to Da: Understanding the Russians. 3d ed.* Yarmouth, ME: Intercultural Press, 2003.

Richmond, Y., and P. Gestrin. *Into Africa: Intercultural Insights*. Yarmouth, ME: Intercultural Press, 1998.

Shahar, L., and D. Kurz. *Border Crossings: American Interactions with Israelis*. Yarmouth, ME: Intercultural Press, 1995.

Wattley-Ames, H. *Spain Is Different*. Yarmouth, ME: Intercultural Press, 1999.

Readings on American Culture

Athen, G. *American Ways: A Guide for Foreigners in the United States. 2d ed.* Yarmouth, ME: Intercultural Press, 2002.

Kim, E. Y. *The Yin and Yang of American Culture: A Paradox*. Yarmouth, ME: Intercultural Press, 2001.

Stewart, E. C., and M. J. Bennett. *American Cultural Patterns: A Cross-Cultural Perspective*. Yarmouth, ME: Intercultural Press, 1991.

Storti, C. *Americans at Work: A Guide to the Can-Do People*. Yarmouth, ME: Intercultural Press, 2004.

Readings on Cultural Adjustment

Cornes, A. *Culture from the Inside Out: Travel and Meet Yourself*. Yarmouth, ME: Intercultural Press, 2004.

Kohls, L. R. *Survival Kit for Overseas Living, 4ᵗʰ ed.* Yarmouth, ME: Intercultural Press, 2001.

Storti, C. *The Art of Crossing Cultures. 2ᵈ ed.* Yarmouth, ME: Intercultural Press, 2001.

Teaching Culture

Byram, M., N. Adams, and D. Stevens. *Developing Intercultural Competence in Practice.* Clevedon, UK: Multilingual Matters, 2001.

DeCapua, A., and A. C. Wintergerst. *Crossing Cultures in the Language Classroom.* Ann Arbor: University of Michigan Press, 2004.

Fantini, A. E. *New Ways in Teaching Culture.* Alexandria, VA: TESOL, 1997.

Hall, J. K. *Teaching and Researching Language and Culture.* New York: Pearson Education, 2002.

Moran, P. R. *Teaching Culture: Perspectives in Practice.* Boston: Heinle & Heinle, 2001.

Stringer, D., and P. Cassiday. *52 Activities for Exploring Values Differences.* Yarmouth, ME: Intercultural Press, 2003.

Wang, M. M., et al. *Turning Bricks into Jade: Critical Incidents for Mutual Understanding among Chinese and Americans.* Yarmouth, ME: Intercultural Press, 2000.

Endnotes

1 See Nydell (1987, 60). Also see Nydell (2002).

2 It is worth pointing out that American cultural values represent a paradox. On the one hand, the majority of Americans will say they value equality. On the other hand, racism still exists in America.

3 My knowledge of Thai culture comes from personal experience, as well as from readings. I recommend a variety of books, including Klausner's (1983) *Reflections on Thai Culture,* Moore's (1992) *Heart Talk,* Heinze's (1982) *Tham Khwan: How to Contain the Essence of Life,* Manivat's (1983) collection of writings by Kukrit Pramoj, Tambiah's (1970) classic study, *Buddhism and The Spirit Cults in Northeast Thailand,* Buddhadāsa's (1970) Theravada Buddhist essays in *Toward the Truth,* Mulder's (1997) *Thai Images: The Culture of the Public World.* I also recommend reading the many translations of Thai short stories and novels, too numerous to list here.

4 From Moore (1992, 83–84).

5 Doi (1973) discusses the psychological makeup of Japanese.

[6] As Fieg (1989, 41) puts it: "Consistent with the Buddhist ideal that ultimate happiness (Nirvana) results from the total detachment of the self from feelings and desires, Thai emotional expression—whether it be positive or negative—is rarely extreme. Instead, Thais have a tendency to neutralize all emotions; even in a moment of elation, there is always the underlying feeling: I don't want to be too happy now or I might be correspondingly sad later; too much laughter today may lead to too many tears tomorrow."

[7] From Wallender (1977, 7).

[8] See From Lewis and Jungman (1986, xxi). Others who discuss the process of cultural adjustment include Adler (1987), Begley (2003), and Storti (2001). Research includes Venrick's (2001) study of his own adjustment processes to Thai culture, Purnell's (2000) study of adjustment processes of Taiwanese students at a small, midwestern college, Ohata's (2004) study of Japanese college students' cultural adjustment and language anxiety, and Hector-Mason's (2004) study of cultural learning experiences of Hispanic adults adapting to life in a small central Texas town.

[9] From Storti (1989, 94).

[10] From Storti (1989, 94).

[11] This quote was discovered in Adler (1987).

[12] Andersen (2003), Hall (1966), McDaniel (2003), and Scollon and Scollon (2001) offer detailed discussion on nonverbal behavior.

[13] See Wylie and Stafford (1977).

[14] This point is based on my own experience and on research by Hoffer (1984).

[15] See Barnlund (1975) for a discussion of touch in Japanese and American cultures.

[16] Watson (1974) has studied touch in cultures around the world; Nydell (2002) writes about touch in Arab countries.

[17] See Hall (1966, 15).

[18] From Nydell (1987, 45).

[19] From Hall (1966, page 15).

[20] This basic idea is discussed Melamed and Barndt (1977).

[21] See Brislin et al. (1986).

[22] See Wang et al. (2000).

[23] See Nicholson and Sakuno (1982).

[24] See Heinze (1982) who has done extensive research on the Thai kwaan. Also see Tambiah (1970), an anthropologist who is an authority on spirit cults in northeast Thailand.

[25] See Marshall (1989) who provides guidelines based on his Peace Corps experience. H. D. Brown (1991) and Rubin and Thompson (1994) have also written books with guidelines and advice for the language learner.

[26] See Storti (2001).

Part 3

Teaching Language Skills

There isn't any listening without someone speaking, and speaking without somebody listening is an empty gesture.

—Bowen, Madsen, and Hilferty 1985, 99

Teaching Students to Comprehend Spoken English

- What does the act of listening include?
- What kinds of listening activities do EFL/ESL teachers use?
- How do EFL/ESL teachers use the media to teach listening?
- What problems do some EFL/ESL teachers have in teaching students to comprehend spoken English?

What Does the Act of Listening Include?

I guide my discussion by focusing on aspects of listening, including active listening, the processing of what we hear to make sense out of it, and two purposes for listening.

Active Listening

Listening is not a passive activity. Rather, listening places many demands on us. When we participate in face-to-face or telephone exchanges, we need to be receptive to others, which includes paying attention to explanations, questions, and opinions. Even when we listen during one-way exchanges—for example, while listening to lectures, radio dramas, films, television news, and musicals—we are active. Consider, for example, how many times you shouted at, laughed at, or agreed with (either out loud or inside your head) a person giving a television commentary. Active listening is even a part of our intrapersonal communication in which we pay attention to our own thoughts and ideas. For example, consider the last time you talked to yourself. "Where did I put my keys? Oh! There they are!"[1]

Processing What We Hear

Another aspect of listening is the way we process what we hear. There are two distinct processes involved in comprehending spoken English: *bottom-up processing* and *top-down processing*. Bottom-up processing refers to decoding a message that the listener hears through the analysis of sounds, words, and grammar, while top-down processing refers to using background knowledge to comprehend a message.[2] For example, imagine that Joe is a tourist in a foreign country. He is staying at the Federal Hotel, and he wanders away to see some local sites, only to discover he is lost. Joe then decides to approach someone, whom he asks, "Excuse me, couldja tell me howta getto to the Federal?" From a bottom-up point of view, the person listening to Joe arrives at meaning by identifying the specific words relevant to the message (such as recognizing that the "Federal" is a hotel), recognizing strings of sounds and being able to segment them (e.g., recognizing that *couldja* is two words, *could you,* and that *howta getto* is *how to get to),* and identifying grammatical and functional clues pertinent to the message (e.g., recognizing that *could you* indicates that a request is about to be made and that *how to get to* indicates asking for directions).

While successful bottom-up processing relies on recognition of sounds, words, and grammar, successful top-down processing hinges on having the kind of background knowledge needed to comprehend the meaning of a message. This can be in the form of previous knowledge about the topic—for example, knowing the hotels in the tourist area. It can also be in the form of *situational knowledge*—for example, knowing there are lost tourists in the area who frequently ask for directions. Finally, background knowledge can be in the form of *schemata* or plans about the overall structure of events and the relationship between them."[3] For example, when someone who looks lost approaches you in a tourist area and says, "Excuse me," you can predict this person is about to ask for directions, location, or something related to being a tourist.

This last kind of background knowledge or schemata relates especially to our real-world experiences and the expectations we have, based on our experiences, about how people behave. The schemata we draw from includes our experience in assigning specific kinds of interaction to an event—for example, knowing how to listen to jokes, stories, and requests. Likewise, it includes the way we categorize knowledge. For example, if we frequently walk through a tourist area, we will know the names of hotels and can group people as tourists and non-tourists. Schemata also includes being able to predict a topic in discourse and infer a sequence of events—for example, expecting that a lost tourist will initiate and move through a conversational routine, including getting our attention, asking for directions, and possibly checking understanding by paraphrasing the directions.

The importance of background knowledge is especially obvious when we consider the language processing problems of foreign students who come to the United States. Many students are considered to be highly talented at bottom-up processing of English, and within their EFL settings they are considered to be very fluent speakers of English. Nonetheless, upon arrival in the United States, some soon discover that they cannot communicate as easily as they had hoped. Here are two examples. The first is that of a student who came from Somalia.[4] This student went to McDonald's® to get something to eat, and when he placed his order at the counter, he was asked, *Would you like this forhereortogo?* He looked at her inquisitively and said nothing, since he could not understand her question. She repeated her question louder, *Forhereortogo?* which did not help. The person behind him then helped him with his bottom-up processing, telling him that the string of words consisted of *For here or to go*, but he still had no idea what the speaker meant. Finally, the person behind him said, *Would you like to take this order out, or would you like to eat it here?* and the student finally understood, having gained the necessary background knowledge to process the culturally based question.

The second example is of an older woman from the People's Republic of China.[5] She was a teacher for a number of years in China, and her dream was to go to the United States to study. She finally did, and during her first week, she was walking across campus when a classmate came toward her. He smiled and said, *Hi!*

What's up? The confused newcomer looked at him for a brief moment, looked to the sky to see what was above her, looked down, and with an unsure voice said, *The sky?* Although this is an extreme example, it, along with the example of the student at McDonald's, shows the importance of background knowledge in comprehending spoken English.

The Purposes of Listening

In addition to bottom-up and top-down processing, we can consider *interactional* and *transactional functions* of language.[6] When language is used to fulfill an interactional communicative function, the focus is on creating harmonious interaction among individuals. As a social phenomenon, interactional use of language centers on such safe topics as the weather, food, and beautiful things. These topics are neutral, or non-controversial, and shift quickly. Because these topics are non-controversial, they promote agreement between speakers and listeners, which in turn creates a harmonious relationship.

Unlike interactional use of language, transactional use focuses attention on the content of the message. Emphasis is on transferring information, and unlike interactional uses of language, it is important for the listener to comprehend the content of the speaker's message. Topics vary from context to context and can include almost any content. Examples of interactional use of language include a doctor advising a patient on how to take a prescription drug or a student listening to a lecture on marriage in the Philippines.

What Kinds of Listening Activities Do EFL/ESL Teachers Use?

An understanding of top-down and bottom-up processes of listening and of the transactional and interactional functions of language provides an awareness of what listeners do as they listen, and this knowledge is useful when we consider the listening activities we have students do in our classrooms. In this section I focus on activities we can use to provide EFL/ESL students with a variety of listening experiences.

Identifying Linguistic Features

The aim of activities that focus on identifying linguistic features is to make students more aware of the linguistic features of spoken English. As such, they center on bottom-up processing. Since the aim is to provide chances for students to develop their perceptual abilities, little attention is given to transactional or interactional purposes. One activity is to give students practice in listening to the way sounds blend in spoken English. The teacher (or a tape-recorded voice) says a phrase, such as *didja,* followed by a sentence, such as *Didja go to the store?* The student then identifies the written version from a list.[7]

The idea of Activity 1 is to show students what sentence stress is and how it influences the rhythm of spoken English. For example, after listening to and marking *He's a terrific actor,* students can see that major words (nouns, main verbs, adverbs, adjectives) receive stress while minor words (pronouns, determiners, articles, prepositions) do not, and that when words have more than one syllable, only one syllable—for instance, *if* in *terrific*—receives primary stress.

---

1. A Stress and Rhythm Listening Activity

Listen to the conversation. Put a mark over each stressed syllable.

A: That was a really good movie!

B: Yeah, Robin Williams. He's a terrific actor. Very funny.

A: What are your favorite Robin Williams movies?

To do Activity 2, the teacher can use any minimal pair (two words that differ only in one sound), making the selection based on sounds that are new or problematic for students. Of course, the teacher can also select pairs that students can easily distinguish so they feel successful. To do this activity, the teacher says the string of words, for example, *Liver. River. River.* Each students puts up one finger each time he or she hears *Liver* and two fingers for *River.* The teacher can challenge the students by increasing the number of words in the string and saying them faster.

> ## 2. A Minimal Pair Listening Activity
> Listen to each word. Each time you hear *river,* put up one finger. Each time you hear *liver* put up two fingers.
>
> 1. river
>
> 2. liver, river
>
> 3. liver, liver, liver

Responding to Requests and Commands

Listen-and-respond activities highlight bottom-up processing because the listener listens to identify specific words and grammatical command structures. One type of activity is Total Physical Response (TPR).[8] Here is an example of a TPR lesson.

> ## 3. TPR
>
> | | |
> |---|---|
> | *Teacher Command:* | Stand up. |
> | *Student Response:* | (Students stand up.) |
> | *Teacher Command:* | Go to the blackboard. |
> | *Student Response:* | (Students walk to the blackboard.) |
> | *Teacher Command:* | Write your name on the board. |
> | *Student Response:* | (Students write their names.) |

While doing TPR with EFL/ESL students, I have found Berty Segal's advice quite useful.[9] Segal suggests that teachers begin by demonstrating the commands, doing them with the students. The teacher can also reduce anxiety by giving commands to the whole class, then to small groups of students, and finally, after the students have lots of practice, to individual volunteers.

There are many possible commands that students can practice.

To create commands, we simply need to select "action" verbs, such as *stand up, sit down, walk, skip, hop, turn, stop, pick up, put down, sing, touch, point, smile, frown, laugh, throw,* and *catch.* These verbs can be combined with nouns and other words to make up commands, each activity emphasizing listening for a purpose. For example, students can listen to the same verb said many times with different nouns, such as *Touch your nose. Touch your chin. Touch your mouth.* or *Point at the clock. Point at the door.* Or students can listen to different combinations of verbs, for instance, *Open your book to page 32. Close your book. Stand up. Point to the door. . . .* Some students appreciate humor, too. For example, I observed a third grade ESL teacher once say, *Jose, put your nose in Maria's armpit.*[10]

Another way to provide ways for students, especially children, to listen and respond is by playing Simon Says. Like TPR, the teacher gives a command. But the listener is only supposed to follow the command if it is preceded by the phrase *Simon says.* Most children love this game. Anxiety levels go down. Attention levels go up.

Another activity liked by both children and adults who are young at heart is the Hokey Pokey. The students and teacher form a large circle, listen to the Hokey Pokey song, and follow the commands: "You put your right foot in. You take your right foot out. You put your right foot in and shake it all about. You do the Hokey Pokey and turn yourself around. That's what it's all about!"[11]

Interacting as a Listener
The goal of interactive listening activities is to focus students' attention on how they can maintain social interactive relations. Both bottom-up and top-down processes can be a part of these activities, depending on the design. One such activity is called Chat. Students view short videotaped segments of interaction in different settings— for example, at the dinner table, the fitness center, a grocery store, the checkout counter. The idea is for students not only to work at comprehending the interaction, but also to consider what a "safe" topic is and how the interaction is maintained. To accomplish this, as students view the videotape, they can:

- Check off those topics that were discussed from a list of possible topics
- Follow along with a written script, highlighting the things listeners do to keep the conversation going (e.g., using head nods and encouraging remarks, such as *uh-huh, What else?* and *No kidding!)*

- Complete a set of multiple choice and true/false questions about the interaction (e.g., True or False? Josh likes to chuckle to show he is listening.)

Eavesdropping is another way to focus students' attention on the function of listening during conversations. The goal is to teach students the value of listening in on conversations and a few strategies for doing so. Activity 4 is an eavesdropping activity from Porter and Roberts.[12] The students are told that they are guests at a party and that they can eavesdrop on conversations. They then listen to short segments of party conversation and complete a worksheet.

---

4. Eavesdropping

You are at a party given by the Director of Studies at your school. A lot of teachers and students are there. You can hear pieces of conversation. Try to guess what the people are talking about. You hear four different conversations. Would you like to join any of them?

Topic   Are you interested?

1. _____

2. _____

3. _____

4. _____

After students complete such eavesdropping activities in class or in the listening lab, I ask them if they would like to try their eavesdropping skills outside the classroom. If they agree, I send them out in teams of two or three. Their task is to observe and capture pieces of conversation, including short dialogues, and to write up their eavesdropping experience and prepare to tell classmates something they learned. Of course, this is much easier in ESL settings, where there are plenty of English language conversations going on (e.g., in college dorms, grocery stores, and restaurants), but it is also possible for EFL students to listen in on English conversations, especially in big cities (e.g., at fast-food restaurants, tourist areas, and department stores). It is worth mentioning that not all students like to eavesdrop. Some consider it an invasion of privacy, and when students object, I respect their wishes not to practice this activity. However, some students have told me how much they like to eavesdrop since they can capture authentic use of English that they can practice in their minds.

Another interactive listening activity is called Matching.[13] Although this activity is a little too outlandish for some, students can be asked to match others' nonverbal behaviors, including head nods, gestures, and facial expressions. The goal is to show the value of observing the behaviors others use as they listen, as well as to focus students' attention on their own use of nonverbal behavior during a conversation. To introduce the concept of matching, I demonstrate by having one student talk on a familiar topic while another listens. At the end of their demonstration, I show a few selected aspects of the listener's behavior, such as quick Japanese head nods. I then have students practice matching other students' behaviors in the same way. Although students sometimes need lots of coaching and coaxing and have to work through fits of laughter, some students soon discover that to be a good listener in another language requires not only knowledge of topics and vocabulary and grammar, but also adapting the nonverbal behaviors we exhibit as we listen.

Comprehending Extended Speech

Transactional in nature, comprehension activities center on comprehending stories, extended speech, and lectures. As with all the activity types in this chapter, there are many possible comprehension activities. One that can be used with beginners and more advanced students is a picture-ordering activity that includes listening to a story and then putting pictures in the order of the events in the story. Students can also draw their own pictures. For example, students can view or listen to a weather forecast and, under the relevant days of the week, draw pictures that represent the forecast.[14]

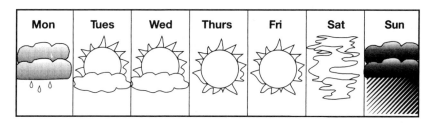

Cloze listening tasks can also be used as comprehension activities. Activity 5 is an example.

---

5. Holidays

Listen to the short lecture. As you listen, read the text. Listen a few times. Then complete each blank with one of the vocabulary words. Keep in mind, there are more words than blanks!

Vocabulary:

restaurants	Hungarians	person's	includes	year
holidays	celebrate	name	birthday	treat

Text:

There are some very interesting _____ in different

countries. _____, for example, have a Name Day.

Each day of the _____ has a person's name. If it is a

_____ Name Day, then he or she has to

_____ friends. This _____ taking friends

out to _____ for meals.

Taking notes can also engage students in listening to extended speech, as in Activity 6.

---

6. The Joy of Traveling

Listen to the travel story three times.

The first time:

What countries did the young woman visit?

What types of transportation did she use?

The second time:

Which country did she like the most?

What are three things the woman says she likes about the country?

The third time:

Listen to the woman's descriptions of the places she visited.

Which place would you like to visit? Why?

Problem Solving

Problem-solving listening activities are transactional because they provide ways for students to comprehend content to solve problems through their use of both bottom-up and top-down processes. There are, of course, a variety of possible activities. In one of my favorite activities,[15] the students are detectives listening to a recorded report about a murder; and as they listen, they complete a grid on the alibis of the suspects. Based on what they hear, their task is to narrow down the suspects to select the murderer. Here is my version of the report students listen to.

> Jerry Gebhard, an ESL teacher, was murdered between 8:00 PM and midnight yesterday at his home near campus. The suspects, his students, described their activities on the night of the murder. Yoko said she had dinner alone from 8:00 to 9:00, and then practiced her flute. Several people heard her playing. She then watched TV for an hour with other students in the dormitory lounge. At 11:00 she was studying in her room. Several students saw her there. Andre said that he was watching TV from 8:00 to 9:00 and was studying alone in his room from 9:00 to 11:00, and then he went to bed. However, a classmate said he saw Andre and Lilia walking away from campus at 9:30. Bahlal said he was at the library from 8:00 until 10:00, then he took a walk with his friend until around 11:00, when he went to his room to study. Several people saw Bahlal at the library. Mohammad said he was talking with Lilia in the dorm hallway from 8:00 to about 9:15, was with another friend until 10:00, watched TV until 11:00, and then went to bed. Lilia claimed she talked with Mohammad from 8:00 to around 9:00 or so, then went to her room to study and sleep.

To add a touch of humor, teachers can use the names of students in their class. See the example of what the grid looks like when it is completed by the students.

Name	8:00–9:00	9:00–10:00	10:00–11:00	11:00–12:00
Yoko	eating dinner alone	playing flute	tv in lounge	studying in room
Andre	tv in lounge	alone in room	alone in room	in bed sleeping
Bahlal	at library	at library	walking with friend	studying in room
Mohammad	with Lilia	with friend	tv in lounge	in bed sleeping
Lilia	with Mohammad	studying in room	studying in room	in bed sleeping

How Do EFL/ESL Teachers Use Media to Teach Listening?

There are many ways in which EFL/ESL teachers can make use of media in our listening classes. Radio, for example, offers songs, advertisements, talk shows, and drama. Television offers an abundance of materials: quiz shows, comedies, reality shows, soaps, cartoons, documentaries, educational programs, news, weather forecasts, movies, award shows, and commercials.[16]

Folk, rock, and popular songs offer students exposure to one form of authentic English through the media, and many students, young and old, enjoy listening to (and singing) songs. EFL/ESL teachers use a variety of different songs, including everything from "The ABC Song" to "Yesterday" by the Beatles. However, most agree that students benefit from the listening experience when the songs are taught so that the lyrics are comprehensible. One way to do this is to provide short lessons on vocabulary and grammar, followed with different listening activities. For example, I observed a teacher have students listen to "Everything I Own" by Bread as part of a lesson on past tense. She had students listen to the song to get the idea, for example, that it is about lost love. She then played the song again, having students perform a fill-in-the-blank task with the past tense verbs they heard.

Singing lines in the song and participating in other ways can also help make the lyrics comprehensible. For example, as children listen to "Old MacDonald,"[17] they can point at pictures of animals, as well as sing animal sounds and the "e-I, e-I, oh."

Old MacDonald

Old MacDonald had a farm
E-I, e-I oh
And on this farm he had a cow
E-I, e-I oh
With a *moo moo* here
And a *moo moo* there
Here a *moo,* there a *moo*
Everywhere a *moo moo.* . . .

As this list of techniques shows, there are also creative things we can do in our classrooms with video clips from TV programs, films, commercials, and teacher-made videotapes of interactions.[18]

Techniques: Processing Authentic Video Materials

Silent Viewing: Students view video material without sound to consider what is going on and guess what speakers are doing and saying.

Soundtrack Only: Students hear the soundtrack without the picture and speculate on what speakers look like, the setting, and the location.

Beginning Only: Students view the beginning of a sequence, then predict what will happen next.

Ending Only: Students view the ending and consider what happened earlier.

Split Viewing (One): Some students view the material without sound. Others listen without viewing. Groups come together to create a fuller understanding of context and content.

Split Viewing (Two): Half the class sits with back to screen. Half can see the screen. Both can hear. Pairs then build a fuller understanding of context and content.

To illustrate how teachers can process authentic video materials, here is an example from my own teaching in Hungary of an episode of an old American situation comedy, *The Wonder Years.* I began by writing a set of questions on the board: How many people are talking? How old do you think they are? What is their relationship? What are they talking about? We then listened to two minutes of the show without a picture and answered the questions written on the board, after which I gave them a new set of questions: What approximate year is it? What are the people doing? What do you think the story is going to be about? I then played the sound and picture of the first five minutes of the show, including the two minutes they had already listened to. After answering the questions, we viewed the show until just before the climax. I then had students meet in groups to write down and announce their predictions about how the show would end. We then viewed the ending to see if any of the predictions were correct and to compare the students' creative endings with the original.

Before ending this section, it is important to add that modern technology provides listening teachers with opportunities to bring a wide variety of media into the classroom or language lab. It is now possible for teachers with financial support to use satellite to bring digital television programs, movies, world news, and much more into the classroom.

What Problems Do Some EFL/ESL Teachers Have in Teaching Students to Comprehend Spoken English?

Problems some EFL/ESL teachers face include the following:

- The "outdated listening lab" problem
- The "How can I judge the authenticity of commercial EFL/ESL listening materials?" problem

The "Outdated Listening Lab" Problem

EFL/ESL teachers may find themselves in a traditional listening lab sitting at their carrels and listening to tapes, rarely speaking with classmates. In these types of programs, the role of the teacher in the listening lab is to broadcast a program to the whole class. The teacher acts as a monitor, listening in on students, correcting errors, and furnishing answers to listening exercises.

This traditional approach doesn't always produce the best results. Students complain that it is sometimes boring, and that they do not necessarily gain much from the experience. Teachers complain that there is little opportunity to interact with students on an individual level or to provide them with practice in listening to authentic English used as a means to communicate meaning between people.[19]

However, it is possible to transform a lab from a traditional one into a place where students can work actively on developing their listening abilities while also making use of the uniqueness of the lab system. In fact, many of the activities previously discussed can be adapted for lab use. For example, the teacher can use magazine pictures of crowded scenes and then create a verbal description of one person from the scene, audiotape this description, and have students listen, imagining they are supposed to meet the person in a crowded place. Teachers then give the picture to students to choose the person from the crowd. Students can do jigsaw listening in a lab. Each student would listen to different alibis, then leave their carrels, meet in small groups, and share their knowledge about the alibis to determine who the murderer is. Then they return to their carrels to listen to an explanation as to who the murderer is and to learn if the explanation matches the group's conclusion. Many such activities, created by the teacher or from the many new listening texts and audio components on the market, are possible. (See Recommended Teacher Resources.)

Lab time can also be devoted to allowing students to select their own listening materials. Here, the teacher acts as a resource by helping students select materials that will be comprehensible and of interest. The advantage of this activity is that it teaches students to take responsibility for their own listening development, and they can work at their own paces and levels. The disadvantage is that such an individualized system does not match all students' learning styles and expectations as to what a listening lab is. Because of these advantages and disadvantages, teachers may want to use a fraction of the scheduled lab time as an open lab or include both regular and elective labs.

Schools also can set up a multimedia lab for students. These labs include traditional listening stations where students can select audio material and textbooks, as well as authentic listening materials such as songs and lyrics or academic lectures with text. These labs feature DVD players, VCRs, and a wide selection of videotaped materials, including movies, documentaries, cartoons, dramas, plays, concerts, and teacher- or student-produced videos on topics of interest. The lab also features computer stations with a variety of software programs, links to the Internet, and other technology (such as language learning games).

At some schools, the cost of maintaining a multimedia lab has been prohibitive, which is unfortunate. However, since most colleges and universities have an interest in educating students in many departments, the advantages outweigh the costs.

The "How Can I Judge the Authenticity of
Commercial EFL/ESL Listening Materials?" Problem

Truly authentic listening experiences focus on varieties of pronunciation and intonation.[20] For example, pronunciation includes simulation of sounds, such as blending two or more words into a single sound, as in *Didja (Did you)*. Pitch and emphatic stress are used to represent a nuance in meaning, and the rhythm of English is set through the use of sentence stress. Major words (e.g., nouns, verbs, adjectives, adverbs) receive sentence stress, while minor words (e.g., articles, prepositions, auxiliary verbs) do not, as in *You'll find the book on the table."*

Authentic listening also includes hearing a variety of grammatical structures, not just one or two said over and over again—the use of fragments or sequences of loosely connected words and clauses, rather than well-formed sentences. It also includes interruptions and two or more people speaking at once (rather than each person taking a distinct turn), as well as one speaker dominating the interaction, lots of attention signals (such as *Mmmmm* and *Uh-huh*), and different examples of background noise.

In the past, in an effort to make language clear to students, some authors/publishers of listening material and texts tried too hard to make English easier to understand. As a result, when students listened to these materials, they heard conversations in which people spoke in complete sentences, conversations without interruptions, and void of background noise. Although there is a benefit to listening to unrealistic spoken language, especially for beginners, more and more, teachers want their students to hear spoken English that is as realistic as possible. When selecting audio materials, be sure to listen to a sample before purchasing/adopting. If you decide you want to use only authentic speech in the classroom, you need to make decisions about whether or not listening material might be too authentic. That is, is the material so authentic that it is difficult for students to understand? If so, seek out more appropriate material.

TEACHER SELF-DEVELOPMENT TASKS

Talk Tasks

1. Have you ever been in a conversation in English in which you lacked the appropriate background knowledge to completely comprehend what you were listening to? Describe your experience. What was the content? What background knowledge did you lack? Why did this lack of knowledge make it difficult for you fully to comprehend the content?

2. What kinds of listening activities have you experienced either as a teacher or as a student? Which activity types in this chapter haven't you experienced? Which would you like to try out in your EFL/ESL classes?

3. Meet with another teacher. Together, select authentic listening material from a published text or the media (e.g., a song, film, TV situation comedy, cartoon, news show, or TV or radio advertisement). Based on the ideas in this chapter on using the media, and on your own ideas, create a step-by-step lesson plan that aims at making this authentic material comprehensible to a group of students with whom you are familiar.

Observation and Talk Tasks

1. Record a conversation between friends. (Make sure you get their permission first.) Select three minutes from this conversation. With other teacher/friends, analyze what goes on in the conversation. What gives the conversation its authenticity?

2. If possible, visit a listening lab. Observe what is going on in the lab. What are students listening to? Are the students all doing the same listening activity? How interested do the students appear to be in the listening activity? Also talk with the teacher in the listening lab. What activities go on in the lab? How does the teacher interact with the students in the lab? Think of your own questions, too.

3. This task has multiple parts.

   a. Study the criteria for authenticity and the worksheet on pages 165–66. What do these words mean: *intonation, pitch, pronunciation, enunciation, assimilation, clause, pace*? Are there any other words or ideas you want to know more about? If possible, look up the words in a specialized dictionary, such as the *Longman Dictionary of Language Teaching and Applied Linguistics*.

b. If possible, discuss the meanings of the words you studied with other teachers.

c. Locate published listening materials that focus on person-to-person interaction in social contexts (rather than, for example, on teaching students to listen to the news). Using the criteria for authenticity and the worksheet on pages 165–66, evaluate the authenticity of these materials. How authentic is the language in the materials?

d. Based on your experience of analyzing the authenticity of the published listening material, consider the appropriateness of the material for different levels of students. Do you think the material is too difficult? Appropriate? Too easy? Why or why not? If possible, share your opinions with other teachers.

e. Listen to the material one more time. This time consider the vocabulary used in the listening material. How difficult is the vocabulary as it relates to the designated level of the student? Appropriate? Too difficult? If too difficult, how might the vocabulary in a listening selection limit students' abilities to process meaning?

f. Do you think that the use of non-authentic listening materials (e.g., exaggerated enunciation) and easy vocabulary can help beginning-level students to develop their listening abilities? If possible, discuss your opinions with other teachers.

Journal Writing Tasks

1. Write what you learned from doing the observation tasks.

2. Consider your own experience in learning to listen in a foreign/second language. Based on your reflections, what listening experiences do you believe helped you to gain in your abilities to comprehend the language? What experiences do you believe did not help you? Do you believe this is the same for other language learners?

3. Write freely on your ideas for teaching students to comprehend spoken English.

Evaluating the Authenticity of Listening Materials

The following criteria provide a way to judge the authenticity of language used in commercial listening materials, by people as they interact in social contexts. Please refer to these criteria while completing the accompanying worksheet.[21]

Intonation: Criteria	Intonation: Questions
Intonation is not authentic when marked by exaggerated and frequent pitch movement. Likewise, it is not authentic when each word receives equal stress.	Does the intonation amuse you? Remind you of an indulgent mother talking to a baby? Is the pitch exaggerated or natural?
Pronunciation: Criteria	Pronunciation: Questions
Pronunciation is not authentic when each word is clearly enunciated. Rather, assimilation (or blending of sounds) is normal.	Does the pronunciation seem artificial? Too correct? Do speakers enunciate all the words? Or do they blend sounds?
Speaker Domination: Criteria	Speaker Domination: Questions
In normal conversations one speaker will dominate the conversation.	Are all speakers saying an equal amount? Or does one person say more than the other?
Complete Sentences: Criteria	Complete Sentences: Questions
Informal speech is characterized by fragmentation. In short, people talk in clauses and single-word utterances.	Do speakers use all complete sentences? Or do they use short loosely connected clauses and words?
Distinct Turns: Criteria	Distinct Turns: Questions
In authentic situations, people do not wait for others to stop talking. They interrupt.	Do speakers wait for others to finish? Or do they sometimes speak at the same time?
Pace: Criteria	Pace: Questions
Authentic speech is characterized by relative rapidity and variability of pace. Uniform pace is not authentic, especially an unusually slow pace.	Are all the speakers speaking at the same pace? Are they talking too slowly?
Background Noise: Criteria	Background Noise: Questions
Normal listening situations include background noise: passing cars, radios, barking dogs, wind in trees.	Is there normal background noise?

Evaluating the Authenticity of Listening Materials Worksheet

Title: _____

Author: _____

Publisher:_____

Level: _____

Overall Evaluation of Authenticity: _____

1————————2————————3————————4————————5
Not authentic   Very authentic

Evaluation of Authenticity of Particular Components

Intonation	1___	2___	3___	4___	5___
Pronunciation	1___	2___	3___	4___	5___
Speaker Domination	1___	2___	3___	4___	5___
Complete Sentences	1___	2___	3___	4___	5___
Distinct Turns	1___	2___	3___	4___	5___
Pace	1___	2___	3___	4___	5___
Background Noise	1___	2___	3___	4___	5___

Recommended Teacher Resources

Listening Textbooks with Audio Components

Biegel, K. *What about You?* New York: McGraw Hill, 2002. (Low-intermediate to Higher-intermediate)

Dunkel, P. A., P. L. Lim, W.. Smatzer, and F. Pialorsi. *Listening and Notetaking. 3d ed.* Boston: Heinle & Heinle, 2005. (High-intermediate)

Espeseth, M. *Academic Listening Encounters: Listening, Note Taking, and Discussion.* New York: Cambridge University Press, 1999. (Intermediate/Advanced).

Foley, B. H. *Listen to Me! Beginning Listening, Speaking & Pronunciation. 2d ed.* Boston: Heinle & Heinle, 1994. (Beginning)

Folse, K. S., and D. Bologna. *Targeting Listening and Speaking: Strategies and*

Activities for ESL/EFL Students. Ann Arbor: University of Michigan Press, 2003. (Intermediate)

Helgesen, M., S. Brown, and D. Smith. *Active Listening*. New York: Cambridge University Press, 1996. (High-intermediate; book 3 of 3)

Nelson, V. *Learning to Listen in English*. New York: McGraw Hill, 1997. (Beginning)

Numrich. C. *Consider the Issues: Listening and Critical Thinking Skills. 3^d ed.* White Plains, NY: Pearson Education, 2004. (High-intermediate/Advanced)

Nunan, D. *Listen In*. Boston: Heinle & Heinle, 1997. (High-beginning)

Sadow, C., and E. Sather. *On the Air: Listening to Radio Talk*. New York: Cambridge University Press, 1998. (Intermediate)

Sanabria, K. *Academic Listening Encounters: Life in Society*. New York: Cambridge University Press, 2004. (Intermediate)

Watson-Delestrée, A. *Basic Telephone Training*. New York: McGraw Hill, 2001.

Readings on Teaching Listening: Concepts and Activities

Anderson, A., and T. Lynch. *Listening*. Oxford: Oxford University Press, 1988.

Buck, G. *Assessing Listening*. New York: Cambridge University Press, 2001.

Field, J. "The Changing Face of Listening." In *Methodology in Language Teaching: An Anthology of Current Practice*, eds. J. C. Richards and W. A. Renandya, 242–47. New York: Cambridge University Press, 2002.

Hadfield, J., and C. Hadfield. *Simple Listening Activities*. New York: Oxford University Press, 1999.

Morley, J. "Aural Comprehension Instruction: Principles and Practices." In *Teaching English as a Second or Foreign Language, 3^d ed.,* ed. M. Celce-Murcia, 69–85. Boston: Heinle & Heinle, 2001.

Nunan, D., and L. Miller, eds. *New Ways in Teaching Listening*. Alexandria, VA: TESOL, 1995.

Sherman, J. *Using Authentic Video in the Language Classroom*. New York: Cambridge University Press, 2003.

Ur, P. *Teaching Listening Comprehension*. New York: Cambridge University Press, 1984.

Endnotes

[1] See Anderson and Lynch (1988), Morley (2001), and Nunan (2002) for more on active listening.

[2] Listening processes are also discussed in Anderson and Lynch (1988), Helgesen (1993), Morley (2001), Nunan (2002), Peterson (2001), and Richards (1990). Peregoy and Boyle (2005) provide a rich discussion on listening processes in ESL K–12 settings, focusing on integration of listening, speaking, reading, and writing.

3 See Richards (1990, 51).

4 See *Cold Water,* a videotape produced by Ogami (1988), to view the Somalia student telling this story.

5 This example comes from my own observations.

6 Brown and Yule (1983) and Richards (1990) discuss the functions of language as they relate to listening.

7 Bowen, Madsen, and Hilferty (1985) offer additional activities to focus attention onto linguistic features of spoken English.

8 Total Physical Response (TPR) was developed by James Asher. His 1982 book, *Learning Another Language through Actions,* outlines his beliefs and teaching practices. Larsen-Freeman (2003) and Richards and Rodgers (2001) also discuss TPR theory and practice.

9 See Segal (1983).

10 This a line from Segal and Sloan's videotape, *TPR and the Natural Approach* (1984).

11 The "Hokey Pokey" can be found on *It's Toddler Time,* produced by Bueffel and Hammett (1982).

12 This listening activity is from Porter and Roberts (1987).

13 I learned about matching behaviors to gain rapport by studying the work of Bandler and Grinder (1975), Lankton (1980), and Rosen (1982).

14 This idea is from Rathet (1994).

15 The idea for this activity comes from Ur (1984).

16 It is important to note that some programs are copyrighted. As Lonergan (1984, 80) points out, "The legal situation concerning the use of video for educational purposes (such as language teaching) can be confusing. It varies not only from country to country, but can also vary from programme to programme. . . . The safest way to avoid infringing copyright is to contact the broadcasting company concerned."

17 The "Old MacDonald" song can be found in *Action Songs for Indoor Days* produced by David White (1978).

18 The techniques discussed here on how to have students process authentic video materials come from Allen (1985), Kajornboon (1989), Kitao (1986), Lonergan (1984), Sherman (2003), and Stempleski (1992).

19 Tanka (1993) points out problems with a traditional notion of a language lab and offers some useful ideas that help create an interactive lab.

20 See Porter and Roberts (1987). My ideas on judging the authenticity of listening materials are directly influenced by the work of Porter and Roberts.

It is through talk that people construe their cultural worlds, display and recreate their social orders, plan and critique their activities, and praise and condemn their follows.

—Frake 1980, 334

Teaching the Conversation Class

- What does it mean to converse in a second language?
- How do EFL/ESL teachers teach conversation to beginners?
- What kinds of activities do EFL/ESL conversation teachers use with post-beginners?
- How do EFL/ESL teachers teach pronunciation?
- What problems do some EFL/ESL teachers have in teaching students to converse in English?

What Does It Mean to Converse in a Second Language?

Conversing in a second language means knowing how to maintain interaction and focus on meaning; use conversational grammar; introduce, develop, and change topics; take turns; apply conversational routines; and adapt style to match the setting/context.[1]

Maintaining Interaction and Meaning

Conversations have both transactional and interactional purposes. When speaking and when the purpose is transactional, the focus is primarily on the meaning of the message. Is your message getting to the listener? For example, imagine explaining how to find your home to a new friend or describing your aches and pains to a doctor. When the speaking purpose is interactional, the focus is on maintaining social relations—greeting, complimenting, and chatting with friends. Are you able to keep the conversation going? Many conversations include both interactional and transactional purposes.

Using Conversational Grammar

To truly communicate, you must also be able to use conversational grammar, which is different from standard grammar because it is based on how people actually talk. It features small chunks, mostly clauses and single words, as opposed to complete sentences. (This is true for both interactional and transactional turns.) Here is an example.

> *Jack:* Hi, what's up?
> *Jane:* Not much.
> *Jack:* Headed to the bookstore?
> *Jane:* Yeah. Have to buy my art course supplies.
> *Jack:* Oh, good! Glad I ran into you! What do we have to buy?
> *Jane:* Colored chalk, ah, sketch pad. Hmmm, charcoal sticks.

Introducing, Developing, and Changing Topics

Carrying on a conversation also requires speakers to introduce, develop, and change topics. This aspect of conversational management can be complex, the selection and development of a topic done through a process of negotiation. This includes opening a conversation with a formulaic expression such as *What's up?* To get past this initial greeting and before going onto another topic, other conversational cues or "formulas" are needed; for example, you may ask the person (or guess from the context) if he or she is busy or free to talk, how much time he or she has, and what topic should be talked about.

In our own language it is natural to select topics to talk about with people we know and people we don't know. But in another language, it is not easy to know how to do this—that is, what is safe to talk about and what isn't. For example, many students who come to the United States to study English are hesitant to talk about a variety of different topics that as Americans we are comfortable talking with strangers about—values or social standards (in certain circumstances), personal or financial needs (in certain circumstances), or the health of our family or self. In many other countries, these topics are not generally discussed with strangers or acquaintances.[2]

Taking Turns

To take part in a conversation also means to take turns, and there are both short and long turns. A short turn includes just one or two utterances, such as in the *What's up?* conversation. A long turn takes place when it is necessary for a speaker to explain or justify something, to provide an anecdote, or to tell a story. Many EFL/ESL students have difficulty taking long turns in a conversation because to do so requires them to take on responsibility for generating a sequence of utterances that gives the listener a good understanding of what they are saying, something that is not always easy to do in a first language, much less a second.[3] Some students have trouble taking both long and short turns, which could be a result of previous language-learning experiences, but possibly also because they lack the strategies in English for taking a turn, such as using interjections like *Mmhmm* to signal a request to speak, and quickly adding something to what a speaker just said.[4] In conversations with multiple participants, EFL/ESL students might wait for a pause in order to contribute; if they are talking to Americans, that pause may not come, which makes knowing how to interrupt another useful strategy.

Carrying Out Conversational Routines

Conversing also means participating in conversational routines, many of which require a sequence of short turns. These routines are used regularly in our daily interactions—for example, paying for a newspaper, greeting a friend in the street, leaving a party, apologizing to a teacher, complimenting a friend, and offering something to a guest. Although all these interactions aren't scripted to a person, there are consistent patterns and rules. For example, consider the following interaction at an American dinner party.

Mrs. Jones: Ann, would you like some more chicken?
Ann: Oh, no thanks! Delicious! I can't eat another bite.
Mrs. Jones: Well, there's plenty. Help yourself!

Now, the same interaction at a dinner party in Beijing.

Mrs. Liu: Ann, some more? (Mrs. Liu reaches for the plate.)
Ann: No, thank you!
Mrs. Liu: I insist. Have some more. Have some more.
Ann: No, thank you.
Mrs. Liu: Oh, come on. Have some more.
Ann: (Silent)
Mrs. Liu: (Puts the chicken on Ann's plate)

While an American routine is to offer something to a guest one or two times, often indicating to the guest to help herself, the pattern in China is often for the guest to refuse the offer several times, waiting for the host to insist. Since there are a wide variety of other such routines associated with daily functions, and these can vary from culture to culture, problems quite often arise for EFL/ESL students, especially when they try to directly transfer a routine from their native cultural experience into their English.

Adapting Style

Conversing also includes the selection of conversational style to match the formality of the situation. Jack Richards provides a good example of how native speakers of English adapt their style when asking someone the time.[5] From informal to formal, language is adapted in social settings in the following ways: *Got the time? What's the time? Do you have the time? Would you know what time it is? Could I trouble you for the time?*

EFL/ESL students have trouble adapting style, sometimes being too formal in an informal setting, in part as a result of applying the style rules from their first language. For example, in the United States some Asian students will use last names in situations that call for first name use, such as Mr. Brown, rather than John. Furthermore, ESL students who are not accustomed to calling older people or those with a higher status by their first names will often avoid addressing them by any name.

On the other hand, in an effort to sound more informal in their use of English, students can really miss the mark. This is what happened to the rural Thai adult I was tutoring some years ago. I was invited to a reception at a hotel in a northeast Thai town, mostly for Americans. I thought this would be a perfect time to expose this young man to conversations beyond ours. So, I invited him to go along. At the reception, he was doing fine, when suddenly, while in the middle of a conversation about Thai food, he smiled, looked at the elderly husband and wife, and said in an eloquent manner, "Please excuse me. I have to take a piss." Of course, no one took offense and even found it amusing, knowing he was learning English. But, it does show the need for us to teach students how to adapt style to different contexts.

How Do EFL/ESL Teachers Teach Conversation to Beginners?

With beginners, especially those students at the survival level, teachers usually limit the scope of the conversations so that these conversations are manageable and the students are successful. One way teachers do this is to control the kinds of questions they ask, using *yes-no*, either-or, and identity questions. As these question types only require students to give single-word answers, they can focus attention on comprehending the meaning in the questions.

Yes-No Questions	Is Piroska's sweater blue? Do Nigerians like to play soccer? Did you get up early? Can you speak French?
Either-Or Questions	Is Piroska's sweater blue or green? Do Nigerians like to play or watch soccer? Did you get up early or late? Which can you speak better, French or English?
Identity Questions	What color is Piroska's sweater? Which sport do Nigerians like to play most? What time did you get up? What languages can you speak?

Teachers also limit the scope of a conversation through the use of what Littlewood calls "quasi-communication" activities,[6] the objective of which is for students to practice using English with reasonable fluency, but without having to be overly concerned with communicating meaning effectively. To create such an activity, some teachers use charts such as the schedule on page 174, which simply requires students to identify words and give short responses to questions.[7]

New York	Pittsburgh	Flight
lv 10:15 AM	ar 11:05 AM	121
lv 12:45 PM	ar 1:35 PM	232
lv 4:40 PM	ar 5:30 PM	330

The schedule offers possibilities to ask a variety of questions: *What time does flight 122 arrive from New York?* (11:05 AM). *Does the flight leaving New York at 4:40 PM arrive in Pittsburgh at 5:35 PM?* (No). *How long does it take to fly from New York to Pittsburgh?* (50 minutes). This same type of questioning activity is also possible with simple class schedules, advertisements, and other basic charts using numbers, prices, and time.

Another quasi-communicative activity is dialogue practice. Most EFL/ESL texts include dialogues. Some teachers write their own short dialogues so they can control the content. At a beginning level, such dialogues can include useful conversational routines. Here is a short example.

Person A: Could I borrow your pen?
Person B: Sure. No problem.
Person A: Thanks.

Teachers sometimes prefer to have students practice dialogues through the use of a technique called Read and Look Up, in which students look down at their line (what they say), look up at the other person, and then say the line (rather than just reading it).[8] With practice, students gain confidence. As beginners gain vocabulary and routines, the task can be made more complex. In this dialogue, students select from the available choices based on levels of formality needed in a situation. Notice that Person B can either accept (+) or turn down (-) the request; Person A then reacts appropriately.

Person A:	*Person B:*
Could I borrow your pen?	Sure, No problem. (+)
May I use your book?	Yeah. Here you go. (+)
Got a pencil?	I'm sorry! I need it right now. (–)

As students become more proficient, teachers also create open-ended dialogues such as this one, allowing students to draw from their memory:

Person A: Could I borrow five dollars?
Person B: _____
Person A: _____

What Kinds of Activities Do EFL/ESL Conversation Teachers Use with Post-Beginners?

Quasi-communicative activities work well with students beyond the beginning level to warm up, review, or teach a new concept. However, with students at this level, it's important to go beyond quasi-communication exercises to give students opportunities to interact freely in English. The sample activities provide students with the kind of language practice that will enable them to express themselves in spoken English, although they also include some reading and writing.

Dialogue Writing, Skits, Role Plays, and Improvisations

One activity many students like because they can consider their own interactive needs is to write their own dialogues. When students act out their dialogues, they become skits, the idea being for students to practice and then perform in front of the class. Role-play activities are similar to skits in that students are expected to act. However, unlike skits, students are not provided with lines but are given a situation and roles to play. It's important to note that while some students are natural performers (actors), others are not and are uncomfortable with these types of activities.

Video drama is similar to role play. However, each role play is videotaped so students can reflect on their use of language. This can lead to improvisation. One teacher, Tracy Forest, has students work in groups to specify the framework (examples my own). She includes specifying when and where the scene takes place (in a cafeteria at noon on a Friday), who is participating in the scene (two close friends), and a recent event shared by the participants (Student B had borrowed $10.00 from Student A and promised to pay it back last week). She also has students describe how they feel about the other person and what is taking place (Student A sees that Student B has money and feels Student B should pay him back.

Student B only has $12.00 and wants to go to a movie with friends that evening). She also has students define what they are doing when the scene begins (standing outside the cafeteria) and decide on an opening line (Student A: "Do you have the $10.00 you borrowed from me?").

Forest points out that the goal of preparation is for the students to create a basic set of facts that will build a conversation, using a wide range of linguistic options. She also points out that although the actual improvisation takes only about five minutes, its success depends on the longer 30 minutes or so of preparation time. Also, the videotape of the performance can provide rich materials for follow-up lessons.[9]

Another use of video requires students to produce their own news broadcast. Sainz,[10] for example, draws students' attention to the five key questions that take place at the beginning of a news story: Who or what is the story about? What happened? When did the event occur? Where did the event take place? Why did the event take place? She also introduces students to different types of news, including world news, local news, sports, cinema, weather, and fashion. Students also watch and complete comprehension exercises from video clips of the news; they make decisions on how they will go about creating their own news broadcast. They write their own news stories (including, as I adapt this activity, news about classmates and their teachers), as well as decide who will deliver the news and play other roles such as sound technicians and set designers. Students then use their created news reports to practice giving the news; after several practice rounds with feedback, they are videotaped. After viewing the tape, the teacher can design lessons that provide constructive feedback for each student on language use.

Buzz Groups

This activity got its name because students sound like a group of busy bees while working on a task. To create a buzz group, the teacher selects a topic that will likely interest students and have some purpose; it's useful to try authentic tasks such as planning an actual trip to a museum or planning a party or picnic. Other topics might be based on questions like "How can the police protect the public against crime?" and "What is a good education?" Here is an example of a buzz group I have used with a variety of EFL/ESL students.

Who's a Good Language Learner?

In your group, make a list of the kinds of things a good language learner does. You will be asked to list these things on the board. To stimulate your thinking before you make your list, answer these questions.

- What do good language learners do in class? At home?
- What do you do that helps you to learn English?

Although some buzz group activities can be done with almost any group of students, some can be contextually designed for a specific group. To illustrate this point here is a buzz group activity, "Who Will Be the Next Student Director of the ALI?" After dividing students into small groups, I gave them this handout.

Who Will Be the Next Student Director of the ALI?

We are going to elect a student director of the ALI. This person will attend some meetings with the director and staff and will be your representative in the director's office.

So, here's your chance to change the ALI. In your group, talk about what you want at the ALI. What do you want to keep? What do you want to change?

A student lounge?	Smaller classes?	More chances to write?
More electives?	More trips?	More homework?
Less homework?	More time on computers?	A pop machine?
Guest speakers?	A more active ALI club?	An ALI baseball team?

Consider other ideas, too! What kind of language program would you really like to have at ALI? After discussing what you want at the ALI, select a member of your group to run for student director. As a group, write a speech for this person to deliver. Help this person to practice the speech. After each of the group's candidates gives his or her speech in front of the student body, we will vote, by secret ballot, for the next ALI student director.

Games and Related Activities

EFL/ESL teachers use games in the conversation class. A variety of games exist—games to teach grammar, vocabulary, spelling, and pronunciation; there are picture, psychology, memory, guessing, card and board games.[11]

One game many people are familiar with is 20 Questions, in which students use English to narrow down possibilities through the use of *yes-no* questions. To play this game, two students identify something in the room—for instance, the teacher's pen, the fan, or the calendar—and their classmates have 20 chances to guess what that object is.

In Paraphrasing Races,[12] the teacher divides students into groups, gives each group a sentence, and allows three minutes for the students to develop as many rephrasings of the sentence as they can. Each acceptable rephrasing is worth one point. The team with the most points wins.

In the Strip Story,[13] students are put into small groups and given one or two lines of a short story. They are told not to show their lines to other students. Instead, they have to negotiate who has the first line, second line, and so on. Slowly, they put the story together. An alternative way to play is to take the strips away after they've read them and have them put the story together from memory. A cartoon version exists in which students put a cartoon sequence together, each describing his or her strip to others without showing it to them.

Teachers sometimes make up their own strip stories while some others discover stories used by other teachers, passed down through the years. Here is an example of one strip story I discovered while teaching at a Thai University.[14]

Who's the Laziest Boy?

An old man was walking along the road.

Suddenly he saw three boys lying on the grass under a tree.

He said, "I'll give a gold coin to the laziest boy. Who's the laziest boy?'

The first boy jumped up, ran over to the old man, and said, "I'm the laziest boy. Give me the coin."

The old man shook his head and said, "No, you aren't. Lie down again."

The second boy held out his hand. "I'm the laziest boy. Give me the coin."

The old man shook his head again. "No, you aren't. Lie down
again."

The third boy said, "Please come over and put the coin in my
pocket."

"Yes," said the old man, "You're the laziest boy!"

And he put the coin into the boy's pocket.

Another activity is a matching game called Same or Different?[15]
Students are divided into pairs and given a set of pictures, Sets A and
B. Some of the pictures in the set are the same and some are different. Without showing the pictures, and within a limited amount of
time, the two students must decide which pictures are the same and
which are different.

Computer-Mediated Communications

Recently, computer technology has come to the conversation class.
There are many ways to engage students in conversation through the
use of computers. One of the first things some people think of is
e-mail.[16] While e-mail provides opportunities for students to communicate, it only partly creates conversation. This can include using
abbreviated speech-like grammar, a question-response-react style,
and content appropriate to informal and formal conversations.
E-mail communication lacks verbal use of language, nonverbal cues,
conversational routines, and conversational turn-taking.

Discussion boards offer another way for students to communicate. To use a discussion board students log on to a website to join an
online community where members can read and post messages on
an electronic discussion board. As Dawn Bikowski and Greg Kessler
point out,[17] some of the benefits of using discussion boards are that
students only need a limited knowledge of computers and the Internet
to communicate whenever and wherever they have access to an
Internet-connected computer. In terms of benefits, each student (not
just the most vocal) has a chance to participate, students may be less
self-conscious and willing to take more risks in communicating their
ideas, and learners have more time to compose their thoughts and
possibly contribute more insightful comments than in face-to-face
conversations. However, as with e-mail, such asynchronous communication (communication between users who are not online at the
same time) as discussion boards only partly provide opportunities for
students to develop their speaking skills. Students do not have the

chance to develop listening, non-verbal, turn-taking, and conversational routines that are a part of face-to-face interaction.

Another way teachers try to engage students in computer-mediated conversation is through the use of Internet chat. To set up an online chat, the teacher and students simply need to have software that allows access to a chat room where small (or large) groups can chat on predetermined or spontaneously generated topics. Unlike e-mail and discussion boards, Internet chat offers students chances to have a live (synchronous) conversation. Although students type on a keyboard and do not see each other or verbalize their thoughts, Internet chat more closely mimics actual conversation in that participants in the conversation respond and react to each other's questions and ideas immediately.[18]

Although the use of computer-mediated communication tools such as discussion boards and Internet chat can be useful to students who want to improve their abilities to communicate in English, there is still the question as to whether or not they help students gain skills in face-to-face conversations. To address this issue, Potchanee Chanrungkanok systematically studied the patterns of interaction in English between Thai students and the teacher when the only preparation for face-to-face discussion was to read materials on a topic.[19] She also studied what happened to their face-to-face interaction when students used a discussion board (or Web board, as they called it) to discuss a topic before meeting face-to-face in the classroom. Further, she studied what happened during class discussion after students had the chance to chat about the topic in an Internet chat room before coming to class. She discovered that when discussion boards and Internet chat preludes oral face-to-face discussion, students were more involved in critical discussion, teaching each other, negotiating meaning without direction from the teacher, and using more complex language. Such findings show that there is value in the use of discussion boards and Internet chat, especially if students have chances to also meet to talk about content.

How Do EFL/ESL Teachers Teach Pronunciation?

Some teachers prefer to have students use a pronunciation text.[20] Many pronunciation texts provide explanations, drawings that illustrate how sounds are made, work on minimal pairs, and lots of practice activities for students in pronunciation of consonant and vowel sounds. More advanced texts focus on intonation patterns, sentence stress placement, emphatic stress placement, and more. While texts are quite useful in teaching pronunciation, it is often necessary to teach beyond the text or develop activities for students. Each class of students has its own pronunciation issues.

Teaching Pronunciation: Creative Activities

Presented here are a few creative activities to teach pronunciation.[21] One activity makes use of minimal pairs (two words pronounced exactly the same except for one difference—e.g., *lice* and *rice, lap* and *lab).* The teacher selects pairs that are problematic for students and lists them on the board. For example, students from Spain might benefit from grappling with these minimal pairs:

List A:	seat	eat	each	sheep
List B:	sit	it	itch	ship

The teacher begins by calling out a word and then students tell the teacher whether it is from list A or B. Once the students understand the rules, they take turns selecting and pronouncing words, while classmates and the teacher tell the speaker the correct answer.[22] This activity is most useful in homogenous classroom settings where the students speak the same first language.

Another activity uses a kazoo to focus on patterns of intonation.[23] With a kazoo, the teacher can avoid words and grammar and focus only on intonation patterns. A number of intonation patterns can be taught—for instance, patterns for declarative sentences, *yes-no* questions, and tag questions. It is possible for the teacher to demonstrate the pattern by humming into the kazoo, as well as to have students practice the patterns without the words. In addition to intonation patterns, a kazoo can be used to show students correct accent placement on words (e.g., ìnteresting rather than interestìng), as well as how sentence stress works (major words, like nouns, main verbs, adjectives, and adverbs receive stress while minor words like prepositions, pronouns, and articles do not receive stress).

To prepare the Pronunciation Computer activity, the teacher needs to collect samples of students' English during classroom activities.[24] The teacher writes these samples (words, phrases, sentences) on the board and numbers each item. The students, who are sitting in a semicircle facing the board, are then told to study the list of language items and to raise their hands if they would like to practice an item. They are also told that the teacher is now a computer and that the students have to turn the computer on and off by saying *start* and *stop.* The point is for students to pick an item from the board and say it before the computer will model the English pronunciation. The job of the pronunciation computer is to stand behind the students and to continue to give the pronunciation of the line given by the student each time the student says it; the computer says it into the student's ear until the student tells the computer to stop.

A number of teachers have discovered that using Carolyn Graham's Jazz Chants is a constructive and fun way to give students practice using natural stress and intonation patterns of conversational American English. Graham has published a number of Jazz Chant books for children and adults over the past 25 plus years.[25] I like Jazz Chants because most students enjoy following the audiotaped chants, appreciate the humor, recognize and use the natural intonation, and are willing to try out new things. For example, I have had no problem getting adults to practice whispering and talking loudly in English when chanting to Graham's jazz chant, *Sh! Sh! Baby's Sleeping!*[26]

Teaching Pronunciation as Communication

Teachers who approach teaching pronunciation as communication use activities that focus on meaning. However, they also build into the activity an aspect of pronunciation. One example activity, created by Marianne Celce-Murcia, focuses students' attention on words using a voiceless *th* sound, such as in *Th*ursday and *th*ird.[27]

As I adapt this activity, students are paired, one student receiving a calendar with notes written on it, especially on dates that begin with *th*, for example, the *thirteenth*. Another student is given written cues for questions he or she should ask the other student: (1) Date of Mary's birthday? (2) Date of the first Thursday? (3) 13th on a Friday? (4) Date of American Thanksgiving? Day of the week? (5) Catherine's brother's third birthday?

Another communicative activity with an added pronunciation component is a version of Bingo. Students are given Bingo boards where the squares include pictures and words based on a minimal pair. For example, if the teacher wants students to practice words with /r/ and /l/, the squares would include words (and possibly pictures) such as *red/lead, ray/lay, crowd/cloud, free/flee, crime/climb*. Of course, each Bingo card has different word combinations. Students take turns pulling words from a bowl, calling out each word while paying attention to pronunciation. They may also use the word in a sentence.[28]

Teaching Students Strategies for Self-Improvement

We can also teach students how to take on responsibility for improvement of their own pronunciation. This list, created by Joan Morley, provides self-improvement strategies teachers can teach students to use.[29]

Strategies to Improve Pronunciation

Strong, Vigorous Practice. Use vigorous practice with strong muscular movements. Use slightly exaggerated mouth movements, overly articulating words. Don't hurry. Take time to articulate as clearly as possible.

Self-Monitored Practice. Listen closely to and monitor yourself on both the sounds and the rate, rhythm, and vocal qualities. Pay attention to stress points, pitch rises and falls, and rhythmic patterns.

Slow-Motion Practice: Half-Speed Practice. Try slow motion, or half-speed, practice for a strong sense of kinesthetic touch-and-movement feedback and for the feeling of articulation.

Loop Practice ("Broken Record" Practice). Use an endless-loop practice of 20 or more strong and vigorous repetitions of a phrase or word with focus on kinesthetic feedback.

Whisper Practice (Silent Practice). Use whispered or silent practice to focus on articulation and the feeling of articulation.

Mirror Practice, Video Practice. Use mirrors to view the articulation of specific sounds. If possible, zoom in on a close-up of your face as you articulate words.

What Problems Do Some EFL/ESL Teachers Have in Teaching Students to Speak in English?

Problems some EFL/ESL teachers face include the following:

- The "students won't talk" problem
- The "error treatment" problem
- The "any native speaker can teach conversation" problem

The "Students Won't Talk" Problem

Some students will not talk in class because they are too shy or anxious. This is not only true for beginners, but also for some students who are fairly advanced in their listening, reading, and writing abilities. Perhaps they are anxious because they have not had many chances to speak or because teachers in the past have been critical of their English. Whatever the reason, when faced with quiet, anxious students, the problem for the conversation teacher is, how can we get these students to talk? Before anything else, we need to gain their trust.[30] The students need to know that we are on their side, that we do not expect them to speak perfect English, and that we realize it takes time and effort for them to learn to converse in English.

As teachers, we also need to provide opportunities for students to feel at ease in the classroom. One way to do this is through warm-up activities. In fact, the objective of using warm-up (or icebreaker) activities is to relax students, to help get them over their classroom apprehensions. There are, of course, a great number of possible ways to warm up students for a conversation class. One way is through the use of techniques drama teachers use to get anxious students to relax and to provide an inviting atmosphere.[31] Here are a few examples.

A Breathing Warm-Up Exercise: The students and the teacher close their eyes, breathe slowly in through their noses for three seconds, hold that breath for nine seconds, then slowly release it through their mouths for six seconds. This is repeated several times.

Walking Warm-Up Exercise: The teacher and students clear away furniture from the center of the room. While standing, they form a circle. They then begin to walk in a circle in their usual way. After a turn or two around the circle, the teacher then calls out commands, such as "Walk like you are chest high in water," "Walk on clouds," "Walk like you were a marionette," and "Walk like you are on hot sand."

A Voice Warm-Up Exercise: While sitting or standing in a circle, the teacher begins by whispering a word or phrase, for example, "Hello!" The next person says the word a little louder, but still in a whisper, the next a little louder, and so on, until the word comes back to the teacher, perhaps even as a shout. A variation is to slow down or speed up the way the word or phrase is said.[32]

The use of quasi-communication activities, such as dialogue practice, can also engage "quiet" students in speaking. As students are able to rely on context and print, they are sometimes more willing to speak. As students become more and more comfortable with these pre-communication activities, we can coax them to participate in the fluency-type activities, such as problem solving, skits, and buzz groups. And, success builds success. From my experience, as students feel the success they have at negotiating meaning, the more risks they are willing to take in expressing their ideas in English.

The "Error Treatment" Problem

Most EFL/ESL teachers now believe that students need to be given an acquisition-rich experience in the classroom, providing them with opportunities to listen to, read, write, and speak a lot of English. Some of these teachers also believe that students will naturally acquire the language through an unconscious process of second language acquisition.[33] As long as language input is comprehensible to the students, they will acquire the grammar of the language on their own. Many of those who believe in acquisition point to the research on the acquisition of grammar by second language learners. This research shows that some grammatical features are acquired early and others later. For example, the *-ing* (progressive), as in "He's going to work" is acquired early while possessive *s*, as in "That's Ann's book," is acquired later. Likewise, the ability to use irregular past tense of verbs, such as *ate, slept, drank,* and *swam,* is acquired before regular past tense. Error treatment may do little to change this natural process.

However, others believe that feedback on language errors can be used as a type of input by students to promote the acquisition process.[34] In short, some educators suggest that error; treatment can provide the kind of feedback that will help the student to work through the different stages of acquisition, especially in EFL settings where students do not have access to much authentic language outside classrooms.

As EFL/ESL teachers, we have choices and consider both sides of the issue. We can decide not to treat language errors, or we can decide to treat them. If we decide to treat them, there are other decisions that need to be made. *When* should errors be treated? *Which* errors should be treated? *Who* should treat them? *How* can they be treated?[35]

As for when to treat errors, they can be treated at the moment the error is made or treatment can be delayed. A problem with instant treatment is that it can disrupt communication. A problem with delaying treatment is the possibility that students who made the errors will not recognize the errors as being their own.

Making decisions about which errors to treat is not an easy task for the teacher. Some teachers base their decision on their estimate of the stage of acquisition of the student—for example, treating irregular past tense verb errors such as "He eated it" (an early stage error) while ignoring regular past tense verb errors (a later stage error). As Allwright and Bailey have said, "The dilemma . . . to English teachers is the question of whether or not treatment of learners' errors . . . will help speed the acquisition of correct form, or simply be futile until the learners reach a stage of development where they can make use of such feedback."[36] Faced with such a dilemma, some teachers take a different approach. Instead of considering the acquisition stage of the student, they base their treatment on whether or not the error interferes with meaning during communication. For example, if there is some confusion over the meaning of "I am very enjoy," the teacher might treat the error: "Do you mean, 'I enjoyed the movie'?"

The teacher also has a choice about who treats the error. Of course, the teacher can treat the error, but so can the student who made the error, or the whole class. One problem in asking students to treat each other's errors is the very real possibility that they will not cooperate.

Even more problematic is how to treat the errors. Returning to an example given in Chapter 2, some teachers will treat the error in ways that are not obvious to the student.[37]

Anna:	I have no brother.
Teacher:	Two sisters? (using rising intonation)
Anna:	Because my mother she dead when I was three years old.
Teacher:	She *died* when you were three?
Anna:	Yes. She dead when I was three years old.

It is possible to make it clear to the student that errors are being treated, as well as offer an activity that draws the student's attention to the error and the correction.[38]

Maria:	I have 30 years.
Teacher:	Which is correct: "I have 30 years" or "I am 30 years old"?
Maria:	I am 30 years old.

Another error treatment activity involves classification. For example, when a student makes an error such as, "I sleep late" (meaning "I slept late"), the teacher can write the error and the correction on the blackboard for the student to see.

Correct	Incorrect
I slept late.	I sleep late.
I am 30 years old.	I have 30 years old.
I'm going to study	I going to study.

The teacher can also do a mini-lesson or conversation to let the student practice the correct form.

Teacher: Jose, did you get up early this morning?
Jose: No, I slept late.
Teacher: Do you sleep late everyday?
Jose: No, I usually get up early. Today I slept late.

The "Any Native Speaker Can Teach Conversation" Problem

Native speakers of English are frequently asked to teach conversation simply because they are native speakers. This idea is based on two assumptions. First, the native speaker is most qualified to expose learners to authentic use of English. Second, those who teach the speaking course do not need special qualifications as teachers (unlike teachers of reading and writing). The idea is that if you are a native speaker of a language, you can teach others to speak it simply by using the language with them.

The first assumption is partially true. Native speakers of English likely expose students to the teacher's culture and fine nuances of English simply by interacting with them. Of course, this depends on how they interact with students. For example, I have observed native speakers who have lived in a country for several years interact with students by using behaviors of the students' culture.

The second assumption is false. As shown in this chapter, teaching students to converse in another language is quite challenging. It requires those who teach it to develop an understanding of what learning to converse in a second or foreign language entails, as well as the ability to make use of activities that provide opportunities for students to speak. In addition, teachers need a great variety of skills in classroom management, as well as in interpersonal and cross-cultural communication.

TEACHER SELF-DEVELOPMENT TASKS

Talk Tasks

1. Have you learned to converse in a foreign or second language? What was the experience like? What problems did you have? Can you relate your experience to the learning experiences of EFL/ESL students?

2. Using the pictures of the four seasons, create a lesson for beginners. Imagine that you will show the pictures on an overhead, and that you, the teacher, will have a conversation with the class about the seasons. To prepare for your conversation, write down a series of *yes-no* questions, either-or questions, and identify questions. See how many possible questions you can list. Consider both dis-

play and referential questions, as well as the content you include in your questions. After listing your questions, meet with another teacher who has also made a list. Compare your lists. Combine your list of questions.

3. Review the activity types in this chapter. Meet with other teachers to answer these questions. Which activities do you like the most? Why? Which have you used as a teacher or experienced as a learner?

4. Do you believe that Internet discussion boards can help EFL/ESL students to improve their speaking skills? Do you believe chat rooms can help students to improve their conversation skills? Ask other EFL/ESL teachers these questions.

Observation and Talk Tasks

1. Listen to a conversation between two EFL/ESL learners. Quickly note examples of the errors the students make. Do you believe that these students will someday speak without making these same errors if given many opportunities to speak English?

2. Record a class you teach. As you listen to the tape, note examples of your error treatment behaviors. Do you treat their errors? If so, how? When? What types of errors? Look for a pattern you use to treat errors. Then, talk with other teachers who have also analyzed how they treat language errors. Do you treat errors in similar ways? Together, generate an alternative plan for treating students' errors. Implement it to see what happens.

3. Observe a friend's conversation class. What kinds of speaking activities does the teacher use? What do you see this teacher doing in the class that you would like to use in your teaching?

Journal Writing Tasks

1. Write down your ideas to teach beginners through the use of *yes-no,* either-or, and fact-type questions and quasi-communication activities. Feel free to draw sketches and list procedures you would use in your teaching.

2. Write about your own experiences in learning to converse in a foreign or second language.

3. What do you think makes students anxious about speaking a foreign or second language? What ideas do you have about reducing students' anxieties?

Recommended Teacher Resources

Some Textbooks Used in Conversation Classes

Becker, M. R. *Samantha: A Soap Opera and Vocabulary Book for Students of English as a Second Language.* Ann Arbor: University of Michigan Press, 1993. (Low-intermediate)

Foley, B. H. *Listen to Me! Beginning Listening, Speaking, and Pronunciation.* Boston: Heinle & Heinle, 1994. (Beginner)

Folse, K. S. *Discussion Starters: Speaking Fluency Activities for Advanced ESL/EFL Students.* Ann Arbor: University of Michigan Press, 1996.

Henrichsen, L. S., B. A. Green, A. Nishitani, and C. L. Bagley. *Pronunciation Matters: Communicative, Story-Based Activities for Mastering the Sounds of North American English.* Ann Arbor: University of Michigan Press, 1999. (Intermediate/Advanced)

King, K. R. *Taking Sides: A Speaking Text for Advanced and Intermediate Students.* Ann Arbor: University of Michigan Press, 1997. (Advanced)

McAndrew, R., and R. Martinez. *Instant Discussion—Photocopiable Lessons on Common Topics.* Boston: Heinle & Heinle, 2003. (Low-intermediate)

McAndrew, R., and R. Martinez. *Taboos and Issues—Photocopiable Lessons on Conversational Topics.* Boston: Heinle & Heinle, 2001. (Intermediate)

Reinhart, S. M., and I. Fisher. *Speaking & Social Interaction. 2^d ed.* Ann Arbor: University of Michigan Press, 2000. (Intermediate)

Wall, A. P. *Say It Naturally—Verbal Strategies for Authentic Communication. 2^d ed.* Boston: Heinle & Heinle, 1998. (High-beginner)

Wong, M. S. *You Said It! Listening/Speaking Strategies and Activities.* New York: Cambridge University Press, 1998. (Intermediate)

Professional Readings on Teaching Speaking: Concepts and Activities

Bailey, K. M., and L. Savage, eds. *New Ways in Teaching Speaking.* Alexandria, VA: TESOL, 1994.

Brown, G., and G. Yule. *Teaching the Spoken Language.* New York: Cambridge University Press, 1983.

Bygate, M. *Speaking.* Oxford: Oxford University Press, 1987.

Goodwin, J. "Teaching Pronunciation." In *Teaching English as a Second or Foreign Language, 3^d ed.*, ed. M. Celce-Murcia, 117–37. Boston: Heinle & Heinle, 2001.

Graham. C. *Jazz Chants: Old and New.* New York: Oxford University Press, 2003. (Beginner through Advanced)

Klippel, F. *Keep Talking: Communicative Fluency Activities for Language Teaching.* New York: Cambridge University Press, 1985.

Lazaraton, A. "Teaching Oral Skills." In *Teaching English as a Second or Foreign Language, 3^d ed.*, M. Celce-Murcia, 103–15. Boston: Heinle & Heinle, 2001.

Morley, J., ed. *Pronunciation Pedagogy and Theory.* Alexandria, VA: TESOL, 1994.

Murphy, J. M. 1991. "Oral Communication in TESOL: Integrating Speaking, Listening, and Pronunciation." *TESOL Quarterly* 25, no. 1 (1991): 51–75.

Riggenbach, H. *Discourse Analysis in the Language Classroom. Volume 1: The Spoken Language.* Ann Arbor: University of Michigan Press, 1999.

Roach, P. *Phonetics.* New York: Oxford University Press, 2001.

Endnotes

[1] My ideas here are influenced by the work of Brown and Yule (1983), Bygate (1987), and Richards (1990).

[2] Barnlund (1975) discusses conversation topics in Japan. The complexity of spoken discourse is evident by reading Gee (1999), Riggenbach (1999), and Scollon and Scollon (2001).

[3] The complexity of turn-taking is evident through reading the collection of articles in Atkinson and Heritage (1984) and Schenkein (1978).

[4] See Wardhaugh (1985).

[5] See Richards (1990, 73).

[6] See Littlewood (1981).

[7] This activity is adapted from Krashen and Terrell (1983, 83).

[8] West (1960) and Fanselow (1987) elaborate on the value of using the technique "Read and Look Up," as well as ways students can use it.

[9] See Forest (1992, 81).

[10] See Sainz (1993).

[11] Several sources describe and illustrate games used in conversational classrooms, including Wright, Betteridge, and Buckby's *Games for Language Learning* (1983), Rinvolucri's *Grammar Games* (1984), and the "Games and Speaking" section in Bailey and Savage's *New Ways in Teaching Speaking* (1994). Sperling (1997) offers websites with games in *The Internet Guide for English Language Teachers.*

[12] This game is described in Harsch (1994).

[13] The Strip Story was created by Robert Gibson (1975).

[14] To the best of my knowledge, a materials writer at The Language Center, Chalalongorn University, Bangkok, in the mid-1970s, created this strip story.

[15] This problem-solving game or versions of it have been described in different publications, including Klippel (1984) and Wright, Betteridge, and Buckby (1983).

[16] Warschauer (1995) explains how teachers have students use e-mail as cross-cultural exchange, as a way for students to interact with each other in a class, and more.

17 See Bikowski and Kessler (2002). Also see Sutherland-Smith (2002) for a discussion of benefits of discussion boards.

18 As Freiermuth points out, "internet chat has produced measurable language gains by students while promoting them with satisfying language learning experiences" (2002, 36). Also see Freiermuth (1998, 2001) and Warschauer (1996, 1997) for more discussion on the benefits and uses of Internet chat.

19 See Chanrungkanok (2004).

20 I highly recommend Henrichsen et al. (1999), *Pronunciation Matters: Communicative Story-Based Activities for Mastering the Sounds of North American English.*

21 A great variety of pronunciation activity ideas can be found in the pronunciation section of Bailey and Savage (1994, 199–262) in Goodwin (2001), Gilbert (1987, 1994), and Hebert (2002). Views and knowledge about pronunciation can be found in Jones (2002), Morley (1991, 1994), Pennington (1989), and Pennington and Richards (1986).

22 Folse (1994) has published a version of this activity.

23 Gilbert (n.d.) discusses the use of the kazoo to teach intonation.

24 "The Pronunciation Computer" was originally designed by Charles Curran (1976) as a part of his counseling-learning approach to second language teaching and learning.

25 Graham's original 1978 book is simply titled *Jazz Chants.* A few of her other books include *Holiday Jazz Chants* (1999), *Jazz Chants Old and New* (2003), and *Children's Jazz Chants Old and New* (2002).

26 This chant is from Graham (1978).

27 See Celce-Murcia (1987, 7).

28 Greenfield (1994) does a similar Bingo activity using street names.

29 See Morley (1987, 86).

30 Trust is important to Curran (1976, 1978) and Stevick (1980). Their work has made it obvious to me that trust is an extremely important aspect of the teaching process.

31 The warm-up activities I give are from Via (1987) and my own experience.

32 Chan (1994) gives a number of pronunciation warm-up activities—for example, having students stretch mouth muscles by making funny faces and waggling the tongue in and out, hitting the teeth, to loosen the tongue.

33 See Krashen (1982, 1985) and Krashen and Terrell (1983).

34 Allwright and Bailey (1991) offer views on error treatment and acquisition. Also see Brown (2000).

[35] See Allwright and Bailey (1991) for a review of literature on the when, what, and how of oral error treatment. Long (1977) offers a discussion on the decision-making process teachers sometimes go through in relation to error treatment.

[36] See Allwright and Bailey (1991, 102).

[37] This example is from Gebhard, Gaitan, and Oprandy (1987, 228).

[38] The error-treatment techniques discussed here are adapted from Fanselow (1977b).

Comprehension may be regarded as relating what we attend to in the world around us—the visual information of print in the case of reading—to what we already have in our heads. And learning can be considered as modifying what we already have in our heads as a consequence of attending to the world around us.

—Smith 1994, 53

Teaching Students to Read for Meaning

- What does reading include?
- How do EFL/ESL teachers teach beginners to read?
- What kinds of reading activities do EFL/ESL teachers use with post-beginners?
- What problems do some EFL/ESL teachers have as reading teachers?

What Does Reading Include?

Reading includes discovering meaning in print and script, within a social context, through bottom-up and top-down processing, and use of strategies and skills.

The Social Context of Reading

As the list of things we read shows, we read a lot of things! We read some of these alone—for example, a newspaper over morning coffee or tea. We also read things and talk about them with others. For example, we might read the movie listings in the newspaper to a friend to select a film to see, or we might read a menu item at a restaurant to the waiter to ask if he or she recommends it. We read some things while sitting, others while walking, and still others while driving. The point is, reading is not done in a vacuum. It is done within a social context.

> *Things We Read*: calendars; addresses on envelopes; numbers and addresses in telephone books; name cards; bank statements; credit cards; maps; diplomas; product warning labels; washing instruction labels; shoe size labels; shopping ads; coupons; money; food product nutrition labels; cereal boxes; messages on coffee cups; graffiti on walls; children's scribbling; letters from friends; business letters; electronic mail; junk mail; postcards; greeting cards; comic books; newspaper columns; magazine articles; advertisements; posters; travel guides; cookbooks; repair manuals; product instruction manuals; notes from mothers; memos; train, bus, and air schedules; place mats in fast-food restaurants; street signs; textbooks, overhead projector notes; syllabi; journal articles; short stories; novels; plays; poems; theater, gallery, and museum programs; store catalogs; song lyrics; film subtitles; subway ads; ads in taxi cabs; job application forms; name tags; names of banks, restaurants, shops, and stores on buildings; pins; t-shirt messages; and messages written by airplanes in the sky

Processing What We Read

Auditory bottom-up and top-down processes involved in listening comprehension were discussed in Chapter 8; these same processes are active in a visual sense when we read.[1] To comprehend written language, we rely on our ability to recognize words, phrases, and sentences (bottom-up or text-driven processing), as well as on our background knowledge related to the content of what we are reading (top-down or conceptually-driven processing). These two processes interact as we read, resulting in a degree of comprehension.

However, bottom-up reading processing is different from listening in that readers need visual strategies, rather than auditory strategies, to process written syntax (for example, word order) and lexicon (words and the meaning of words). In addition, they need to be able to process orthography (letters), decode words, as well as have an ability to process reading phonology (for example, the intonation used in reading when we read aloud inside our heads or to an audience).

Certainly, the reading process is much more complex than what I introduce here. However, I can provide one very important idea, backed by research findings, about how EFL/ESL students learn to process what they read that can be quite useful to EFL/ESL teachers: Students learn to process what they read by reading. In other words, the more they read, the better they become at processing what they read. This is because as they process text, they build a wider vocabulary, knowledge of the second language, the world, and text types.[2] The implications are that EFL/ESL teachers need to have students read a variety of texts and to read as extensively as possible.

Strategies Used by Readers to Comprehend Text
What do fluent readers say they do to comprehend reading materials?[3] A list follows.

- Skip words they do not know
- Predict meaning
- Guess the meaning of unfamiliar words from the context
- Do not constantly translate
- Look for cognates
- Ask someone what a word means
- Have knowledge about the topic
- Draw inferences from the title
- Make use of all information in the paragraph to comprehend unfamiliar words
- Try to figure out the meaning of a word by the syntax on the sentence
- Read things of interest
- Study pictures and illustrations
- Purposefully reread to check comprehension

In addition to what good readers say about their own strategies for comprehending reading materials, research on the eye movements of fluent readers shows another reason for success: They read most words on a page, including 80 percent of the content words and 40 percent of the function words. They do not simply sample a small piece of text and try to guess what the rest of the text is about. Instead, good readers read in a very precise way. Even when reading fast, they identify the majority of the words.[4] Also, readers who consistently read with success do not read just once in a while but spend much time reading, as many well-known studies have reported.

Skills Used to Read

In addition to the strategies readers use to make sense of print, successful readers also learn basic reading skills.[5] They can *skim* a text to get the general idea of a passage. For example, good readers can read a newspaper headline and the first paragraph or two to determine what the story is about and whether they want to read the article. Successful readers can *scan* things they read to locate facts or specific information—for example, to locate a number in the phone book or a file from a list on a computer screen.

Successful readers can also read for *thorough comprehension*. This means they read to understand the total meaning of a passage. This kind of reading is often done in academic and other settings where complete comprehension is necessary. In addition, successful readers can *read critically*. Critical reading requires that readers evaluate what they read and consider whether or not they share the author's point of view or are convinced by the author's argument or position. Finally, successful readers *read extensively*. This means they read broadly in areas of interest, such as mystery novels, or in a field of study, such as history or cooking.

How Do EFL/ESL Teachers Teach Beginners to Read?

Before being able to skim, scan, read for thorough comprehension, read critically, and read extensively in English, students need opportunities to build their bottom-up processing abilities in the language. In other words, they need time and practice building knowledge of sentence structure and vocabulary, as well as experiencing reading within meaningful contexts.[6]

This can be done in several ways. One way, of course, is to use texts, and there are a number of beginning-level grammar and vocabulary texts on the market. Most of these books include lots of exercises, charts, graphs, illustrations, and photos.[7] Reading texts written for beginners also offer students tightly controlled grammatical structures and vocabulary while providing stories relevant to a particular reading audience (e.g., young adults).

EFL/ESL students at the beginning level can also benefit from teacher-created vocabulary-building activities, especially if these activities are based on the students' immediate, or at least felt, needs.

Teachers also create activities that provide contexualized reading experiences. One way is with pen pals. Students in one class write to students in another, or the teacher can link students across schools, even countries. These letters can be handwritten, or, if available, e-mail offers speed and often an exciting way for students to communicate. The letters from students become the reading text; when students truly connect, the letters offer students a valuable reading and learning experience. If students' oral skills are more developed than their reading skills, they can generate their own reading texts by recording their life stories, which the teacher (or advanced students) can transcribe and edit. These stories then become reading material for the students.

What Kinds of Reading Activities Do EFL/ESL Teachers Use with Post-Beginners?

As students gain in their processing abilities, teachers can have them do activities to develop their skills to skim, scan, read for thorough comprehension, read critically, and read extensively.

Skimming Activities

Readers skim to gain a general impression of a book, story, essay, or article and to determine whether to read it more carefully. The activities[8] illustrate ways that students can practice this. The first example asks the reader to skim a passage and then identify the best title.[9]

The Best Title

Read the passage quickly. Then select the best title.

Mary Ashworth couldn't believe it! She had purchased a lottery ticket six months ago, put it in her wallet, and forgot about it. One day while at the store, she found the ticket and decided to see if she had won. To her amazement, she had won top prize of two million dollars! She remarked enthusiastically, "I really couldn't believe it! I almost threw the ticket away without checking to see if I won anything!"

Which title is best?

a. The Good Shopper   c. Six Months Ago

b. The Lucky Lottery Winner d. The Lost Wallet

A second example of a skimming activity is more extended; students are given a topic and expected to select relevant books, newspaper articles, magazine articles, and other reading materials from a library collection. To prepare, the teacher collects reading materials on a variety of narrowed topics, such as sports of Chinese origin, Italian fashion, computer games, and travel in Eastern Europe. The teacher also adds readings (comprising about half the total readings) on closely related topics, such as sports in Latin America, New York fashion, computer programs used in business, and travel in Western Europe. The teacher sets up the class library, asks each student to select a specific topic from a list, and has students locate and skim readings from the class library, searching for readings on their topic. The idea is to see how many of the topic-specific readings the student can discover.

Scanning Activities

While skimming is quick reading to find the general idea, scanning is quick reading to locate specific information.[10] For example, we scan telephone books, catalogs, dictionaries, event calendars, book indexes, menus, a wide variety of print on the Internet—basically any source in which we need to locate specific information. Here is an example of a scanning activity that uses classified ads.

Scanning the Classified Ads

Scan the newspaper classified ads to find answers to the following questions.

1. Which number would you call if you were interested in buying a car?
2. If you wanted to house-sit, which number would you call? Do you have to like cats?
3. If you know someone who wants a student to do lawn work, who would you tell him to call?
4. Imagine you would like to live in a house rather than an apartment. How many houses are for rent?
5. How many apartment rentals include utilities? How many do not?
6. Who would you call if you were interested in finding a new apartment?
7. Could you buy a computer for less than $800? What would this computer include?
8. Which employment listing seems like the best opportunity for a student? Do any of the jobs interest you?
9. What is the phone number for the dormitory office at Moore Hall?

For Sale	Apartments	New! New! New!	Looking for a mature

For Sale

Dell Inspiron 4000, 2 years old, Windows 2000 professional, CD and DVD drive, loaded with memory & programs. $600. Must sell to pay tuition. Call Jason, evenings: 724-463-1969.

1998 Honda Accord, 53,000 miles, auto, 4-door, A/C, P/W, power lock. Must see and drive. $5,300.

Wanted

Apartment for Fall semester. Call John at 412-678-9917.

Student needs part-time work. Have home repair experience. Will do lawn work. Call Matt: 724-465-2234.

Looking for Spanish tutor. Larry 724-349-2583.

Apartments

1-bedroom apartment for two students, no smokers, furnished, $220.00/month. 724-349-2786.

1 female needed to fill 4-person apartment close to campus. Fall and spring. $1,500/semester. Utilities included. Call 714-676-5888.

2-bedroom duplex. Fall and spring. 412-682-7786.

Apt. for three. One-half mile from campus, large yard, fully furnished, off-street park. $2,000/semester, includes utilities. 724-357-6751.

Need responsible older student to house-sit. Must love cats. 724-463-2224.

New! New! New! Diamond Apartments. Available now. 357-2489.

Need apartment for the summer? 2-person, 2 bedroom, 1 block from campus. Only $500/both summer sessions.

Summer apartment, own room, $350 for ten weeks. Utilities included. Call Betty at 724-357-4547.

Moore Hall, single dorm rooms available. Fall and Spring. 724-357-6665.

Employment

Need extra cash? Psychologist needs 50 students. 412-456-9981 or jsmith@iup.edu

Needed: Secretary 357-2282.

Looking for a mature older graduate student to manage apartment. Call Steve, 357-0800.

B&B Cruise Ships now hiring. Earn big $$$ and travel the world. No experience necessary. 800-875-4000.

The Hiring Help Line will help you find a good job: *www.hiringhelp.com*

Personals

Happy Birthday, Frank! All my love! Jill.

Looking for good home for 1-year-old cat. Loving, litter trained. Call Janet 723-365-0871.

Yuki, I'm sorry! I miss and love you!

Another way to give students practice with scanning is to have a contest. Students form teams, and each student receives a handout that includes facts. I sometimes use fact sheets on different countries—for example, on China's 14 coastal port cities.[11] Equipped with a long list of questions and answers, the teacher throws a question out to the class. The first team to answer the question correctly gets two points. If a team gets the answer wrong, it loses a point. The team with the most points wins.

Reading for Thorough Comprehension: Activities

Unlike skimming and scanning, activities that aim at having students read for thorough comprehension require students to read meticulously. The goal is for the students to understand the total meaning of a reading selection, and there are a number of techniques teachers can use to get students to interact with the reading material:[12]

- Students study the title and skim to capture the main idea.
- Students read two paragraphs and predict what will follow.
- Students do several different scanning tasks, such as underlining past tense verbs in red and adverbs indicating sequence (e.g., *first, second, next,* etc.) in blue, circling words they do not recognize, and putting stars next to words that seem important. After each task, they briefly discuss what they underlined, circled, or starred.
- After students have a sense of what the reading material is about, they read silently while answering true-false or multiple-choice questions.
- Students meet in groups, consider the text, write down questions, and give them to another group to answer.
- Students draw pictures of the main characters in a story or draw pictures that illustrate the story line.
- Students, working in groups, reconstruct material previously cut into pieces (also called a jigsaw task).
- Students read a story with the conclusion missing, then write their own endings.
- Students give the reading material a new title.
- Students put a set of pictures or photos in order to show the story line or content.
- Students meet in groups to summarize an article and to separate main ideas from supporting ideas and examples.
- Students listen to the teacher discuss how the piece of writing is organized.

This list illustrates some of the activities teachers use in reading classes, and there are, of course, other ways to teach reading, as well as ways to creatively combine a number of reading activities into a single lesson. And it is through such a combination of activities that students have opportunities to read thoroughly. With this in mind, here is a reading lesson I designed for a lower-intermediate ESL class, including a story I wrote and a combination of activities.

Through this example, I encourage you to write your own stories and activities for students in your classes.

> My wife, Yoko, and I got up very early on Saturday. We had a busy day ahead of us. Before leaving the house, we shut the windows. Then we noticed our cat, Kiku, sitting comfortably on a chair. "This won't do," Yoko said. "We better put Kiku outside for the day."
>
> Yoko said goodbye to Kiku just before she got into the car. The cat didn't look happy. He wanted to go back into the house to rest comfortably on the chair! But this was impossible. At least, this is what we thought!
>
> We then drove to see my mother at a retirement home. But my mother wasn't home. Se we walked in the garden. Yoko spent some time at the small white fountain in the middle of the garden.
>
> After we walked in the garden, we drove to the countryside to join relatives at a family reunion. Yoko talked with Aunt Nita and my cousin Ann for a long time. She also talked with Uncle Gene, who always seems to be wearing white slacks and shoes.
>
> We left the reunion early to go to a wedding party. Our friend Agnes is from Poland, and she married her childhood sweetheart, Wojtek. They had a wonderful time, although they missed their families in Poland on such an important day.
>
> Finally, late at night, we went home. And guess what! We found Kiku in the hall of the house! How did that cat do that!?

Here are the activities students did.

- Students answered questions before they read (e.g., *How many of you have ever had a cat as a pet? How many cats? What do cats like to do?*).
- Students studied a blown-up photo of Kiku the cat next to a drawing of a chrysanthemum while listening to an explanation about the meaning of Kiku's Japanese name, meaning chrysanthemum.
- Students looked at the reading while tracing some of the script with their finger, spelling out words. As a class, they wrote the same words in the air with their index fingers.

- Students looked for words they had studied the week before, such as *fountain, garden, and countryside.*
- Students underlined verbs in the past tense, and then counted the number of past tense verbs.
- One student read the story silently and responded true or false to such statements as (1) Kiku is a dog, (2) Yoko and her husband visited three places, (3) Yoko and her husband visited his mother after going to a picnic.
- While in groups, students read each paragraph together and then had one person in each group summarize it.
- After students finished reading the summaries, they arranged seven drawings into the same order as the events in the story.
- As a group, students answered the following question: *How did Kiku get back in the house?* Then each group gave their answer to the whole class.
- As a class, students gave the story possible titles while the teacher wrote them on the board.

Critical Reading

There are at least three things to remember when asking students to do critical reading. First, students still need to do the kinds of activities that lead to full comprehension, as discussed earlier. Second, students need to make judgments about what they read: *Do I agree with the author's point of view? How is my view different? Does the author persuade me to change my view? Is the author's evidence strong?* Third, we need to be careful about what we ask students to make judgments on. In other words, we need to select content that is not only interesting to the students as readers, but also something they can relate to. For example, young adults from Japan, Mexico, and California will likely be more interested in reading and giving opinions about earthquake survival than will people in places not affected by earthquakes. Likewise, young students are apt to have better-informed opinions about popular rock stars and youth fashion than the average adult would.

Extensive Reading

The goal of extensive reading is to improve reading skills by processing a quantity of materials that can be comprehended and pleasurable. Teachers who implement extensive reading set up an open library (in the classroom or school library) where students can select from an assortment of reading materials.[13] The teacher's job is to guide the reader to materials that are comprehensible, letting the students make their own choices.

As a part of the extensive reading experience, teachers often ask students to report on what they have read. One way to do this is to have students interview each other through the use of question prompts. For example, if a student reads a short story, the question prompts might include:[14]

- What is the story title?
- What kind of short story is it?
- Did you like the story?
- Why did you like it, or why not?
- Would you recommend the story?
- Who is the story's author?
- What is the main message in the story?

Computer-Mediated Reading

Reading done on the computer includes all the reading activity types previously discussed. In fact, it is possible to buy books that have accompanying CD-ROMS and DVDs that include reading texts and activities that students will skim, scan, read critically, and read extensively. However, computer technology provides students with ways to discover reading materials on the Internet, as well as activities they do with them. For example, there are websites that link students to newspapers,[15] such as the Bangkok Post (*www.bangkokpost.net*), China News Service (*www.chinanews.com*), Los Angeles Times (*www.latimes.com*), and The Jerusalem Post (*www.jpost.com*). Likewise, logging on to *www.pathfinder.com* brings up a variety of links to magazines, such as *Time.com, Teen People.com, People.com,* and *Fortune.com.* In addition, such websites as Dave's ESL Cafe (*www.eslcafe.com*) offer a variety of interactive reading materials, such as the ESL Graffiti Wall and ESL Idea Page.

One benefit of computers is that students can become more autonomous learners, especially if they are taught to use the Internet to discover authentic and personally interesting reading materials.[16] Regarding vocabulary and reading, programs such as TextLadder help teachers and students to scan readings for frequently used vocabulary. Through analysis of frequently used words in a text, students without sufficient vocabulary size to comprehend authentic text in English can first use a program to scan the text to see if it will be comprehensible.

What Problems Do Some EFL/ESL Teachers Have as Reading Teachers?

Problems some EFL/ESL teachers face include the following:

- The "background knowledge" problem
- The "getting students to read" problem

The "Background Knowledge" Problem

Students' ability to comprehend the content of reading material depends in part on their knowledge about the topic of the reading selection. To increase students' potential comprehension, the teacher can lead a variety of pre-reading activities that build background knowledge.

One activity is to have a short discussion about the topic. For example, the teacher might lead off discussion with the following set of questions before asking students to read an article on the lifestyles of sumo wrestlers: *How many of you have ever watched sumo on TV? What happens during a match? What are some of the rules in sumo? What do you know about the lifestyles of sumo wrestlers?* If time is limited, written reading previews could be used. Similar to a movie preview, a reading preview introduces the student to the main idea of the reading. Pictures, sketches, or photographs can also be used to introduce the topic of a reading.

Another pre-reading activity is to take a field trip to a historical or cultural site or event or to watch a film or video clip about the topic of the future reading. For example, students could watch part of a videotaped sumo match and view a short documentary on the lives of famous contemporary sumo wrestlers.

The "Getting Students to Read" Problem

In some EFL/ESL teaching settings, students do not necessarily value reading. It is a constant struggle for teachers to get students to read in and out of class. When faced with such an attitudinal or motivational problem, teachers are often at a loss about what to do.

Although there is no single or simple way to change students' attitudes toward reading, there are things teachers can try.[17] First, we can begin with the following assumption: "People learn better when what they are studying has considerable meaning for them . . . when it really comes out of their own lives . . . when it is something that they can in some way commit themselves to or invest themselves in."[18] Second, we can work at discovering what brings meaning to the life of each student in our classes. We can do this by observing students: What do they talk about? Show interest in? Carry around with them? Some nonreaders will read if the reading matches their interest, such as learning to develop photos or learning to cook. When given the right conditions, problem readers will spend time reading because they have an invested interest in learning something they consider to be important or useful.

Third, we can do our best to introduce students to readings that match their interests, mostly through extensive reading activities. By putting together a library collection that includes the readings and content in which students express interest, we can most easily guide students toward materials that interest them. Such a collection for adults includes mysteries, how-to books, old letters, grammar books, catalogs, sports magazines, newspaper clippings, poems, application forms, menus, academic books, and adventure stories.

TEACHER SELF-DEVELOPMENT TASKS

Talk Tasks

1. Meet with others who are interested in teaching reading. Ask each other questions about learning to read. Here are a few questions to get you started: How did you learn to read your native language? Have you learned to read a second language? How did your teacher manage the reading lessons? Do you think there were differences in learning to read your first and second languages? If so, what are some of these differences?

2. Meet with a friend. Work through the following steps:

   a. Make a list of materials that students can use to practice scanning.
   b. Locate one of these materials.
   c. Create a scanning activity.

3. Meet with a friend. Work through these steps:

   a. Locate a reading passage. If you are now teaching a reading class, you might want to select material you plan to teach or are required to teach.
   b. Study the list (given earlier in this chapter) of techniques teachers can use to have students interact with reading materials.

      c. Based on the list of techniques to have students interact with reading materials, and on your own creative ideas, generate a detailed reading lesson that contains at least five different reading activities to help students process the passage you selected.

      d. Find others who have done this same activity. Give each other copies of your lesson plans.

Observation and Talk Tasks

1. Try one of the reading lessons created in Talk Task 2 or 3. Record the lesson. Then select three two-minute sections from the tape to listen to. As you listen, note alternative ways you could teach the same aspect of the lesson.

Journal Writing Tasks

1. Study the activity types discussed in this chapter. Which do you like the most? Why? Which types have you used as a teacher or experienced as a learner?
2. Write about your experiences in learning to read a second language.
3. Select one of the problems from the section What Problems Do Some EFL/ESL Teachers Have as Reading Teachers? Write about why this is a problem for some teachers, and perhaps for yourself as a teacher.

Recommended Teacher Resources

Professional Readings on Teaching Reading:
Concepts and Activities

Aebersold, J. A., and M. L. Field. *From Reader to Reading Teacher*. New York: Cambridge University Press, 1997.

Alderson, J. C. *Assessing Reading*. Cambridge: Cambridge University Press, 2000.

Birch, B. M. *English L2 Reading: Getting to the Bottom*. Mahwah, NJ: Lawrence Erlbaum, 2002.

Day, R. R., and J. Bamford. *Extensive Reading in the Second Language Class-room*. New York: Cambridge University Press, 1998.

Grabe, W., and F. L. Stoller. "Reading for Academic Purposes: Guidelines for the ESL/EFL Teacher." In *Teaching English as a Second or Foreign Language*, 3d ed., ed. M. Celce-Murcia, 187–203. Boston: Heinle & Heinle, 2001.

Grellet, F. *Developing Reading Skills: A Practical Guide to Reading Comprehension Exercises.* New York: Cambridge University Press, 1981.

Peregoy, S. F., and O. F. Boyle. *Reading, Writing, and Learning in ESL: A Resource Book for K–12 Teachers. 4th ed.* New York: Pearson Education, 2005.

Hadfield, J., and C. Hadfield. *Simple Reading Activities.* New York: Oxford University Press, 2000.

Smith, F. *Understanding Reading.* New York: Holt, Rinehart and Winston, 1994.

Professional Readings on Teaching Vocabulary

DeCarrico, J. S. "Vocabulary Learning and Teaching." In *Teaching English as a Second or Foreign Language, 3d ed.,* ed. M. Celce-Murcia, 285–99. Boston: Heinle & Heinle, 2001.

Folse, K. S. *Vocabulary Myths: Applying Second Language Research to Classroom Teaching.* Ann Arbor: University of Michigan Press, 2004.

Hunt, A., and D. Beglar. "Current Research and Practice in Teaching Vocabulary." In *Methodology in Language Teaching: An Anthology of Current Practice,* eds. J. C. Richards and W. A. Renandya, 258–66. New York: Cambridge University Press, 2002.

Nation, P., ed. *New Ways in Teaching Vocabulary.* Alexandria, VA: TESOL, 1994.

Read, J. *Assessing Vocabulary.* Cambridge: Cambridge University Press, 2000.

Textbooks for Reading Classes

Kay, J., and R. Gelshenen. *Adventures in Literature: New Pathways to Reading.* Ann Arbor: University of Michigan Press, 2004. (Intermediate)

Robledo, R., and H. Dolores. *Read to Succeed I: Academic Reading from the Start.* New York: Houghton Mifflin, 2005. (High-beginner)

Silberstein, S., B. K. Dobson, and M. A. Clarke. *Reader's Choice, 4th ed.* Ann Arbor: University of Michigan Press, 2002. (Advanced)

Upton, T. A. 2004. *Reading Skills for Success: A Guide to Academic Texts.* Ann Arbor: University of Michigan Press, 2004. (Advanced)

Valcourt, G., and L. Wells. *Mastery: A University Word List Reader.* Ann Arbor: University of Michigan Press, 1999. (Intermediate to High-intermediate)

Teaching Reading: Series Readers

Anderson, N. J. *Active Skills for Reading.* Boston: Heinle & Heinle, 2003. (Series of three books from High-beginning through High-intermediate)

Collins, T. *Access Reading—Reading for Your World.* Boston: Heinle & Heinle, 2004. (Series of four books from Beginning to Intermediate)

Draper, C. G. *Great American Stories.* White Plains, NY: Longman, 2001. (Series of three books from Intermediate to Advanced)

Heyer, S. *All New Easy True Stories: A Picture-Based Beginning Reader.* White Plains, NY: Longman, 2004. (One of six books in a *True Stories* series from Beginning through High-intermediate)

McCloske, M. L., and L. Stack. *Visions: Language through Literature and Content.* Boston: Heinle & Heinle, 2004. (Three books—A, B, & C—support middle/high school newcomer transition into mainstream classrooms.)

Yedlin, J., and C. Linse. *Visions: Basic Language and Literacy.* Boston: Heinle & Heinle, 2004. (Book one of the Vision series.)

Endnotes

[1] Many sources address second language reading processes. Some include Aebersold and Field (1997), Alderson (2000), Birch (2002), Carrell and Eisterhold (1983), Carrell, Devine, and Eskey (1988), Grabe (2002), and Peregoy and Boyle (2005).

[2] See Day and Bamford (1998) and Krashen (1988, 1993).

[3] Most of this list is from Papalia (1987, 72).

[4] See Grabe (2002).

[5] The way I categorize reading skills has been influenced by Day (1993), Grellet (1981), and Silberstein, Dobson, and Clarke (2002).

[6] See Birch (2002) and Eskey (1986) for discussions on how L2 readers process text.

[7] Three very different beginning-level grammar books include *Beginning Interactive Grammar* by McKay (1993), *Clear Grammar 1* by Folse (1998), and *Grammar Work* by Breyer (1995). Grammar activities can also be found in *New Ways in Teaching Grammar,* edited by Pennington (1995).

[8] In a book of this scope, I can only give a few example activities. Other activities can be found in Aebersold and Field (1997), Day (1993), Grellet (1981), and in published EFL/ESL reading texts.

[9] The idea for this activity came from Grellet (1981, 69–70). The passage and titles are my own.

[10] Silberstein, Dobson, and Clarke (2002), Day (1993), and Grellet (1981) provide an abundance of ideas on how to teach scanning skills.

[11] EFL teachers can obtain from the tourist information center fact sheets about the country they are visiting or living in.

[12] Ideas from Papalia (1987) and Fanselow (1987) are included in this list of teaching techniques.

[13] Graded readers (Beginner through Intermediate) for children and adults can be a part of the extensive library materials. (See Recommended Teacher Resources.)

14 These prompts were designed by Kluge (1993), who also offers procedures for setting up and carrying out interviews.

15 These and other links to newspapers can be found in Sperling (1997).

16 Based on their personal observations, Brandl (2002) and Galavis (1998) point out that the Internet-based reading can teach students to be more independent readers.

17 The three ways are also discussed in the article "Teaching Reading through Assumptions about Learning" (Gebhard 1985).

18 See Stevick (1978, 40).

We cannot teach students to write by looking only at what they have written. We must also understand how that came into being, and why it assumed the form it did. . . . We have to do the hard thing, examine the intangible process, rather than the easy thing, evaluate the tangible product.

—Hairston 1982, 84

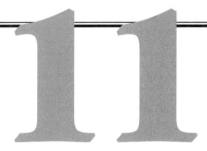

Teaching Students How to Process Writing

- What does writing include?
- How do EFL/ESL teachers teach beginners to write?
- What kind of writing activities do EFL/ESL teachers use with post-beginners?
- What problems do some EFL/ESL teachers have as writing teachers?

What Does Writing Include?

The usual things associated with writing are word choice, use of appropriate grammar (such as subject-verb agreement, tense, and article use), syntax (word order), mechanics (such as punctuation, spelling, and handwriting), and organization of ideas into a coherent and cohesive form. However, writing also includes a focus on audience and purpose, as well as a recursive process of discovering meaning.

Audience and Purpose

When we put pen to paper or fingers to keyboard, we usually have a specific audience in mind who will read what we wrote. On a personal level, we write notes and letters to friends, relatives, and lovers. We also write diary entries to ourselves. As teachers, we write memos to colleagues, notes to students, and reports to parents and administrators. We might also write articles and newsletter items about teaching and learning for other teachers; conference papers to deliver at professional meetings; reading materials for students; and grant proposals to government agencies, corporations, or a private funding source.

A Recursive Process of Creating Meaning

When we write, especially something that is fairly complex, we do not ordinarily write a perfect letter, memo, essay, or proposal in a single draft. Rather, we go through a process of creating and recreating this piece of writing until we discover and clarify within ourselves what we want to say and until we are able to express this meaning in a clear way.[1]

To prepare to write, some of us make lists, sketch, cluster our related ideas, or outline our thoughts. Some of us prefer to think about our topic, create mental notes and images, then begin to write. As we write, we put ideas into draft form, and as we do this, we create meaning.

As we write, we also take breaks to read the draft, reflecting on whether our writing reveals our intended meaning. We might also consider our purpose and audience, and as we read what we wrote, we cross out paragraphs, sentences, and words; reorder the way we present ideas; and make notes about how to revise our writing. We continue to write and read and draft changes until we are satisfied with the piece of writing. If the piece of writing is important enough, we ask a trusted friend to read it and give us feedback. We then use this feedback as a way to further revise our writing.

How Do EFL/ESL Teachers Teach Beginners to Write?

Teachers generally agree that beginning-level EFL/ESL writers need to learn the basic conventions of writing. This includes being able to identify and write letters, words, and simple sentences, as well as learning to spell and punctuate. Teachers use a variety of activities to teach these conventions.[2]

One basic activity is tracing letters, words, and sentences. Although such a task may seem trivial, it can teach students letter recognition and discrimination; word recognition; and basic spelling, punctuation, and capitalization rules. Students, for example, can use pencils to trace letters and words written in an appropriate size and shape on tablet-style sheets used to teach American children. In addition, students can use their index finger to trace letters and words cut from felt. This can be especially useful for those whose learning modality is more kinesthetic than visual. Some students also benefit from saying the letters and words aloud as they trace them.

Another widely used activity is called Copy and Change. Students are given a passage and asked to copy it. But they are also required to change one aspect of the passage—for example, to change the subject from *he* to *she* and make accompanying changes (for instance, all references to *him* need to be changed to *her*). This activity can be done using other grammatical features, such as changing verb tense from present to past time and changing the subject from singular to plural form.

A similar activity involves teaching students a grammatical pattern and functional rules. For example, we can teach students that we use simple present tense to describe everyday routines, and we can provide a model sentence pattern, such as this one:

Subject +	Adverb +	Pres. Tense Verb +	Object +	Preposition +	Time
I	usually	eat	lunch	at	noon.

Based on this pattern, students make up new sentences by exploring different grammatical conventions, such as investigating the use of other adverbs of frequency *(never, rarely, seldom, sometimes, often, frequently, always)*, as well as changing the verb *(have, go out for, make)*, object (breakfast, dinner, a snack), or time (3:00 AM, 8:30 PM).

Another beginning-level activity is to have students unscramble muddled sentence parts. For example, students are given a list of words—such as *school, goes, friend, everyday, my, to*—and they are asked to form a sentence.

After students gain some of the conventions of grammar, mechanics, spelling, and punctuation, they can take on more demanding tasks. One idea is to have students plan a party by making two lists: Things to Do and Things to Buy. Students work in groups or pairs to create their two lists and practice related tasks, such as writing invitation notes and addressing envelopes.[3]

Another activity for advanced beginners is to read and write public notices, such as the ones on supermarket or dormitory bulletin boards. I have had ESL students in beginning-level classes practice with reading notices I bring to class and copy notices they see on bulletin boards and bring them to class. We also prepare for and role-play telephone conversations to practice asking questions related to a notice. Based on their reading, copying, and conversation experience, students write their own notices. It is interesting that some students have been able to make connections with the larger community outside the classroom through actual use of their notices, thus expanding their language learning opportunities. For example, one student started a haircutting business, another found a job doing lawn care, and another found a free ride to a distant city.

What Kind of Writing Activities Do EFL/ESL Teachers Use with Post-Beginners?

After students have gained some control over the convention of writing, they can focus more easily on communicating their ideas through writing. There are a variety of writing activities students can do.

Composition Writing

As writing teachers, we have students write short stories, descriptions, arguments, and more. Quite often we find ourselves giving a composition assignment, such as to write about the character of a person we know, and we immediately focus on vocabulary and grammar that can be used to complete this assignment. When the composition is completed, we read each student's work and mark the errors with red ink. We might also write comments in the margins, such as *Very interesting* or *Good use of the present tense.* But is it enough to give an assignment, to let the students write, and then to evaluate the product of their work? No, it is not. In fact, as writing teachers, we are advised to take students through a nonlinear process whereby, as writers, they can discover and rediscover their ideas as they attempt to put meaning into prose.

Our role is to provide chances for students to develop workable strategies for getting started (finding topics, generating writing ideas, focusing, planning content and organization), for drafting (working through multiple drafts), for revising (deleting, adding, reorganizing, modifying), and for editing (working out problems with word choice, grammar and mechanics, and sentence structure). To accomplish this, we are encouraged to have students work through a process of prewriting, drafting, revising, and editing.[4] Although each of these activities does not take place in a linear fashion, let's look at each separately.

Prewriting Experiences

Brainstorming begins with the introduction of a topic by the teacher or students, after which students call out ideas associated with the topic while the teacher (or a student or two) writes the ideas on the board. Although there is no right or wrong association in this activity, some EFL/ESL students will shy away from calling out their ideas. As such, some teachers have students brainstorm first in small groups, then as a whole class. Brainstorming can also be done by the writer. Similar to brainstorming is an activity called *clustering* (or word mapping), in which students' associations are clustered together and stem off of the central word.[5]

Another prewriting activity is *strategic questioning,*[6] where students consider their topic through a series of questions, such as *What do you know about your topic?* and *What do you still need to learn?* Students consider what they know and need to learn about their writing topic. *Sketching* is a visual idea-generating strategy, useful, for example, when visualizing descriptions or showing the plot of a story. When *free-writing,* students put their ideas into writing,[7] then write continuously for a set amount of time (e.g., eight minutes) and do not stop writing. They write whatever comes to mind, even if it's *The teacher is crazy!* Then students read and consider what they wrote, after which they free-write again. Freed from worrying about grammar and word choice, students generate lots of raw material for their essays.

Prewriting: Ways to Get Started

Brainstorming. Based on a topic of interest, students call out as many associations as possible while the teacher (or students) jots them down.

Clustering. Using a key word placed in the center of a page (or board), a student (or teacher) jots down all the free associations students give related to the word, clustering similar words.

Strategic Questioning. Students answer a set of questions designed to guide their writing, such as *What do you want to write about? What is your goal? What do you know about this topic? What do you need to find out? What interests you or surprises you about this topic? Who might want to read what you are about to write?*

Sketching. Students draw a series of sketches that represent ideas for an essay—for example, the plot of a short story.

Free-writing. Students write nonstop on a topic for a set time (e.g., eight minutes). They stop to read and consider what they wrote and then write nonstop again for another set amount of time.

Exploring the Senses. Suitable for generating ideas for descriptive essays, the teacher guides students through their senses by asking them to visualize, hear, smell, and feel a person or place.

Interviewing. Students interview each other or go outside the classroom to interview people on a particular topic.

Information Gathering. Students collect information about a topic through library research.

I developed a prewriting activity, Exploring the Senses, to facilitate idea gathering for descriptive essays on a place or person.[8] I begin by having students relax (sometimes doing deep-breathing exercises). I then take them through a series of "daydreaming" experiences by guiding them to see, hear, smell, touch, and feel a place or to see, listen to, smell, and have feelings about a particular person. As I do this, I do not get too specific but rather act as a guide and create an opportunity for the students to capture their own descriptions: "See the person. Zoom in on this person's face. Study the face. (Silence.) Now back away from the person. Look at this person from

different positions, as if you are walking around the person."
(Silence.) After several minutes as a visual guide, I switch the students' experience to another sense: "Now, sense what it is like to be with this person. What feelings do you have when you are with this person?" I also guide students through smelling, touching, and listening experiences.

Teachers can have students experience a combination of prewriting activities. After taking students though the activity exploring the senses, I have students list their visual, auditory, kinesthetic, tactical, and other sensual experiences. If students are willing, I then have them meet in groups, each taking turns describing their person or place, after which I take them through a free-writing experience.

Drafting

After students have generated ideas, they start writing. This can be done in a number of ways. One way is to have students do component writing in which they write different sections of their texts within a certain period of time. Another way is to have students do one-sitting writing in which they are encouraged to write a draft of their entire essay, from beginning to end, in one sitting. Another way is through leisurely writing in which students begin a draft in class and finish it at their leisure at home.[9]

Revising

Once students have generated a draft, they can consider revision of the content and organization of their ideas. However, this is not necessarily easy for students to do. Some students have a limited understanding about what revision includes, and some lack the patience needed to go through a time-consuming and sometimes frustrating revision process. However, there are things teachers can do to teach students the concept of revision.

In the university ESL writing courses I teach, I make revision a required part of the students' essay-writing experience, but I also teach them how they can explore the revision process. Here are the instructions I use when I teach narration:

1. Write and hand in three versions of your essay. Mark the essay you like the most with an asterisk (*) next to the title. Add a note explaining why you like it the most.
2. Here are some ways you can revise. Consider changing one or a combination of the following: (a) the beginning, (b) the climax, (c) the events in the steps that build up to

the climax, (d) the sex of the main character, (e) the "person" in which the story is told (e.g., from first person, *I*, to second person, *he* or *she*), (f) the setting in which the study takes place (for instance, from an inner-city high school to a summer camp), and (g) any major content or organization change you would like to make.

Editing

Editing requires recognizing problems in grammar (e.g., subject-verb disagreement, improper pronoun use, incorrect verb tense), syntax (e.g., fragments and run-on sentences), and mechanics (e.g., spelling and punctuation errors). Editing is not problematic in the way that revision is because most students are willing to work hard at editing their work. However, it does take much time, knowledge, experience, and commitment to become a good editor; some students (and teachers) can become so preoccupied with editing that they equate good writing with correct grammar, syntax, word choice, and mechanics rather than with the expression of meaning, of which editing is simply a part.

Nonetheless, teaching students how to edit their work is important, and teachers approach this task in a variety of ways. Some teachers go through each student's paper, circling errors and writing notes, such as "wrong tense" or "awkward sentence." Although we teachers have good intentions and spend hours marking papers, students do not always appreciate our efforts and can even be confused by many corrections and comments. Realizing this, some teachers select one or two aspects of the student's work, such as a particular grammatical error and punctuation problem, and mark only these errors. There are, of course, other ways to respond to students' work, and these are discussed in the problem section at the end of this chapter.

Language-Play Writing

Some EFL/ESL teachers use language-play activities in writing classes. I consider such activities as "play" because they can be fun and still engage students in writing. There are, of course, a great number of language-play writing activities, and here I only provide two examples.

One activity is called the How Does It End? activity. The teacher has students read the first part of a short story, preferably something that builds suspense but is not very long, and then asks them to complete the story. For example, I use an English translation of a German short story by Kurt Kusenberg called "Odd Tippling."[10] In this story a hiking traveler stops at a tavern to have a glass of wine. After ordering the first glass, the town mayor shows up and tells the traveler he has to pay a fortune for the wine. The traveler is surprised and argues with the mayor, but to no avail. Frightened and confused, the traveler decides to order a second and then a third glass, and to his amazement, he discovers that the third glass had created a totally new situation, that he was no longer in debt but rather owned the tavern and inn. Surprised, the traveler decides to have a fourth glass of wine.

I cut the end of the story off, and having students read all but the ending, I give a homework assignment, to write their own ending to the story, telling what happens to the traveler after ordering the fourth glass of wine. During the next class I have students read each other's endings, as well as write a group ending to the story. After having students read their group ending to the class, we read the author's ending, sometimes amazed at how close some individuals and groups came to matching the author's ending, as well as appreciating the creative, playful, and sometimes more interesting, endings of the students.

Another play activity aims at challenging students to communicate descriptions of people in writing. Students are divided into pairs and are given a picture that has lots of people in it. Each pair is asked to select one person in the picture to describe. After describing the person's physical appearance, the pairs exchange their pictures and written descriptions. The objective is to identify the person in the picture who the students described.

Newsletter Writing

Some classes (or schools/institutes) engage students in publishing their own newsletter. Such newsletters come out once a semester or every few months, and students can take on a variety of roles. The teacher can solicit or ask volunteer students to write columns for the newsletter on local cultural events, trips they took, and news about class members and teachers. Likewise, the newsletter can include students' creative writing, for example, short stories, poetry, or an editorial. They might also include announcements, test schedules, and other procedural-type news. Teachers usually try to have as many students as possible contribute their writing and participate in the production of the newsletter. As teachers and students who have taken the effort to publish their own newsletter will tell you, participants can gain a great sense of accomplishment and pride and learn lessons about writing with a purpose and to an audience, in this case one that they know will read and appreciate their efforts.

Pen Pals

A way to provide a genuine writing experience for students is through pen pals. There are a number of pen-pal organizations, and it is possible for teachers to establish their own pen-pal connections. For example, I established a pen-pal alliance between students in a Hungarian high school and native English-speaking students in a rural Pennsylvania school. Based on my experience with pen pals, I suggest that a one-to-one assignment of pen pals be made. For example, Andrea (an EFL student in Hungary) might be matched with Yoko (a Japanese ESL student in the United States).

Once the connection is established, one class needs to initiate a letter. If the students are fairly low level, a short generic letter can be written by the whole class and sent to each pen pal. Students can study letter format, including how and where to write the date and examples of ways to open and close letters. Basic get-acquainted questions can be included, such as *What's your name? How old are you? How many brothers and sisters do you have?* and *What do you like to do?* Of course, students can introduce their own questions, which the teacher can help them with as a group or individually.

Specific days for writing to pen pals (e.g., once every two months) can be set aside in the schedule. Students can bring letters they got from their pen pals to class and voluntarily read them to classmates, pass them around for others to read, or put them on an overhead for the class to read together. Of course, it is also possible to use e-mail to exchange and share letters in class.

Dialogue Journal Writing

A dialogue journal is a written conversation between two or more people.[11] Through the use of notebooks or computers, the two write back and forth to each other on a regular basis on topics of their choice. Quite often the teacher and each student in the class write back and forth, and there are benefits to such a one-to-one exchange. It is possible to get to know the students, better understand their language problems, and create a personal way to motivate each student. It can also teach students that we write to an audience, that we think about the reader as we write.

If it is impossible for the teacher to write to each student, an alternative is to respond to close-knit groups. Each student still writes to the teacher, but the teacher's response is in a single entry to the entire group.[12] Here is an example.

> Dear Mario, Carlos, Mohammed, and Yoko,
>
> It's always a delight to read your journal entries! Mario, I really enjoyed hearing about your trip to the zoo! How did you get the monkey to pose like that? Could I see other pictures you took? Andrea, your weekend sounded very frustrating! Everything went wrong, huh? How could you have forgotten to take sunscreen! Is your back still red? I hope you are over the pain. As I have similar skin—that is, I burn easily—I know what you are going through.
>
> Carlos, I don't agree with your idea about memorizing word lists. This takes more time than it's worth. I suggest you keep a vocabulary notebook. Each day add three new words. Write down example sentences with the words in them. You can also draw sketches to illustrate them and can include different forms of the word. For example, if the word is a noun, also include the adjective and adverb forms of the word if they exist. You might also include your own definition of the word.
>
> Mohammed, your interest in cultural-adjustment processes really captures my interest. I'm happy you liked the documentary we viewed in class on the stages of cultural adjustment. Do you have any interesting stories about adjustment to other cultures? In fact, I would be pleased to read any of your group's cultural-adjustment stories!
>
> Yoko, how about you! I miss reading your journal entries! I hope that you are feeling better and ready to correspond with me again!
>
> Enjoy!
>
>   Your teacher

Although a teacher-student dialogue exchange has many benefits, there are also problems. First, as experienced teachers know, writing to each student or even to groups of students can be an extraordinary amount of work for the teacher, even impossible if the teacher has a large class. Second, many students believe that the teacher probably cannot relate to their view of the world so they write about what they think are the teacher's interests and do not consider discussing what genuinely interests them. Third, there is the problem of status. Some teachers want to really reach students, but even when the teacher tries hard to establish a special rapport, some EFL/ESL students will resist. This is especially true for students who are from countries such as Asia where the culturally based rules demand that students place the teacher on a hierarchical level above the student. In brief, it would be impolite for the students to complain, criticize, or openly write about a topic that could cause the teacher to lose face or that could upset their harmonious relationship.

Considering these factors, an alternative is to have students communicate with each other through journals. This is what Karen Bromley does with "buddy journals," which she uses to connect immigrant and American children in sharing language and literacy.[13] With journals students can feel free to establish rapport based on shared interests, problems, and tastes without worrying about status or about pleasing the teacher or taking his or her time.

Computer-Mediated Writing

As with other language skills, computer technology has opened up new ways for teachers and students to process writing. To begin, many teachers and students now have access to e-mail, including chat rooms, and some teachers have made creative use of this technology. Nancy Krooenberg, for example, wanted to increase students' thinking and communicative writing skills by using chat room technology. She linked two classes of multinational students and involved them in a one-topic discussion through a chat-mode where students used the computer simultaneously to discuss the topic. She let students come up with a topic to discuss, after which she had them discuss the opposing sides to the issue.[14]

An activity the whole class can do is a chain-story activity in which the teacher e-mails a partial sentence, such as *It was a dark, stormy night and . . .* to one of the students in the class. Then, that student completes the line and begins a new one, then sends the e-mails to a classmate. The story continues to move from student to student until it is complete.[15]

Some teachers have students keep electronic portfolios of their writing. The content of the portfolios are often similar to traditional portfolios and include a variety of different writing by the student— short stories, letters, essays, book critiques, poetry, academic papers, jokes, dialogues, short plays. However, the electronic medium offers chances for students to add sound, images, video clips, graphics, or other multimedia.[16]

What Problems Do Some EFL/ESL Teachers Have as Writing Teachers?

Problems some EFL/ESL teachers face include the following:

- The "teaching the less-proficient writer" problem
- The "I can't write English" problem
- The "teacher response" problem
- The "Serving Generation 1.5 learners with their writing" problem

The "Teaching the Less-Proficient Writer" Problem

To teach less-proficient writers, it helps to identify how they process writing differently from the proficient writer.[17] Unlike proficient writers, less-proficient writers tend to jump right into the writing task without using prewriting strategies to generate ideas and organize thoughts. In addition, rather than quickly getting organized thoughts onto paper, they might take much time to write down their ideas, as well as focus primarily on surface level aspects of writing, struggling with form over meaning.

The Composing Behaviors of EFL/ESL Writers

Proficient Writers:
- Think about the task. Use a variety of prewriting strategies.
- Have a sense of audience. Will consider audience while composing.
- Once organized, get ideas onto paper quickly.
- At drafting stage, pay attention to meaning over form.
- Concerned with higher levels of meaning along with surface level.
- Will revise at all levels (word, sentence, paragraph, entire text).
- Will revise by adding, deleting, reordering ideas.
- Generate several drafts, each with some revision.

Less-Proficient Writers:
- Start off confused, without using prewriting strategies.
- Have vague or little awareness of audience.
- Take much time to get ideas onto paper.
- Work primarily at the sentence level, struggling with form.
- Concerned with vocabulary choice and sentence structure.
- Will revise primarily at the word and sentence level. Revise surface-level items (spelling, grammar, punctuation, etc.).
- Are bothered by confusion over revision. Tend to avoid adding, deleting, and reordering ideas.
- Revise primarily only the first draft.

Unlike proficient writers, less-proficient writers will revise primarily at the word and sentence level, using the revision process to edit grammar, syntax, spelling, and punctuation. Their revisions do not usually show many additions, deletions, substitutions, or reordering of ideas; when revision is done, it occurs primarily on the first draft. Perhaps this is because there is often confusion associated with revision, and unlike proficient writers, less-proficient writers seem to lack patience to work through the confusion in the process of clarifying meaning.

Understanding the writing behaviors of proficient and less-proficient writers is a start. The question then becomes how teachers can provide opportunities for less-proficient writers to improve their writing skills. We need to give less-proficient writers more of everything—"More time, more opportunity to talk, listen, read, and write; more instruction and practice in generating, organizing, and revising ideas; more attention to the rhetorical options available to them; and more emphasis on editing for linguistic form and style."[18] In short, we need to do more than simply take less-proficient writers through a process of producing a piece of writing. We also need to give our full attention to them, to show them how to plan a piece of writing through prewriting activities (discussed earlier in this chapter), how to draft and revise (discussed later in this chapter under The Teaching Response Problem), and how to edit their writing.

We can also create interesting and authentic writing challenges for them that include a real audience. If less-proficient writers lack audience awareness it's because the nature of the writing activities aren't authentic. Some students simply do not respond well to such artificial assignments, but they might respond differently to a real audience, such as a pen pal or newsletter readers.

The "I Can't Write English" Problem[19]

Some students simply do not like to write. In fact, I get some highly emotionally charged responses when I ask students how they feel about writing: "I really don't like to write. It's boring." "Writing is so difficult. I always feel my English is terrible. It make me sad." Such negative attitudes are problematic in EFL/ESL writing classrooms. When students believe they cannot write, or have a defeatist attitude toward writing, they disengage themselves from the writing process.

It is important for us, as teachers, to identify students who have negative attitudes toward writing. To do this, we "need to be researchers who observe, listen, and learn from students."[20] Talking to students informally about writing, listening to stories about their writing experiences and their views of themselves as writers, not only offers us knowledge about the student as writer but can make students more aware of themselves and their attitudes, possibly leading to change.

In addition, to explore ways to give students a more positive perspective about their writing, we can demystify the writing process. We can point out that no person's writing is perfect, that writing is often hard work, and that the point of writing is to express our ideas. To demystify the process, we can lead students through prewriting, drafting, and revising activities, and we can join them. We can let students read our drafts and revisions, including those that are partially developed. By doing this, students can see that writing is indeed a process of development that takes time and effort.

Another way to provide students with a positive perspective about their writing and themselves as writers is to ask them to put together a portfolio of their best writing. When students can see their best work together in one place, they often feel very good about themselves, even proud of their efforts. And we can reward students for doing their best to develop a piece of writing. One way to reward students is to have class members read each other's portfolios and recommend a piece of writing for a class "publication." When students see their writing in print, along with other writers, they quite often are delighted.

The "Teacher Response" Problem

Writing teachers often spend many hours reading and marking students' papers, offering revision suggestions and feedback on language errors. We correct, circle, underline, and write notes like "preposition problem." But students quite often do not pay attention to our comments and corrections. When what we do does not seem to work, or when we simply want to explore new ways of responding to students' work, we can try out alternative ways to respond to students' writing. In this section, I offer some of the ways that EFL/ESL writing teachers can respond to students' writing.

Writing teachers need to recognize if they treat an initial draft as if it were a final draft, applying a prescriptive, grammar-focused stance, the response is likely to fail. A grammar-focused teacher should respond to student drafts in ways that are appropriate to the development of a piece of writing. One way to do this is to require students to hand in two or three drafts of their writing. The teacher can then respond to each draft of writing in different ways.[21] For example, on some students' early drafts, the teacher can comment on how the students can revise their work, using such remarks as, "Did your topic change here? You need to add a transition." "What are ways to capture the reader's attention at the start of your essay?" and "I like the content of the five points. But try reordering them. See if you like the change." On a later draft, the teacher can respond to surface-level errors, such as grammatical, spelling, punctuation, and syntactical errors. It is worth pointing out that students say they appreciate and gain something from the teacher's responses, especially if these responses are clear in their intent.

In addition to written responses, teachers can work with students on developing their written work through one-to-one conferences. Teachers and students often point out the value of such conferences, especially when the teacher and student focus on specific aspects of the student's writing and the student has chances to negotiate meaning. One way to provide focus is to have the student prepare for the conference by writing questions, comments, and explanations before the conference. The teacher can also prepare by reading the student's draft before the conference while taking side notes on problems (e.g., with revision) that can be addressed during the conference. A way to encourage students to negotiate meaning is to let the student begin the conference (rather than the teacher) by describing what he or she wants to accomplish in the piece of writing and the noticeable problems in doing this. As the student talks, the teacher can paraphrase, thus providing a recognized version of what the student has said and a way for the student to reflect and discover new things in his or her writing. If the student does not react well to a paraphrasing approach, which is the case for some students, another way to engage the student in negotiation is through collaboration. For example, the teacher and student can take turns generating ways to revise the student's paper. The teacher might suggest the student rewrite the essay in first person, the student might suggest writing a new conclusion, the teacher might suggest that the student use the final paragraph to begin the essay, and so on. At any point in this turn-taking process, the student should feel free to ask questions, add details, and explore additional ideas.

Peer response groups offer another way for students to get feedback on their writing. Here is a set of procedures for conducting a peer-group response session.[22]

1. Provide students with guidelines.
2. Model appropriate responses to students' drafts.
3. Group students.
4. Have students photocopy essay drafts for group members.
5. Have students read each other's drafts. Have them write on the draft or complete a peer review sheet.
6. Have students discuss their peers' drafts.

Guidelines include advice for the draft reader and the author. "Do not quarrel with other readers' reactions," "Describe your reactions as you read the paper," and "Be specific by pointing to a particular item in the paper" provide necessary advice to the reader. Advice to the writer includes, "If you want comments on a specific part of your paper, ask for them"; "Listen carefully"; "Do not argue, reject, or justify"; and "Remember that comments from readers are only suggestions. This is your paper, and you make the final decisions about how to write it."

Providing a model can also help clarify what the students are expected to do. Some teachers show example drafts with specific written comments on an overhead projector, as well as have the whole class read and respond to the same draft of an essay. Peer response sheets are also useful. Since these sheets include questions about specific aspects of the essay, using them can provide a way for readers to give relevant feedback to writers. I provide an example of a peer review sheet I have used with university freshman ESL writers.

Although readers do not have to complete every item, I encourage them to do this, if for no other reason than to provide another option.

Peer Review Sheet

After reading the paper, complete the following sentences.

1. I think the best part of your paper is _____.
2. You could reorganize your ideas by _____.
3. I think you could change or omit _____.
4. I do not understand _____.
5. You could add _____.
6. You are good at _____.

I also provide another peer review sheet I have used for Student-to-Student Writing Conferences. This one includes more specific tasks for the readers.

Student-to-Student Writing Conferences

1. Pair up with a classmate. Take turns reading your own piece of writing aloud. Feel free to stop in the middle of reading to make fast changes or take notes.
2. Exchange papers. Read each other's writing silently.
3. Taking turns, each reader should summarize the other's writing in the following way:

    a. Tell quickly what you found to be the main idea, main feeling, or center of gravity.
    b. Summarize the piece into a single sentence.
    c. Choose one word from the writing that best summarizes it.

4. Each reader should write answers to these questions:

    a. Does the writer capture your attention? Why?
    b. Are the ideas well organized? How does the writer organize the ideas in the piece of writing?
    c. Are there words that seem powerful? Which words? Are there words that seem weak or repeated too often? Which words?

> d. Does the writer use transitions to go from one idea to the next idea? Can you identify them? Can the writer identify them for you?
> e. Does the piece of writing have paragraph development?
> f. Is there anything else to say about the piece of writing?

The "Serving Generation 1.5 Learners with Their Writing" Problem

Some ESL high school and university composition teachers in the United States have expressed frustration with teaching composition to Generation 1.5 students. Many of these long-term U.S. residents and English learners are fluent, even native-like in their use of spoken English, but they still have ESL-type language errors in their writing. Depending on their previous experiences with learning to compose in English, many have a rather negative attitude toward writing, believing that they will never master writing in English.

My response to those teachers who want to know how to work with Generation 1.5 learners is fairly basic and is based on my experience as a college composition teacher, as well as on the experiences of teachers who have taught 1.5 learners.[23]

1. Recognize that Generation 1.5 learners have long-term experience in the United States. Learn about what experience they have had in school and in their personal lives, including their cultural heritage.
2. Draw from their experience. Can you help them to tap into their cultural heritage? Include assignments that allow these 1.5 writers to draw on the familiar. (For example, many African cultures keep historical records through storytelling; many Hmong enjoy storytelling and song writing.)
3. Recognize that although the student's spoken English might sound close to a native speaker, the student likely does not have native-like intuition as a writer.
4. Work one-to-one with the student; conference with the student over his or her writing.[24]
5. Teach the student how to write; don't simply show the student how to get through an assignment. This means explaining the process of developing an essay through prewriting, composing, revising, and editing stages, as well as offering constructive feedback as the student works through the process.

6. Spend time working with the student on both grammar and rhetoric (for example, how to organize sections in an essay; how to make smooth transitions from one idea to the next).

TEACHER SELF-DEVELOPMENT TASKS

Talk Tasks

1. What do writing experts mean when they say, "writing is a recursive process of creating meaning"? Ask other teachers this question.
2. What activities do I suggest writing teachers use with beginning writers? Meet with another teacher. Add an additional three activities that a teacher might use to teach beginners.
3. Study the list of prewriting activities I suggest teachers use to provide a genuine writing experience for students. Which have you used, or which would you like to use? Find out what prewriting activities other teachers have used.
4. Study the kinds of activities I suggest teachers use to provide a genuine writing experience for students. Which have you used, or which would you like to use? Find out what activities other teachers use or would like to use.

Observation and Talk Tasks

1. Interview a writing teacher. Find out what his or her beliefs are about teaching students to write. Then observe his or her class. Are this teacher's beliefs reflected in the classroom writing activities?
2. Ask a writing teacher if you can observe his or her class. Take detailed descriptive notes that focus on the activities the teacher has students do in class. After the class, consider what you saw this teacher do that you would like to do in your own teaching.
3. Locate an EFL or ESL student. Ask this student to describe how he or she composes. It might help to ask, "How do you write an essay from beginning to end?" Keep the student talking by paraphrasing what he or she says, adding comments like "Very interesting! Tell me more!" and showing interest with facial and other nonverbal expressions. After talking with the student, consider what he or she told you. Does he or she consider the audience? Pay attention to expressing meaning in early drafts? Reorganize, delete, and add? Generate several drafts? Does the student see writing as a

developmental process? Interpret what the student said. Would you classify him or her as a proficient writer? What advice (if any) would you give to this writer?

Journal Writing Tasks

1. Write about you own experiences in learning to write. Did your teachers treat writing as a process of development? Why or why not?
2. Reflect on how you compose. Do you do the kinds of things writing experts say proficient writers do?
3. Write about your observation and interviewing experiences from doing the observation and talk tasks.

Recommended Teacher Resources

Recommended Writing Textbooks

Blanton, L. L., and L. Lee. *Composition Practice 1. 3ᵈ ed.* Boston: Heinle & Heinle, 2001. (High-beginner/Low-intermediate)

Ingram, B., and C. King. *From Writing to Composing: An Introductory Composition Course.* New York: Cambridge University Press, 2004. (High-beginner to Low-intermediate)

Leki, I. 1998. *Academic Writing: Exploring Processes and Strategies.* New York: Cambridge University Press, 1998. (Advanced)

Swales, J. M., and C. B. Feak. *Academic Writing for Graduate Students: Essential Skills and Tasks. 2ᵈ ed.* Ann Arbor: University of Michigan Press, 2004.

Withrow, J., G. Brookes, and M. C. Cummings. *Inspired to Write.* New York: Cambridge University Press, 2004. (High-intermediate/Advanced)

Resources on Teaching Writing

Burton, J., and M. Carroll, eds. *Journal Writing.* Alexandria, VA: TESOL, 2001.

Casanave, C. P. *Controversies in Second Language Writing: Dilemmas and Decisions in Research and Instruction.* Ann Arbor: University of Michigan Press, 2003.

DeLuca, G., L. Fox, M. A. Johnson, and M. Kogen, eds. *Dialogue on Writing: Rethinking ESL, Basic Writing, and First-Year Composition.* Mahwah, NJ: Lawrence Erlbaum, 2002.

Ferris, D. R. *Treatment of Error in Second Language Student Writing.* Ann Arbor: University of Michigan Press, 2002.

Goldstein, L. M. *Teacher Written Commentary in Second Language Writing Classrooms.* Ann Arbor: University of Michigan Press, 2005.

Kroll, B. "Considerations for Teaching an ESL/EFL Writing Course." In *Teaching English as a Second or Foreign Language, 3ᵈ ed.*, ed. M. Celce-Murcia, 210–32. Boston: Heinle & Heinle, 2001.

Leki, I. ed. *Academic Writing Programs*. Alexandria, VA: TESOL, 2001.

Liu, J., and J. G. Hansen. *Peer Response in Second Language Writing Classrooms*. Ann Arbor: University of Michigan Press, 2002.

Peregoy, S. E., and O. F. Boyle. *Reading, Writing and Learning in ELS: A Resource Book for K–12 Teachers*. 4th ed. Boston: Pearson Education, 2005.

White, R. V., ed. *New Ways in Teaching Writing*. Alexandria, VA: TESOL, 1995.

Endnotes

[1] A number of EFL/ESL writing researchers have addressed the recursive process that writers go through to create meaning. Among these researchers are Richards (1990), Raimes (1985), Zamel (1982, 1983), and Silva and Matsuda (2001).

[2] Olshtain (2001), Raimes (1983), and White (1995) describe and illustrate a number of activities for beginning EFL/ESL writers.

[3] I discovered this listing activity in Olshtain (2001).

[4] A number of EFL/ESL writing professionals agree that learning to write includes developing an effective nonlinear process. These professionals include DeLuca, et al. (2002), Kroll (2001), Raimes (1985), Silva and Matsuda (2001), and Zamel (1982, 1987).

[5] These prewriting strategies are discussed in Kroll (2001), Richards (1990), and Scarcella and Oxford (1992). The Sketching and Exploring the Senses activities are created out of my own experience as a writing teacher.

[6] Strategic questioning is discussed in Richards (1990).

[7] Freewriting was originally discussed by Elbow (1973).

[8] I created the Exploring the Senses prewriting activity while studying Neurolinguistic Programming (NLP). NLP offers a way to guide people through hypnotic trance states that can, with regard to prewriting, offer writers new ways to understand their own experience. Introductory books include Bandler and Grinder's *Patterns of the Hypnotic Techniques of Milton H. Erickson* (1975) and Lankton's *Practical Magic* (1980).

[9] These three ways to generate drafts are discussed in Scarcella and Oxford (1992).

[10] "Odd Tippling" by Kusenberg can be found in Lewis and Jungman's 1986 collection, *On Being Foreign: Culture Shock in Short Fiction*.

[11] A number of teachers have written about the use of dialogue journals. Pioneers include Dolly (1990), Peyton and Reed (1990), and Peyton (1993).

[12] Rinvolucri (1995) also explains how the teacher can write to groups rather than to each student.

[13] See Bromley (1995).

[14] See Krooenberg (1994–95).

[15] I have done chain-story activity in my composition classroom. Belisle (1996) reminds us that this activity can be done electronically as well.

[16] Kahtani (1999), whose ideas I use here, elaborates on the use of electronic portfolios.

[17] The characteristics I assign to less-proficient (and proficient) writers are based on research done by Lapp (1984), Raimes (1985), and Zamel (1983, 1983), as well as on my own experience. These characteristics are tentative and meant to be heuristic in nature, as it would be a mistake to over-generalize patterns of writing behavior based on our limited kowledge.

[18] See Raimes (1985, 248).

[19] Ideas in this section on the affective side of the writing process are also expressed by Thomas (1993).

[20] See Thomas (1993, 15).

[21] The idea of treating writing from a developmental point of view and responding to writing in ways appropriate to the development of the piece of writing is most convincingly made by Zamel (1985) and Ferris (1995, 2002).

[22] The procedures and guidelines I illustrate are based on my experience as a writing teacher and on those given by Nelson and Murphy (1992–93); also see Liu and Hansen (2002) for research and practical ideas on peer response in L2 contexts.

[23] I talked with several high school and college teachers who consistently work with K–12 learners and have read the work of experienced K–12 teachers. I especially draw from Freeman and Freeman (2003), Harklau (1999), and Thonus (2003), and I especially thank Agnes Malicka for sharing her experience with teaching Generation 1.5 learners.

[24] See Thonus (2003) for detailed suggestions about how to conference with Generation 1.5 students over their writing.

Appendixes

Appendix A
A Selection of Professional Journals

Annual Review of Applied Linguistics

Published annually, this journal provides a comprehensive, up-to-date review of research in key areas in the broad field of applied linguistics. Each issue is thematic, covering the topic by means of critical summaries, overviews, and bibliographic citations. Every fourth or fifth issue surveys applied linguistics broadly, offering timely essays on language learning and pedagogy.

Cambridge University Press
40 West 20th Street
New York, NY 10011-4211
800-872-7423
www.journals.cup.org

Applied Linguistics

This journal promotes principled and multidisciplinary approaches to research on language and language-related concerns by encouraging enquiry into the relationship between theoretical and practical studies. It publishes research in language with relevance to real-world problems.

Oxford University Press
2001 Evans Road
Cary, NC 27513
www.oup.com

Applied Psycholinguistics

Published quarterly, this journal includes articles on the psychological processes involved in language. Articles address the development, use, and impairment of language in all modalities, spoken and written, with a particular emphasis on cross-linguistic studies.

Cambridge University Press
40 West 20th Street
New York, NY 10011-4211
www.journals.cup.org

Asian EFL Journal

Published quarterly, this free electronic journal examines issues within the Asian EFL linguistic context and considers how traditional educational approaches are integrated with or contrasted against what is new in the field. It seeks new insights into key issues that are emerging and of contemporary interest.

www.asian-efl-journal.com

College ESL

Published biannually, this journal focuses on theory and practice in teaching ESL at the college level, especially to urban immigrant and refugee adults in college and pre-college settings.

Editor, *College ESL*
Instructional Resource Center
The City University of New York
535 East 80th Street
New York, NY 10021

Essential Teacher

Published quarterly, this journal focuses on practical experienced-based teaching ideas and reflection on teaching. Established in 2004, it offers short articles and columns aimed at an international audience. This journal is free with membership to TESOL (see Appendix B).

TESOL
700 South Washington Street, Suite 200
Alexandria, VA 22314
www.tesol.org

ELT Journal

Published quarterly by Oxford University Press in association with the British Council, this English language teaching journal maintains an international scope. Practical articles are written by experienced EFL/ESL teachers and teacher educators. Article titles, abstracts, and key concepts appear free online through the *ELT Journal* website.

> Journal Customer Service
> Oxford University Press
> 2001 Evans Road
> Cary, NC 27513
> *jnl.orders@oup.usa.org* (subscriptions)
> *http://eltj.oupjournals.org*

English for Specific Purposes Journal

Published three times each year, this journal includes articles that address language teaching and learning within specific contexts.

> Customer Service Department
> 6277 Sea Harbor Drive
> Orlando, FL 32887-4800
> *www.elsevier.com/locate/esp*

English Teaching Forum

Published quarterly, this journal includes practical articles on teaching EFL/ESL. Articles focus on the theory and practice of teaching English and include methods, techniques, and ideas useful in the classroom.

> *English Teaching Forum*
> U.S. Department of State, SA44
> 301 4th Street SW, Room 304
> Washington, DC 20547
> *orders@gpo.gov* (subscriptions)
> *http://exchanges.state.gov/forum*

Foreign Language Annals

Published six times each year by the American Council on the Teaching of Foreign Language (ACTFL), this journal serves the interests of teachers, administrators, and researchers in foreign language teaching.

Contributions:
Editor, C/O ACTFL
6 Executive Plaza
Yonkers, NY 10701-6801
headquarters@actfl.org
www.actfl.org

Hands-on English

Published six times a year, this periodical is specifically for teachers and tutors who want practical ideas for teaching ESL to adults.

Hands-on English
P.O. Box 256
Crete, NE 68333
www.handsonenglish.com

JALT Journal

Published semiannually by the Japan Association of Language Teachers, this journal includes research-oriented articles on teaching and learning EFL.

JALT Central Office
Urban Edge Bldg 5F
1-37-9 Taito, Taito-Ku
Tokyo, 110-0016
Japan
http://jalt-publications.org/jj/

Journal of Second Language Writing

Published quarterly, this journal includes articles on topics related to teaching writing in the second language classroom, especially theoretically grounded research reports on implications for teaching.

Publisher:
Elsevier Science Inc.
655 Avenue of the Americas
New York, NY 10010-5107
Editorial Office:
Ilona Leki
Journal of Second Language Writing
Department of English
301 McClung Tower
University of Tennessee
Knoxville, TN 37996-0430
www.jslw.org

Language Learning

Published quarterly in association with the University of Michigan (founding publisher), this academic journal publishes articles in applied linguistics and language learning.

Language Learning
Journal Customer Services
Blackwell Publishing
350 Main Street, Malden, MA 02148
subscrip@blackwellpublishing.com (subscription)
www.blackwellpublishing.com

The Modern Language Journal

Published quarterly, this journal promotes scholarly exchange among teachers and researchers of all modern foreign languages and SL. It publishes documented essays, quantitative and qualitative research studies, response articles, and editorials that challenge paradigms of language learning and teaching. The *Modern Language Journal Electronic Index 1916–1996* is available online.

Blackwell Publishing
350 Main Street
Malden, MA 02148
subscrip@bos.blackwellpublishing.com (subscriptions)
www.blackwellpublishing.com/journal.asp?ref = 0026-7902

PASAA

Published annually by Chulalongkorn University, this journal includes research and practical articles on teaching and learning English in Thai-speaking context.

> PASAA
> Department of Research
> Language Institute
> Chulalongkorn University
> Prem Burachat Building
> Phaya-Thai Road, Bangkok 10330
> Thailand

Prospect

Published three times per year by the National Centre for English Language Teaching and Research, this Australian journal of TESOL includes articles on applied linguistics and teaching concerns related to the adult ESL field.

> Sales and Marketing Manager
> NCELTR
> Macquarie University
> Sydney, NSW 2109
> Australia
> *www.nceltr.mq.edu.au/prospect/prospect.htm*

RELC Guidelines

Published twice a year by the South Asian Ministers of Education Organization (SEAMEO), this periodical provides a forum for EFL teachers to share their new ideas for language teaching with a wide audience of language teachers in Southeast Asia and other parts of the world.

> *RELC Guidelines*
> SEAMEO Regional Language Centre
> 30 Orange Grove Road
> Singapore 258352
> Republic of Singapore
> 65-6885-7830
> 65-6734-2753 (fax)
> *ceciliakong@relc.org.sg*
> *www.relc.org.sg/pub_frame.htm*

RELC Journal
Published three times per year by the South Asian Ministers of Education Organization (SEAMEO), this journal disseminates information and ideas on theories, research, methods, and materials related to language learning and teaching.

> *RELC Journal*
> SEAMEO Regional Language Centre
> 30 Orange Grove Road
> Singapore 258352
> Republic of Singapore
> 65-6885-7830
> 65-6734-2753 (fax)
> *www.relc.org.sg/pub_frame.htm*

Second Language Research
Published quarterly, this journal publishes theoretical and experimental papers concerned with second language acquisition and second language performance. It promotes interdisciplinary research which links acquisition studies to related non-applied fields such as neurolinguistic, theoretical linguistics, and first language developmental psycholinguistics.

> Hodder Arnold Journals
> 338 Euston Road
> London, NW1 3BH
> United Kingdom
> *www.secondlanguageresearch.com*

Studies in Second Language Acquisition
Published quarterly by Cambridge University Press, this journal includes articles related to second language acquisition and foreign language learning and teaching.

> Cambridge University Press
> 40 West 20th Street
> New York, NY 10011-4211
> 800-872-7423 or 212-924-3900
> *www.journals.cup.org*

System

Published quarterly, this international journal is devoted to the applications of educational technology and applied linguistics to problems of foreign language teaching and learning. Attention is paid to all languages and to problems associated with the study and teaching of ESL/EFL.

Elsevier Inc.
360 Park Avenue South
New York, NY 10010
212-989-5800
www.elsevier.com/wps/find

TESL Canada Journal

Published twice yearly, this journal is for practicing teacher educators, graduate students, and researchers. It includes articles concerning diverse aspects of the teaching and learning of ESL/EFL, including syllabus and curriculum design, testing and evaluation, psycholinguistics, applied linguistics, teacher training, and computer-assisted language learning.

TESL Canada
P.O. Box 44105
Burnaby, BC V5B 4Y2
Canada
www.tesl.ca/journal.html

TESL Reporter

Published quarterly, this journal has short practical articles on teaching and learning EFL/ESL.

Circulation Manager/*TESL Reporter*
BYU-H #1940
Laie, HI 96762
campbelm@byuh.edu (subscriptions)
http://w3.byuh.edu/academics/lang/teslr.htm

TESOL Quarterly

Published quarterly by TESOL, this journal represents contemporary thinking in the field and includes original research, reviews of research, and practical applications of theory and research to teaching EFL/ESL.

TESOL
700 South Washington Street, Suite 200
Alexandria, VA 22314
www.tesol.org

Appendix B
List of Publishers of Materials of Interest to EFL/ESL Teachers

This appendix lists selected publishers of EFL/ESL resources, including the addresses, telephone numbers, fax numbers, and/or websites of offices where further information and publication catalogs may be requested.

Alta Book Center Publishers
Alta Book Center
14 Adrian Court
Burlingame, CA 94010
800-258-2375; 650-692-1285
info@altaesl.com
www.altaesl.com

Berty Segal Cook, Inc.
1749 E. Eucalyptus
Brea, CA 92621
714-529-5359
714-529-3882 (fax)
bertysegal@sbcglobal.net
www.tprsource.com

Blackwell Publishing
P.O. Box 20
Williston, VT 05495
800-216-2522
802-864-7626 (fax)
www.Blackwellpublishing.com

The Brookings Institution Press
The Brookings Institution
1775 Massachusetts Avenue NW
Washington DC 20036
800-275-1447; 202-797-6000
202-797-6004 (fax)
bibooks@brookings.edu
www.brook.edu/press/books/ordform.htm

Cambridge University Press
40 West 20th Street
New York, NY 10011
800-872-7423; 212-924-3900
212-691-3239 (fax)
information@cup.org
www.cup.org

Delta Systems Co., Inc.
1400 Miller Parkway
McHenry, IL 60050-7030
800-323-8270; 815-363-3582
800-909-9901; 815-363-2948 (fax)
custsvc@delta-systems.com
www.delta-systems.com

ERIC Clearinghouse on Language and Linguistics
4646 40th Street, NW
Washington DC 20016-1859
202-362-0700; 800-276-9834
202-362-3740 (fax)
eric@cal.org
To subscribe to ERIC/CLL Language Link:
   join-langlink@caltalk.cal.org
www.cal.org/ericcll/ (Center for Applied Linguistics)

Georgetown University Press
3240 Prospect Street, NW
Washington DC 20007
202-687-5889
202-687-6340 (fax)
gupress@georgetown.edu
http://press.georgetown.edu/

Intercultural Press
P.O. Box 700
Yarmouth, ME 04096
866-372-2665; 207-846-5168
207-846-5781 (fax)
books@interculturalpress.com
www.interculturalpress.com/shop/index.html

Multilingual Matters
Frankfurt Lodge, Clevedon Hall
Victoria Road, Clevedon BS21 7HH
United Kingdom
+44 (0) 1275- 876519
+44 (0) 1275-871673 (fax)
info@multilingual-matters.com
www.multilingual-matters.com

Oxford University Press
ESL Department
198 Madison Ave
New York, NY 10016-6314
800-451-7556; 212-726-6000
cusserv.us@oup.com
www.oup-usa.org

Pearson Education ESL
Headquarters, Pearson Education
One Lake Street
Upper Saddle River, NJ 07458
201-236-7000
communications@pearsoned.com
www.pearsoned.com

Pro Lingua Associates
P.O. Box 1348
Brattleboro, VT 05302-1348
800-366-4775
802-257-5117 (fax)
Info@ProLinguaAssociates.com
www.prolinguaassociates.com

RELC (Regional English Language Centre, Southeast Asia)

SEAMEO Regional Language Centre
30 Orange Grove Road
Singapore 258352
Republic of Singapore
65-6885-7830
65-6734-2753 (fax)
ceciliakong@relc.org.sg
www.relc.org.sg/pub_frame.htm

TESOL (Teachers of English to Speakers of Other Languages)

700 South Washington Street, Suite 200
Alexandria, Virginia 22314
888-547-3369; 703-836-0774
703-836-7864/6447 (fax)
info@tesol.org
www.tesol.org

Thomson Heinle

20 Park Plaza
Boston, MA 02116
877-633-3375
www.heinle.com

The University of Michigan Press ESL

839 Greene Street
Ann Arbor, MI 48104
866-804-0002 (product help)
esladmin@umich.edu
www.press.umich.edu/esl/

Bibliography

Aebersold, J. A., and M. L. Field. *From Reader to Reading Teacher*. New York: Cambridge University Press, 1997.

Adler, P. S. "Culture Shock and the Cross-Cultural Learning Experience." In *Toward Internationalism*, eds. L. F. Luce and E. C. Smith. Rowley, MA: Newbury House, 1987.

Alderson, J. C. *Assessing Reading*. New York: Cambridge University Press, 2000.

Allen, M. *Teaching English with Video*. White Plains, NY: Longman, 1985.

Allen, P., M. Fröhlich, and N. Spada. "The Communicative Orientation of Language Teaching: An Observation Scheme." In *On TESOL '83*, eds. J. Handscombe, R. A. Orem, and B. P. Taylor, 231–52. Washington, DC: TESOL, 1984.

Allwright, D., and K. M. Bailey. *Focus on the Language Classroom*. Cambridge, UK: Cambridge University Press, 1991.

Alpert, R., and R. Haber. "Anxiety in Academic Achievement Situations." *Journal of Abnormal and Social Psychology* 61 (1960): 207–15.

Altman, H. B. "What Is Second Language Teaching?" In *The Second Language Classroom*, eds. J. E. Alatis, H. B. Altman, and P. M. Alatis, 5–19. New York: Oxford University Press, 1981.

Andersen, P. A. "In Different Dimensions: Nonverbal Communication and Culture." In *Intercultural Communication: A Reader*, eds. L. A. Samovar and R. E. Porter, 239–52. Belmont, CA: Wadsworth, 2003.

Anderson, A., and T. Lynch. *Listening*. Oxford: Oxford University Press, 1988.

Anderson, N. J. "Cognitive Styles and Multicultural Populations." *Journal of Teacher Education* 39 (1988): 2–9.

Arcario, P. "Post-Observation Conferences in TESOL Teacher Education Programs." Doctoral dissertation, Teachers College, Columbia University, 1994.

Asher, J. *Learning Another Language through Actions*. Los Gatos, CA: Sky Oaks, 1982.

Atkinson, J. M., and J. Hertiage, eds. *Structures of Social Action: Studies in Conversation Analysis*. Cambridge: Cambridge University Press, 1984.

Bailey, K. M. "Diary Studies in Teacher Education Programs." In *Second Language Teacher Education*, eds. J. C. Richards and D. Nunan, 215–26. New York: Cambridge University Press, 1990.

Bailey, K. M., A. Curtis, and D. Nunan. *Pursuing Professional Development.* Boston: Heinle & Heinle, 2001.

——. "Undeniable Insights: The Collaborative Use of Three Professional Development Practices." *TESOL Quarterly* 32, no. 3 (1998): 546–56.

Bailey, K. M., and D. Nunan, eds. *Voices from the Language Classroom.* New York: Cambridge University Press, 1996.

Bailey, K. M., and L. Savage, eds. *New Ways in Teaching Speaking.* Alexandria, VA: TESOL, 1994.

Bandler, R., and J. Grinder. *Patterns of the Hypnotic Techniques of Milton H. Erickson.* Cupertino, CA: Meta Publications, 1975.

Barnlund, D. C. *Public and Private Self in Japan and the United States.* Yarmouth, ME: Intercultural Press, 1975.

Barns, D. *From Communication to Curriculum.* Harmondsworth, UK: Penguin, 1975.

Becker, H. *Teaching ESL K–12: Views from the Classroom.* Boston: Heinle & Heinle, 2001.

Begley, P. A. "Sojourner Adaptation." In *Intercultural Communication: A Reader,* eds. L. A. Samovar and R. E. Porter, 406–11. Belmont, CA: Wadsworth, 2003.

Belisle, R. "E-Mail Activities in the ESL Writing Class." *The Internet TESL Journal* 2, no. 12 (1996). *www.aitech.ac.ip/~iteslj.*

Bèrubè, B. *Managing ESL Programs in Rural and Small Urban Schools.* Alexandria, VA: TESOL, 2000.

Bikowski, D., and G. Kessler. "Making the Most of Discussion Boards in the ESL Classroom." *TESOL Journal* 11, no. 3 (2002): 21–26.

Birch, B. M. *English L2 Reading.* Mahwah, NJ: Lawrence Erlbaum, 2002.

Bowen, D. J. H., H. Madsen, and A. Hilferty. *TESOL: Techniques and Procedures.* Rowley, MA: Newbury House, 1985.

Brandl, K. "Integrating Internet-Based Reading Materials into the Foreign Language Curriculum: From Teacher to Student-Centered Approaches." *Language Learning Technology* 6, no. 3 (2002): 87–107.

Breen, M., and C. N. Candlin. "The Essentials of Communicative Curriculum in Language Teaching." *Applied Linguistics* 1, no. 2 (1980): 89–112.

Breyer, P. P. *Grammar Work.* Englewood Cliffs, NJ: Prentice Hall, 1995.

Brinton, D., and C. Holten. "What Novice Teachers Focus On: The Practicum in TESL." *TESOL Quarterly* 23 (1989): 343–50.

Brinton, D. M. "The Use of Media in Language Teaching." In *Teaching English as a Second or Foreign Language,* ed. M. Celce-Murcia, 454–72. Boston: Heinle & Heinle, 1991.

Brislin, R. W., et al. *Intercultural Interactions: A Practical Guide.* Beverly Hills, CA: Sage Publications, 1986.

Brock, C. A. "The Effects of Referential Questions on ESL Classroom Discourse. *TESOL Quarterly* 20, no. 1 (1986): 47–59.

Bromley, K. "Buddy Journals for ESL and Native-English-Speaking Students." *TESOL Journal* 4, no. 3 (1995): 7–11.

Brown, G., and G. Yule. *Teaching the Spoken Language.* Cambridge: Cambridge University Press, 1983.

Brown, H. D. *Breaking the Language Barrier.* Yarmouth, ME: Intercultural Press, 1991.

———. *Principles of Language Learning and Teaching.* White Plains, NY: Longman, 2000.

Buddhadāsa, B. *Toward the Truth.* Philadelphia: Westminster Press, 1970.

Bueffel, E. G., and C. T. Hammett, prods. *It's Toddler Time.* Long Branch, NJ: Kimbo Educational Record, 1982.

Bullough, R. V., and K. Baughman. "Continuity and Change in Teacher Development: First Year Teachers after Five Years." *Journal of Teacher Education* 44, no. 2 (1993): 86–93.

Burns, A. "Collaborative Action Research and Curriculum Change in the Australian Adult Migrant English Program." *TESOL Quarterly* 30 (1996): 591–98.

———. *Collaborative Action Research for English Language Teachers.* Cambridge: Cambridge University Press, 1999.

Burns, A., and S. Hood, eds. *Teachers' Voices 2: Teaching Disparate Learner Groups.* Sydney, AUS: National Centre for English Language Teaching and Research, 1997.

Bygate, M. *Speaking.* Oxford: Oxford University Press, 1987.

Calderhead, J., ed. *Teachers' Professional Learning.* London: The Falmer Press, 1988.

Canale, M., and M. Swain. "Theoretical Bases of Communicative Approaches to Second Language Teaching and Testing." *Applied Linguistics* 1, no. 1 (1980): 1–47.

Carrell, P. L., J. Devine, and D. Eskey, eds. *Interactive Approaches to Second Language Reading.* New York: Cambridge University Press, 1988.

Carrell, P. L., and J. Eisterhold. "Schema Theory and ESL Reading Pedagogy." *TESOL Quarterly* 17 (1983): 553–73.

Celce-Murcia, M. "Teaching Pronunciation as Communication." In *Current Perspectives on Pronunciation,* ed. J. Morley, 1–12. Alexandria, VA: TESOL, 1987.

Celce-Murcia, M., and J. M. Goodwin. "Teaching Pronunciation." In *Teaching English as a Second or Foreign Language,* ed. M. Celce-Murcia, 136–53. Boston: Heinle and Heinle, 1991.

Chan, M. "Pronunciation Warm-Up." In *New Ways in Teaching Speaking,* eds. K. M. Bailey and L. Savage, 199–201. Alexandria, VA: TESOL, 1994.

Chanrungkanok, P. "A Naturalistic Study of Integration of Computer-Mediated Communication into Oral Discussion in an EFL College Classroom in Thailand." Doctoral dissertation, Indiana University of Pennsylvania, 2004.

Clarke, M. A. "On Bandwagons, Tyranny, and Common Sense." *TESOL Quarterly* 16, no. 4 (1982): 437–48.

———. *A Place to Stand: Essays for Educators in Troubled Times.* Ann Arbor: University of Michigan Press, 2003.

Clarke, M. A., and S. Silberstein. "Problems, Prescriptions, and Paradoxes in Second Language Teaching." In *Enriching ESOL Pedagogy,* eds. V. Zamel and R. Spack, 3–16. Mahwah, NJ: Lawrence Erlbaum, 2002.

Conrad, K. B., and T. Conrad. "Creating an ESL Computer-Mediated Class Memory Book." *TESOL Journal* 11, no. 3 (2002): 47–48.

Conrad, T. "An Exploration of Transformative Intercultural & Intracultural Interaction among Middle-School Students of a Dual Language Spanish/English Class." Doctoral dissertation, Indiana University of Pennsylvania, 2000.

Crandall, J. "They DO Speak English: World English in U.S. Schools." In *ERIC/CLL New Bulletin.* Washington, DC: ERIC Clearinghouse on Languages and Linguistics, 2003.

Crookes, G. "Action Research for Second Language Teachers: Going beyond Teacher Research." *Applied Linguistics* 14, no. 2 (1993): 130–44.

Crystal, D. *English as a Global Language. 2ᵈ ed.* Cambridge: Cambridge University Press, 2003.

Cummins, J. "Knowledge, Power, and Identity in Teaching English as a Second Language." In *Educating Second Language Children: The Whole Child, the Whole Curriculum, the Whole Community,* ed. F. Genesee, 33–58. New York: Cambridge University Press, 1994.

Curran, C. *Counseling-Learning in Second Languages.* Apple River, IL: Apple River Press, 1976.

———. *Understanding: A Necessary Ingredient in Human Belonging.* Apple River, IL: Apple River Press, 1978.

Day, R. R. *New Ways in Teaching Reading.* Alexandria, VA: TESOL, 1993.

Day, R. R., and J. Bamford. *Extensive Reading in the Second Language Classroom.* New York: Cambridge University Press, 1998.

DeLuca, G., et al., eds. *Dialogue on Writing: Rethinking ESL, Basic Writing, and First-Year Composition.* Mahwah, NJ: Lawrence Erlbaum, 2002.

Dobbs, J. *Using the Board in the Language Classroom.* New York: Cambridge University Press, 2001.

Doi, T. *The Anatomy of Dependence.* Tokyo: Kodansha International, 1973.

Dolly, M. R. "Adult ESL Students' Management of Dialogue Journal Conversation." *TESOL Quarterly* 24, no. 2 (1990): 317–21.

Duncan, J. *Technology Assisted Teaching Techniques.* Brattleboro, VT: Pro Lingua Associates, 1987.

Dwyer, M. A. "Creating and Sustaining Change for Immigrant Learners in Secondary Schools." *TESOL Journal* 7, no. 5 (1998): 6–11.

Edge, J. *Continuing Cooperative Development: A Discourse Framework for Individuals as Colleagues.* Ann Arbor: University of Michigan Press, 2002.

Eisenman, G., and H. Thornton. "Telementoring: Helping New Teachers through the First Year." *T.H.E. Journal* 26, no. 9 (1999): 79–82.

Elbow, P. *Writing without Teachers.* New York: Oxford University Press, 1973.

Esbenshade, E. "My Learning through Journaling: Forgiveness as a Source of Power and the Communication of Voice in the Classroom." In *Teachers' Inquiry as Professional Development,* eds. K. E. Johnson and P. G. Golombek, 108–17. New York: Cambridge University Press, 2002.

Eskey, D. "Theoretical Foundations." In *Teaching Second Language Reading for Academic Purposes,* eds. F. Dubin, D. Eskey, and W. Grabe, 3–23. Reading, MA: Addison-Wesley, 1986.

Fanselow, J. F. "Beyond Rashomon: Conceptualizing and Observing the Teaching Act." *TESOL Quarterly* 11, no. 1 (1977a): 17–41.

———. *Breaking Rules: Generating and Exploring Alternatives in Language Teaching.* White Plains, NY: Longman, 1987.

———. *Contrasting Conversations: Activities for Exploring Our Beliefs and Teaching Practices.* White Plains, NY: Longman, 1992a.

———. "Let's See: Contrasting Conversations about Teaching." *TESOL Quarterly* 22, no. 1 (1988): 113–30.

———. "Over and Over Again." In *GURT '83: Applied Linguistics and the Preparation of Second Language Teachers: Toward a Rationale,* eds. J. E. Alatis, H. H. Stern, and P. Strevens, 168–76. Washington, DC: Georgetown University Press, 1983.

———. "Postcard Realities." In *On Becoming a Language Educator: Personal Essays on Professional Development,* eds. C. P. Casanave and S. R. Schecter, 157–72. Mahwah, NJ: Lawrence Erlbaum, 1997.

———. "The Treatment of Error in Oral Work." *Foreign Language Annals* 10 (1977b): 583–93.

———. *Try the Opposite.* Tokyo: Simul, 1992b.

Farrell, T. S. C. "Anxiety: The Hidden Variable in the Korean EFL Classroom." *Language Teaching* 1, no. 1 (1993): 16–18.

———. "ESL/EFL Teacher Development through Journal Writing." *RELC Journal* 29, no. 1 (1998): 92–109.

———. "Exploring Teaching in the PAC Journal." *The PAC Journal* 1, no. 1 (2000): 1–5.

———. *Reflecting on Classroom Communication in Asia.* White Plains, NY: Longman, 2004.

Ferguson, C. "Toward a Characterization of English Foreigner Talk." *Anthropological Linguistics* 17, no. 1 (1975): 1–14.

Ferris, D. "Student Reactions to Teacher Response in Multiple-Draft Composition Classrooms." *TESOL Quarterly* 29 (1995): 33–53.

———. *Treatment of Error in Second Language Student Writing.* Ann Arbor: University of Michigan Press, 2002.

Fieg, J. P. *A Common Core: Thais and Americans.* Yarmouth, ME: Intercultural Press, 1989.

Flaitz, J., ed. *Understanding Your International Students: An Educational, Cultural, and Linguistic Guide.* Ann Arbor: University of Michigan Press, 2003.

Folse, K. S. *Clear Grammar 1: Activities for Spoken and Written Communication.* Ann Arbor: University of Michigan Press, 1998.

——. "Minimal Pairs." In *New Ways in Teaching Speaking*, eds. S. Stempleski and P. Arcario, 79–92. Alexandria, VA: TESOL, 1994.

Forest, T. "Shooting Your Class: The Videodrama Approach to Language Acquisition." In *Video in Second Language Teaching*, eds. S. Stempleski and P. Arcario. Alexandria, VA: TESOL, 1992.

Frake, C. *Language and Cultural Description*. Stanford: Stanford University Press, 1980.

Freeman, Y., and D. Freeman. "Struggling English Language Learners: Keys to Academic Success." *TESOL Journal* 12, no. 3 (2003): 5–10.

Freiermuth, M. R. "Internet Chat: Collaborating and Learning via E-Conversations." *TESOL Journal* 11, no. 3 (2002): 36–40.

——. "Native Speakers or Non-Native Speakers: Who Has the Floor? On-line and Face-to-Face Interaction in Culturally Mixed Small Groups." *Computer Assisted Language Learning* 14, no. 2 (2001): 169–99.

——. "Using a Chat Program to Promote Group Equity." *CA ELL Journal* 2 (1998): 16–24.

Freund, B. "Young Radio Amateurs Speak English." *English Teachers Journal* 51 (1997): 70–71.

Fuller, F. F. "Concerns of Teachers: A Developmental Characterization." *American Educational Research Journal* 6 (1969): 207–26.

Fuller, F. F., and O. H. Bown. "Becoming a Teacher." In *Teacher Education: The Seventy-Fourth Yearbook of the National Society for the Study of Education*, ed. K. Ryan, 25–51. Chicago: The National Society for the Study of Education, 1975.

Galavis, B. "Computer and the EFL Class: Their Advantages and Possible Outcome, the Autonomous Learner." *English Teaching Forum* 36, no. 4 (1998): 1–27.

Garber, C. A., and G. Holmes. "Video-Aided Written/Oral Assignments." *Foreign Language Annals* 14 (1981): 325–31.

Gebhard, J. G. "Awareness of Teaching through Action Research: Examples, Benefits, Limitations." *JALT Journal* 27, no. 1 (2005b): 53–69.

——. "Awareness of Teaching: Approaches, Benefits and Tasks." *English Teaching Forum* 30, no. 4 (1992): 2–7.

——. "The Cyclic Process of Action Research." *Thai TESOL Forum* 15, no. 3 (2002): 20–23.

——. "Interaction in a Teaching Practicum." In *Second Language Teacher Education*, eds. J. C. Richards and D. Nunan, 118–31. New York: Cambridge University Press, 1990.

——. "Seeing Teaching Differently: The Teacher as Observer." *The Language Teacher* 15, no. 5 (1991): 17–20.

——. "Teacher Development through Exploration: Principles and Activities." *TESOL-EJ* 10, no. 4 (2005a).

——. "Teaching Reading through Assumptions about Learning." *English Teaching Forum* 23, no. 3 (1985): 16–20.

Gebhard, J. G., and A. Ueda-Motonaga. "The Power of Observation: Make a

Wish, Make a Dream, Imagine All the Possibilities." In *Collaborative Language Learning and Teaching,* ed. D. Nunan, 178–91. Cambridge: Cambridge University Press, 1992.

Gebhard, J. G., J. M. Fodor, and M. Lehmann. "Teacher Development through Exploration: Principles, Processes, and Issues in Hungary." In *Studies in English Theoretical and Applied Linguistics,* eds. J. Andor, J. Horvàth, and M. Nikolov, 250–61. Pècs, HUN: Lingua Franca Csoport, 2003.

Gebhard, J. G., and R. Oprandy. *Language Teaching Awareness: A Guide to Exploring Beliefs and Practices.* New York: Cambridge University Press, 1999.

Gebhard, J. G., S. Gaitan, and R. Oprandy. "Beyond Prescription: The Student Teacher as Investigator." *Foreign Language Annals* 20, no. 3 (1987): 227–32.

Gee, J. P. *An Introduction to Discourse Analysis: Theory and Method.* New York: Routledge, 1999.

Gibson, R. "The Strip Story: A Catalyst for Communication." *TESOL Quarterly* 9 (1975): 149–54.

Gilbert, J. "Intonation: A Navigation Guide for the Listener." In *Pronunciation Pedagogy and Theory: New Views, New Directions,* ed. J. Morley, 36–48. Alexandria, VA: TESOL, 1994.

———. "Nonverbal Tools for Teaching Pronunciation." University of California, Davis, n.d. Photocopy.

———. "Pronunciation and Listening Comprehension." In *Current Perspectives on Pronunciation,* ed. J. Morley, 29–40. Alexandria, VA: TESOL, 1987.

Good, T. L., and J. E. Brophy. *Looking into Classrooms.* New York: Harper & Row, 1987.

Goodwin, J. "Teaching Pronunciation." In *Teaching English as a Second and Foreign Language, 3d ed.,* ed. M. Celce-Murcia, 117–37. Boston: Heinle & Heinle, 2001.

Grabe, W. "Dilemmas for Development of Second Language Reading Abilities." In *Methodology in Language Teaching,* eds. J. C. Richards and W. A. Renandya, 276–86. New York: Cambridge University Press, 2002.

Graham, C. *Children's Jazz Chants: Old and New.* New York: Oxford University Press, 2002.

———. *Holiday Jazz Chants.* New York: Oxford University Press, 1999.

———. *Jazz Chants.* New York: Oxford University Press, 1978.

———. *Jazz Chants: Old and New.* New York: Oxford University Press, 2003.

Greene, M. *Teacher as Stranger: Educational Philosophy for the Modern Age.* Belmont, CA: Wadsworth, 1973.

Greenfield, R. "Minimal Pairs with Street Names." In *New Ways in Teaching Speaking,* eds. K. M. Bailey and L. Savage, 218–19. Philadelphia, PA: John Benjamins, 1994.

Grellet, F. *Developing Reading Skills: A Practical Guide to Reading Comprehension Exercises.* New York: Cambridge University Press, 1981.

Hall, E. T. *The Silent Language*. New York: Anchor Books, 1966.

Halliday, M. A. K., and R. Hasan. *Cohesion in English*. London: Longman, 1976.

Harklau, L. "ESL versus Mainstream Classes: Contrasting L2 Learning Environments." In *Enriching ESOL Pedagogy*, eds. V. Zamel and R. Spack, 127–57. Mahwah, NJ: Lawrence Erlbaum, 2002.

Harklau, L., K. M. Losey, and M. Siegal, eds. *Generation 1.5 Meets College Composition: Issues in Teaching of Writing to U.S.-Educated Learners of English*. Mahwah, NJ: Lawrence Erlbaum, 1999.

Harsch, K. "Paraphrasing Races." In *New Ways in Teaching Speaking*, eds. K. M. Bailey and L. Savage, 97–98. Alexandria, VA: TESOL, 1994.

Hebert, J. "PracTESOL: It's Not What You Say, but How You Say It!" In *Methodology in Language Teaching: An Anthology of Current Practice*, eds. J. C. Richards and W. A. Renandya, 188–200. New York: Cambridge University Press, 2002.

Hector-Mason, A. "Cultural Processes and Cultural Learning Experiences: How Hispanic ESL Adults Adjust to Life in a Small Central Texas Town." Doctoral dissertation, Indiana University of Pennsylvania, 2004.

Heinze, R. I. *Tham Khwan: How to Contain the Essence of Life*. Kent Ridge, SGP: Singapore University Press, 1982.

Helgesen, M. "Creating Active Effective-Listeners." *Language Teacher* 17, no. 8 (1993): 13–14.

Henrichsen, L. *Distance Learning Programs*. Alexandria, VA: TESOL, 2001.

Henrichsen, L., et al. *Pronunciation Matters: Communicative, Story-Based Activities for Mastering the Sounds of North American English*. Ann Arbor: University of Michigan Press, 1999.

Higgins, C. "Ownership of English in the Outer Circle: An Alternative to the NS-NNS Dichotomy." *TESOL Quarterly* 37, no. 4 (2003): 615–44.

Hoffer, B. L. "English Sociokinesics." *Die Neueren Sprachen* 83, no. 5 (1984): 544–54.

Holten, C. A., and D. M. Brinton. "You Shoulda Been There: Charting Novice Teacher Growth Using Dialogue Journals." *TESOL Journal* 4, no. 4 (1995): 23–26.

Hull, G., et al. "Remediation as Social Construct: Perspectives from an Analysis of Classroom Discourse." In *Enriching ESOL Pedagogy*, eds. V. Zamel and R. Spack, 159–91. Mahwah, NJ: Lawrence Erlbaum, 2002.

Hymes, D. "On Communicative Competence." In *Sociolinguistics: Selected Readings*, eds. J. Pride and J. Holmes. Harmondsworth, UK: Penguin, 1972.

———. "Competence and Performance in Linguistic Theory." In *Language Acquisition: Models and Methods*, eds. R. Huxley and E. Ingram. London: Academic Press, 1971.

Isbell, K., and J. Reinhardt. "Web Integration: A Model for Task-Based Learning." In *Technology-Enhanced Learning Environments*, ed. E. Hanson-Smith, 45–55. Alexandria, VA: TESOL, 2000.

Jersild, A. T. *When Teachers Face Themselves*. New York: Teachers College Press, 1955.

Johnson, K. E. "Learning to Teach: Instructional Actions and Decisions of Preservice ESL Teachers." *TESOL Quarterly* 26 (1992): 507–34.

———. "Portfolio Assessment in Second Language Teacher Education." *TESOL Journal* 6, no. 2 (1996): 11–14.

Johnson, K. E., and P. R. Golombek. *Teachers' Narrative Inquiry as Professional Development*. New York: Cambridge University Press, 2002.

Jones, R. H. "Beyond 'Listen and Repeat': Pronunciation Teaching Materials and Theories of Second Language Acquisition." In *Methodology in Language Teaching: An Anthology of Current Practice*, eds. J. C. Richards and W. A. Renandya, 178–87. New York: Cambridge University Press, 2002.

Jung, S. K., and B. Norton. "Language Planning in Korea: The New Elementary English Program." In *Language Policies in Education: Critical Issues*, ed. W. Tollefson. Mahwah, NJ: Lawrence Erlbaum, 2002.

Kachru, B. *The Alchemy of English*. Oxford: Pergamon Press, 1989.

———. "Teaching World Englishes." *Indiana Journal of Applied Linguistics* 15, no. 1 (1986): 85–95.

Kahtani, S. "Electronic Portfolios in ESL Writing: An Alternative Approach." *Computer Assisted Language Learning* 12, no. 3 (1999): 261–68.

Kajornboon, B. "Video in the Language Class." *PASAA* 19, no. 1 (1989): 41–52.

Kitao, K. "Using Authentic Video Materials in the Language Classroom." *Cross Currents* 12, no. 2 (1986): 17–28.

Klausner, W. J. *Reflections on Thai Culture*. Bangkok, THA: The Siam Society, 1983.

Klippel, F. *Keep Talking: Communicative Fluency Activities for Language Teaching*. New York: Cambridge University Press, 1984.

Kluge, D. E. "Your Turn at the Mike." In *New Ways in Teaching Reading*, ed. R. R. Day, 9–11. Alexandria, VA: TESOL, 1993.

Ko, K. S. "Gumkmin Hakgyo Yeong-eo Gyoyuk-ui Segyejeok Donghyang-gwa Geugwaje" ("The Trend of Primary English Education in the World and the Issues"). *English Teaching* 46 (1993): 165–87.

Korean Ministry of Education. *Chodeung Hakgyo Yeong-eo Gyoyuk Jeongchaek Jaryojip (The English Education Policies in Elementary Schools)*. Seoul, KOR: Ministry of Education, 1997.

Krashen, S. D. "Do We Learn by Reading? The Relationship between Free Reading and Reading Ability." In *Linguistics in Context: Connecting Observation and Understanding*, ed. D. Tannon, 269–98. Norwood, NJ: Ablex, 1988.

———. *The Input Hypothesis: Issues and Implications*. New York: Longman, 1985.

———. *The Power of Reading: Insights from the Research.* Englewood, CO: Libraries Unlimited, 1993.

———. *Principles and Practice in Second Language Acquisition.* Oxford: Pergamon, 1982.

Krashen, S. D., and T. Terrell. *The Natural Approach: Language Acquisition in the Classroom.* Oxford: Pergamon Press, 1983.

Kroll, B. "Considerations for Teaching an ESL/EFL Writing Course." In *Teaching English as a Second or Foreign Language, 3d ed.*, ed. M. Celce-Murcia, 219–32. Boston: Heinle & Heinle, 2001.

Kroonenberg, N. "Developing Communicative and Thinking Skills via Electronic Mail." *TESOL Journal* 4 (1994–1995): 24–27.

Kusenberg, K. "Odd Tippling." In *On Being Foreign: Culture Shock in Short Fiction*, eds. T. Lewis and R. Jungman, 51–53. Yarmouth, ME: Intercultural Press, 1986.

Lankton, S. *Practical Magic: A Translation of Basic Neuro-Linguistic Programming into Clinical Psychotherapy.* Cupertino, CA: Meta Publications, 1980.

Lapp, R. E. "The Process Approach to Writing: Toward a Curriculum for International Students." University of Hawaii at Manoa, 1984. Working Papers, ESL Department.

Larsen-Freeman, D. *Techniques and Principles in Language Teaching. 2d ed.* New York: Oxford University Press, 2003.

Lessow-Hurley, J. *The Foundations of Dual Language Instruction.* White Plains, NY: Longman, 1996.

Lewis, T. J., and R. E. Jungman. *On Being Foreign: Culture Shock in Short Fiction.* Yarmouth, ME: Intercultural Press, 1986.

Lieberman, A. Foreword to *Contrasting Conversations: Activities for Exploring Our Beliefs and Teaching Practices*, by J. F. Fanselow. White Plains, NY: Longman, 1992.

Littlewood, W. *Communicative Language Teaching.* Cambridge: Cambridge University Press, 1981.

Liu, J., and J. G. Hansen. *Peer Response in Second Language Writing Classrooms.* Ann Arbor: University of Michigan Press, 2002.

Lonergan, J. *Video in Language Teaching.* Cambridge: Cambridge University Press, 1984.

Long, M. "Teacher Feedback on Learner Error: Mapping Cognitions." In *On TESOL 77*, eds. H. D. Brown, C. Yorio, and R. H. Crymes, 278–94. Alexandria, VA: TESOL, 1977.

Long, M. L., and C. Sato. "Classroom Foreigner Talk Discourse: Forms and Functions of Teachers' Questions." In *Classroom Oriented Research in Second Language Acquisition*, eds. H. Seliger and M. Long, 268–86. Rowley, MA. Newbury House, 1983.

Lorayne, H., and J. Lucas. *The Memory Book.* New York: Dorset Press, 1974.

Maley, A., and A. Duff. *Drama Techniques in Language Learning.* New York: Cambridge University Press, 1982.

Manivat, V. *Kukrit Prajoj: His Wit and Wisdom.* Bangkok, THA: Editions Duang Kamol, 1983.

Marshall, T. *The Whole World Guide to Language Learning.* Yarmouth, ME: Intercultural Press, 1989.

Marzio, M. "Getting 'Real' with Video and CD-ROM: Real English at the Marzio School." In *Technology-Enhanced Learning Environments,* ed. E. Hanson-Smith, 67–81. Alexandria, VA: TESOL, 2000.

Maurice, K., K. Vanikieti, and S. Keyuravong. "Putting Up a Reading Board and Cutting Down the Boredom." *English Teaching Forum* 27, no. 2 (1989): 29–31.

McCoy, L. R. "Means to Overcome the Anxieties of Second Language Learners." *Foreign Language Annals* 12, no. 3 (1979): 185–89.

McDaniel, E. R. "Japanese Nonverbal Communication: A Reflection of Themes." In *Intercultural Communication: A Reader, 10th ed.,* eds. L. A. Samovar and R. E. Porter, 253–61. Belmont, CA: Wadsworth, 2003.

McKay, I. S. *Beginning Interaction Grammar.* Boston: Heinle & Heinle, 1993.

McKay, S. L. *Teaching English Overseas: An Introduction.* New York: Oxford University Press, 1992.

Melamed, L., and D. Barndt. "Exercises Focusing on Non-Verbal Communication." *TESL Talk* 8, no. 4 (1977): 31–38.

Melvin, B. S., and D. F. Stout. "Motivating Language Learners through Authentic Materials." In *Interactive Language Teaching,* ed. W. Rivers, 44–56. New York: Cambridge University Press, 1987.

Migliacci, N. "New Ways of Using Video Technology in English Language Teaching." *ESL Magazine* 5, no. 3 (2002): 22–24.

Moore, C. G. *Heart Talk.* Bangkok, THA: White Lotus, 1992.

Morely, J. "Aural Comprehension Instruction: Principles and Practices." In *Teaching English as a Second or Foreign Language, 3d ed.,* ed. M. Celce-Murcia, 69–86. Boston: Heinle & Heinle, 2001.

———. "The Pronunciation Component in Teaching English to Speakers of Other Languages." *TESOL Quarterly* 25 (1991): 481–520.

———, ed. *Current Perspectives on Pronunciation.* Alexandria, VA: TESOL, 1987.

———. *Pronunciation Pedagogy and Theory: New Views, New Directions.* Alexandria, VA: TESOL, 1994.

Mulder, N. *Thai Images: The Culture of the Public World.* Bangkok, THA: Silkworm Books, 1997.

Murphy, J. M. "Reflective Teaching in ELT." In *Teaching English as a Second or Foreign Language, 3d ed.,* ed. M. Celce-Murcia, 499–514. Boston: Heinle & Heinle, 2001.

Nash, R. J., and D. A. Shiman. "The English Teacher as Questioner." *English Journal* 63 (1974): 38–44.

Nelson, G. L., and J. M. Murphy. "Writing Groups and the Less Proficient ESL Student." *TESOL Journal* 2, no. 2 (1992–1993): 23–25.

Nicholson, P., and R. Sakuno. *Explain Yourself: An English Conversation Book for Japan.* Kyoto, JPN: PAL, 1982.

Numrich, C. "On Becoming a Language Teacher: Insights from Diary Studies." *TESOL Quarterly* 30, no. 1 (1996): 131–53.

Nunan, D. *Language Teaching Methodology: A Textbook for Teachers.* Hertfordshire, UK: Prentice Hall, 1991.

——. *The Learner-Centered Curriculum.* New York: Cambridge University Press, 1988.

——. "Listening in Language Learning." In *Methodology in Language Teaching: An Anthology of Current Practice,* eds. J. C. Richards and W. A. Renandya, 238–41. New York: Cambridge University Press, 2002.

——. "The Teacher as Decision-Maker." In *Perspectives on Second Language Teacher Education,* eds. J. Flowerdew, M. Brock, and S. Hsia, 135–65. Kowloon, HKG: City Polytechnic of Hong Kong, 1992.

Nydell, M. K. *Understanding Arabs: A Guide for Westerners.* Yarmouth, ME: Intercultural Press, 1987.

——. *Understanding Arabs: A Guide for Westerners.* 2d ed. Yarmouth, ME: Intercultural Press, 2002.

Ogami, N., prod. *Cold Water.* Yarmouth, ME: Intercultural Press, 1988. Videotape.

Ohta, K. "Cultural and Personal Aspects of Language Learning Anxiety: A Case Study of Seven Japanese Individuals' Reflective Accounts of Language Learning Anxiety." Doctoral dissertation, Indiana University of Pennsylvania, 2004.

Olshtain, E. "Functional Tasks for Mastering the Mechanics of Writing and Going Just Beyond." In *Teaching English as a Second or Foreign Language, 3d ed.,* ed. M. Celce-Murcia, 207–18. Boston: Heinle & Heinle, 2001.

Ovando, C. J., and V. P. Cullier. *Bilingual and ESL Classrooms: Teaching in Multicultural Contexts.* New York: McGraw Hill, 1985.

Oxford, R. "Anxiety and the Language Learner." In *Affect in Language Learning,* ed. J. Arnold, 58–67. New York: Cambridge University Press, 1999.

——. *Language Learning Strategies: What Every Teacher Should Know.* Boston: Heinle & Heinle, 1990.

Papalia, A. "Interaction of Reader and Text." In *Interactive Language Teaching,* ed. W. Rivers, 70–82. New York: Cambridge University Press, 1987.

Pearson-Hamatani, E. P. "Without a Dictionary." In *New Ways in Teaching Reading,* ed. R. R. Day, 217–18. Alexandria, VA: TESOL, 1993.

Pennington, M. C. "Teaching Pronunciation from the Top Down." *RELC Journal* 20, no. 1 (1989): 20–38.

——, ed. *New Ways in Teaching Grammar.* Alexandria, VA: TESOL, 1995.

Pennington, M. C., and J. C. Richards. "Pronunciation Revisited." *TESOL Quarterly* 20 (1986): 207–25.

Peregoy, S., and O. F. Boyle. *Reading, Writing and Learning in ESL: A Resource Book for K–12 Teachers.* 4*th* ed. New York: Pearson, 2005.

Peterson, P. W. "Skills and Strategies for Proficient Listening." In *Teaching English as a Second or Foreign Language,* ed. M. Celce-Murcia, 87–100. Boston: Heinle & Heinle, 2001.

Peyton, J. K. "Dialogue Journals: Interactive Writing to Develop Language and Literacy." *ERIC Digest,* April 1993.

Peyton, J. K., and L. Reed. *Dialogue Journal Writing with Nonnative English Speakers: A Handbook for Teachers.* Alexandria, VA: TESOL, 1990.

Platt, J., H. Weber, and H. M. Lian. *The New Englishes.* London: Routledge and Kegan Paul, 1984.

Porter, D., and J. Roberts. "Authentic Listening Activities." In *Methodology in TESOL,* eds. M. L. Long and J. C. Richards, 177–87. Rowley, MA: Newbury House, 1987.

Purnell, D. "Cultural and Language Adjustment Processes of Taiwanese Students at a Small, Midwestern College." Doctoral dissertation, Indiana University of Pennsylvania, 2000.

Raimes, A. *Techniques in Teaching Writing.* New York: Oxford University Press, 1983.

———. "What Unskilled ESL Students Do as They Write: A Classroom Study of Composing." *TESOL Quarterly* 19 (1985): 229–58.

Rathet, I. "English by Drawing: Making the Language Lab a Center of Active Learning." *TESOL Journal* 3, no. 3 (1994): 22–25.

Reid, J. M. "The Learning Style Preferences of ESL Students." *TESOL Quarterly* 21, no. 1 (1987): 87–111.

———. *Learning Styles in the ESL/EFL Classroom.* Boston: Heinle & Heinle, 1995.

Reynolds, J. "Video Jigsaw." *TESOL Journal* 10, no. 4 (2001): 28–29.

Richard-Amato, P. A. *Making It Happen.* White Plains, NY: Longman, 2003.

Richards, J. C. "Beyond the Textbook: The Role of Commercial Materials in Language Teaching." *RELC Journal* 24, no. 1 (1993): 1–14.

———. *Beyond Training.* New York: Cambridge University Press, 1998.

———. *The Language Teaching Matrix.* New York: Cambridge University Press, 1990.

Richards, J. C., and B. Ho. "Reflective Thinking through Journal Writing." In *Beyond Training,* eds. J. C. Richards, 153–70. New York: Cambridge University Press, 1998.

Richards, J. C., B. Li, and A. Tang. "Exploring Pedagogical Reasoning Skills. In *Beyond Training,* ed. J. C. Richards, 86–102. New York: Cambridge University Press, 1998.

Richards, J. C., and C. Lockhart. *Reflective Teaching in Second Language Classrooms.* New York: Cambridge University Press, 1994.

Richard, J. C., J. Platt, and H. Platt. *Longman Dictionary of Language Teaching and Applied Linguistics.* 3*d* ed. White Plains, NY: Pearson-Longman, 2003.

Richards, J. C., and T. Rodgers. *Approaches and Methods in Language Teaching. 2ᵈ ed.* New York: Cambridge University Press, 2001.

Richards, J. C., and W. A. Renandya, eds. *Methodology in Language Teaching: An Anthology of Current Practice.* New York: Cambridge University Press, 2002.

Riggenbach, H. *Discourse Analysis in the Language Classroom. Volume 1: The Spoken Language.* Ann Arbor: University of Michigan Press, 1999.

Rinvolucri, M. *Grammar Games.* Cambridge: Cambridge University Press, 1984.

———. "Language Students as Letter Writers." *ELT Journal* 49 (1995): 152–59.

Rivers, W., ed. *Interactive Language Teaching.* New York: Cambridge University Press, 1987.

Rodgers, C. "Reflection in Second Language Teacher Education" (three book reviews). *TESOL Quarterly* 32, no. 3 (1998): 610–13.

Rosen, S. *My Voice Will Go with You: The Teaching Tales of Milton H. Erickson.* New York: W.W. Norton, 1982.

Rowe, M. "Wait Time: Slowing Down May Be a Way of Speeding Up." *Journal of Teacher Education* 37, no. 1 (1986): 43–50.

Rubin, J., and I. Thompson. *How to Be a More Successful Language Learner.* Boston: Heinle & Heinle, 1994.

Ryan, P. "Exploring Elementary Teachers' Experiences with English Language Learners." Doctoral dissertation, Indiana University of Pennsylvania, 2004.

Sainz, M. J. "Good Evening, and Welcome to This Edition of the News." *TESOL Journal* 3, no. 1 (1993): 41–42.

Sano, T., and T. Miyano, prods. *Faces of Japan: Cram School.* Tokyo Telejapan Inc., 1988.

Savignon, S. *Communicative Competence: Theory and Classroom Practice.* New York: McGraw Hill, 1997.

———. "Communicative Language Teaching for the Twenty-First Century." In *Teaching English as a Second or Foreign Language, 3ᵈ ed.,* ed. M. Celce-Murcia, 13–28. Boston: Heinle & Heinle, 2001.

Scarcella, R. C., and R. L. Oxford. *The Tapestry of Language Learning: The Individual in the Communicative Classroom.* Boston: Heinle & Heinle, 1992.

Schenkein, J., ed. *Studies in the Organization of Conversational Interaction.* New York: Academic Press, 1978.

Scollon, R., and S. W. Scollon. *Intercultural Communication. 2ᵈ ed.* Malden, MA: Blackwell, 2001.

Segal, B., prod. *Teaching English through Action.* Brea, CA: Berty Segal, 1983. Videotape.

Segal, B., and H. Sloan, prods. 1984. *TPR and the Natural Approach.* Brea, CA: Berty Segal, 1984. Videotape.

Sherman, J. *Using Authentic Video in the Language Classroom.* New York: Cambridge University Press, 2003.

Short, D. "Expanding Middle School Horizons: Integrating Language, Culture, and Social Studies." *TESOL Quarterly* 28, no. 3 (1994): 581–607.

Silberstein, S., B. K. Dobson, and M. A. Clarke. *Reader's Choice. 4th ed.* Ann Arbor: University of Michigan Press, 2002.

Silva, T., and P. Matsuda, eds. *On Second Language Writing.* Mahwah, NJ: Lawrence Erlbaum, 2001.

Smith, F. *Understanding Reading.* New York: Holt, Rinehart, and Winston, 1994.

Smith, L. "Some Distinctive Features of EIL vs. ESOL in English Language Education." In *Readings in English as an International Language,* ed. L. Smith. Oxford: Pergamon Press, 1983.

Sperling, D. *The Internet Guide for English Language Teachers.* Upper Saddle River, NJ: Prentice Hall Regents, 1997.

Stempleski, S. "Teaching Communication Skills with Authentic Video." In *Video in Second Language Teaching,* eds. S. Stempleski and P. Arcario, 7–24. Alexandria, VA: TESOL, 1992.

———. "Video in the Classroom: Making the Most of Movies." *ESL Magazine* 3, no. 2 (2000): 10–12.

Stevick, E. W. "Control, Initiative, and the Whole Learner." In *Collected Papers in Teaching English as a Second Language and Bilingual Education.* New York: NYS ESOL BEA, 1978.

———. *My Understanding of Teaching Languages: A Way and Ways.* Paper presented at the TESOL Convention, Honolulu, Hawaii, 1982.

———. *Teaching Languages: A Way and Ways.* New York: Newbury House, 1980.

Storti, C. *The Art of Crossing Cultures.* Yarmouth, ME: Intercultural Press, 1989.

———. *The Art of Crossing Cultures. 2d ed.* Yarmouth, ME: Intercultural Press, 2001.

Sutherland-Smith, W. "Integrating Online Discussion in an Australian Intensive English Language Course." *TESOL Journal* 11, no. 3 (2002): 31–35.

Tambiah, S. J. *Buddhism and the Spirit Cults in Northeast Thailand.* Cambridge: Cambridge University Press, 1970.

Tanka, J. 1993. "Teaching Listening in the Language Lab: One Program's Experience." *TESOL Journal* 3, no. 1 (1993): 15–17.

Thomas, J. "Countering the 'I Can't Write English' Syndrome." *TESOL Journal* 2, no. 3 (1993): 12–15.

Thonus, T. "Serving Generation 1.5 Learners in the University Writing Center." *TESOL Journal* 12, no. 1 (2003): 17–24.

Tudor, I. "Teacher Roles in the Learner-Centered Classroom." *ELT Journal* 47, no. 1 (1993): 22–30.

Ur, P. *Teaching Listening Comprehension.* New York: Cambridge University Press, 1984.

Venrick, R. "Cultural Adjustment: The Language and Cultural Problems of

Expatriates in Thailand." Doctoral dissertation, Indiana University of Pennsylvania, 2001.

Verplaetse, L. S. "How Content Teachers Interact with English Language Learners." *TESOL Journal* 7, no. 5 (1998): 24–29.

Via, R. "'The Magic if' of Theater: Enhancing Language Learning through Drama." In *Interactive Language Teaching*, ed. W. M. Rivers, 110–23. New York: Cambridge University Press, 1987.

Wallace, M. J. *Action Research for Language Teachers*. Cambridge: Cambridge University Press, 1998.

Wallender, D. *The Bridge, Fall*. Excerpts from a volunteer's journal, 1977.

Wang, M. M., et al. *Turning Bricks into Jade*. Yarmouth, ME: Intercultural Press, 2000.

Wardhaugh, R. *How Conversation Works*. Oxford: Basil Blackwell, 1985.

Warschauer, M. "Comparing Face-to-Face and Electronic Discussion in the Second Language Classroom." *CALICO Journal* 13, no. 2 (1996): 7–26.

———. "Computer-Mediated Collaborative Learning: Theory and Practice." *Modern Language Journal* 81 (1997): 470–81.

———. *E-Mail for English Teachers*. Alexandria, VA: TESOL, 1995.

West, M. *Teaching English in Difficult Circumstances*. London: Longman, 1960.

White, A., ed. *New Ways in Teaching Writing*. Alexandria, VA: TESOL, 1995.

White, D., prod. *Action Songs for Indoor Days*. Los Angeles: Tom Thumb Records, 1978.

Wong, L. A. "The Descriptive Analysis of the Varieties of Singapore English as Recreated by Singapore Writers of Fiction." Doctoral dissertation, Indiana University of Pennyvania, 1992.

Wright, A., D. Betteridge, and M. Buckly. *Games for Language Learning*. Cambridge: Cambridge University Press, 1983.

Wright, T. *Roles of Teachers and Learners*. Oxford: Oxford University Press, 1987.

Wylie, L. W. *Beaux Gestes: A Guide to French Body Talk*. Cambridge, MA: Undergraduate Press, 1977.

Yahya, N. "Keeping a Critical Eye on One's Own Teaching Practice: EFL Teachers' Use of Reflective Teaching Journals." *Asian Journal of English Language Teaching* 10 (2000): 1–18.

Zamel, V. "The Composing Processes of Advanced ESL Students: Six Case Studies." *TESOL Quarterly* 17 (1983): 165–90.

———. "Recent Research on Writing Pedagogy." *TESOL Quarterly* 21 (1987): 697–715.

———. "Responding to Student Writing." *TESOL Quarterly* 19 (1985): 79–91.

———. "Writing: The Process of Discovering Meaning." *TESOL Quarterly* 16 (1982): 165–90.

Index